Information Society Studies

We are often told that we are 'living in an information society' or that we are 'information workers'. But what exactly do these claims mean, and how might they be verified? In this ambitious methodological study, Alistair Duff cuts through the rhetoric to get to the bottom of the so-called 'information society thesis'.

Duff presents the argument that there are in reality several 'information society theses', each with its own disciplinary origin and tradition. One talks about an 'information economy'. Another, the Japanese theory of the 'informationised society', measures communication flows, while a third focuses on IT and the 'information revolution'. This book brings together the various schools and examines them systematically in a comparative setting. It represents one of the first in-depth treatments of the field as a whole.

Wide-ranging in coverage, this work will be of interest to scholars in information science, communication and media studies, and social theory. It is a key text for the newly unified specialism of Information Society Studies and an indispensable guide to the future of research into the social role of information.

Alistair S. Duff lectures on the information society in the Department of Print Media, Publishing and Communication, Napier University, Edinburgh. He is the founder of the Ameritech Information Society Lecture, an annual congress of leading scholars in the field of Information Society Studies.

Routledge Research in Information Technology and Society

Information Society Studies

Alistair S. Duff

London and New York

First published 2000
by Routledge
11 New Fetter Lane, London EC4P 4EE

Simultaneously published in the USA and Canada
by Routledge
29 West 35th Street, New York, NY 10001

Routledge is an imprint of the Taylor & Francis Group

© 2000 Alistair Duff

Typeset in Garamond by
Prepress Projects, Perth, Scotland
Printed and bound in Great Britain by
St. Edmundsbury Press Ltd., Bury St. Edmunds, Suffolk

British Library Cataloguing in Publication Data
A catalogue record for this book is available
from the British Library

Library of Congress Cataloging in Publication Data
Duff, Alistair
    Information Society Studies/Alistair Duff.
    Includes bibliographical references and index.
    ISBN 0–415–21551–X (alk. paper)
    1. Information Science. I. Title
    HM851.D84 2000
    020–dc21
    CIP

Contents

Tables

Figures

Preface

This monograph is offered as a contribution to the young field I call Information Society Studies, and particularly to its methodology. Its objective is to find out whether the ways which have been used to support the information society thesis – i.e. the claim that advanced nations have turned into information societies – are in any degree successful. Now some readers may not be impressed by the failure to embed the information society thesis in particular historic and economic circumstances, to read it as an ideological ricochet from crises of one kind or another. I would certainly acknowledge that such reductionist approaches have some value. Indeed, when I embarked upon the research from which this book grew, the aim was to examine the information society in *all* its aspects and relations. However, it soon became clear that my vocation was to focus strictly on methodological fundamentals, since, in spite of the voluminous information society literature, these had never before been systematically addressed. Information Society Studies is in any case not bound to any one approach: it is irreducibly an interdisciplinary specialism. My own academic background, a curious combination of analytical social philosophy and information science, seemed to privilege me with a helpful vantage point from which to tackle the basic question: is there such a thing as an information society?

Before beginning, I wish to clarify one other matter. The following pages contain some sharp criticism of Fritz Machlup's pioneering work on knowledge production. Without exactly 'decanonising' this work, I have suggested that its influence upon the development of Information Society Studies has been excessive. However, my antithetical stance should not be taken as evidence that I have failed to recognise Machlup's stature. I am well aware of his greatness not only as an economist, but also as a man. Indeed, anyone who has the courage to stand up to the bully-boys of the Right, as did Machlup in the America of the 1950s, has my abiding respect. I am also absolutely certain that Machlup himself would not have wanted his posthumous reputation to alter the course of any scholarly investigation.

Alistair Duff
Edinburgh
December 1999

Acknowledgements

Many have helped me in various ways with this book. They include, in no particular order, Alistair McCleery, Paul Burton, Jack Meadows, Ian Johnson, Rennie McElroy, Frank Webster, Marjory Carnegie, Ian Gunn, David Duff, and Daniel Bell.

Copyright acknowledgements

Where necessary and where possible, permission was obtained from copyright holders for the many materials analysed in this book. In some cases illustrative material appeared to require multiple copyright permissions. Apologies are offered if any unintentional oversights have occurred.

Edward Elgar Publishing: Table 4.2; Figure 4.2
Elsevier Science: Tables 3.4–3.6; Figures 3.4, 3.5, 4.1
Japanese Ministry of Posts and Telecommunications: Tables 3.2, 3.3; Figures 3.2, 3.3, 3.6, 3.7
Library of Congress: Table 2.4
National Science Foundation: Table 2.3
Organization for Economic Cooperation and Development: Table 5.5
Princeton University Press: for extensive quotations and illustrations from *The Production and Distribution of Knowledge in the United States* by Fritz Machlup (1962)
Professor Emeritus Daniel Bell: for quotations from many writings
Professor Ian Miles: Table 4.1
Research Institute of Telecommunications and Economics: Table 3.1; Figure 3.1
United States Department of Commerce, Bureau of the Census: Tables 2.2, 2.4, 2.6, 2.7
United States Department of Commerce, Office of Telecommunications: Figure 5.1
United States Department of Education: Tables 2.1, 2.2, 2.8
United States Department of Labor, Bureau of Labor Statistics: Tables 2.8, 5.1–5.4, 5.6, 5.7
University of Tokyo Press: Tables 3.4–3.6; Figures 3.4, 3.5

1 Introduction

Introduction

> The Information Society is here! ... It may sound like a cliché, but the Information Society is here.
>
> (Lehtonen 1988: 104)

Researchers in many disciplines, social commentators and columnists, policy-makers at both the national and international level, and even that useful epistemological construct 'the man on the Clapham omnibus'[1] seem to be agreed that we are witnessing the onset of a new era: the 'information age'. Scholars have been particularly diligent in investigating the ethical and social problems allegedly faced by citizens of the information society: online pornography, threats to privacy, intellectual property violations, and the increasing gap between 'info rich' and 'info poor', to name only a few. However, while all this thought and activity may be laudable, the *grounds* for the existence of this putative new social formation remain rather unclear. Commenting on the second edition of a well-regarded textbook on the information society, a prominent British information scientist notes that the book's author 'very reasonably emphasises the difficulty of deciding exactly what the term means, and, hence, of determining whether we are really members of such a society' (Meadows 1996: 278). Indeed, it is the case that 'the serious academic study of information society issues is still relatively under-developed', and that 'many of the claims made about the information society are not subjected to serious scrutiny' (Preston and Wickham 1997: vi). However, if something is repeated often enough it is sooner or later accepted as the truth, and this seems to have happened to the 'information society thesis'; it has become, as Jaako Lehtonen says, a cliché.

The aim of this book is to try to establish whether the assertion that 'the information society is here' can really be justified. This chapter begins by tracing the literary roots of the term 'information society', to discover from where this bewitching descriptor originally came. The next section charts the term's recent behaviour in academic literature and the press, and demonstrates bibliometrically that 'information society' has indeed become a widely influential concept, and, if not a new 'paradigm', then at least a new framework for research and speculation. I then outline the parameters of the problem at the heart of the present investigation: is there a methodology which can truly justify the information society thesis? It will be assumed as axiomatic that there is nothing as important as facts: does, then, the information society thesis rest squarely or even obliquely on them, and if so, what precisely are they, and in what way or ways does it do so? It will be argued below, specifically, that there are several logically distinct but usually conflated *versions* of the information society thesis. In the chapters that follow, each of these versions is expounded and evaluated, both in its own right and in relation to the other versions. The investigation is thus offered as a basic methodological contribution to the budding interdisciplinary field of Information Society Studies.[2]

The roots of the information society concept

The origins of the term 'information society' are not well understood. If one ignores the many vague or patently anachronistic claims which have appeared, one is left with two cogent theories. Both locate the invention in the early 1960s, and both also link it closely to the idea of the 'information industry'. However, there is disagreement over whether it is authors in Japan or the USA who should be credited. Here the main arguments for both schools are examined.[3]

The case for American provenance

The key document in the case for US provenance is Fritz Machlup's *The Production and Distribution of Knowledge in the United States* (1962). In an allusion typical of this school of thought, A.E. Cawkell says that 'Fritz Machlup, an American economist, started it all, although he called it "The Knowledge Industry" ' (1986: 87). Cawkell acknowledges that Machlup did not himself actually ever use the term 'information society', but argues that he should be credited with its invention on the grounds that the 'idea of an "Information Society" was *implicit* in Fritz Machlup's work in 1962' (Cawkell 1984: 63, my italic). That is to say, the case for American provenance reduces to a claim concerning the coining of the term 'knowledge industry', and thus depends upon the legitimacy of equating *knowledge* with *information*, and *industry* with *society*.

In his book, Machlup had propounded the view that 'all information in the ordinary sense of the word is knowledge' (1962: 15). Moreover, while he did not speak of the 'information industry', he did refer to computers and an assortment of other technologies as the 'information machine industry'. It may therefore be possible to infer that the idea of information industries was *implicitly* there. However, the conflation of *industry* and *society* cannot be defended. No doubt the former implies the latter in the trivial sense that one cannot have industries in the absence of some kind of society, but it does not at all follow that every economist who has written on an industry or group of industries has *ipso facto* been engaged in an act of sociological origination. A society is, after all, a complex formation in which industry is only one of many components. Thus the question remains: who actually invented 'information society'?

The first actual usage of the term identified by Cawkell comes in a 1975 OECD conference paper by Edwin Parker and Marc Porat, but this is certainly too late a date. In *The Coming of Post-Industrial Society* (1974; first published 1973), Daniel Bell had already mentioned the term, albeit choosing, at this stage in the development of his thought, not to adopt it. He wrote:

> The question has been asked why I have called this speculative concept the 'post-industrial society', rather than the knowledge society, or the information society, or the professional society, all of which are somewhat apt in describing salient aspects of what is emerging.
>
> (Bell 1974: 37)

The wording here seems to imply that 'information society' was already a live option as a possible descriptor for the emergent social formation. Susan Crawford (1983) indeed traces the term back to 1970, when the American Society for Information Science (ASIS) organised its annual meeting around the theme of 'The Information Conscious Society'. Eugene Garfield has argued (1979: 209) that 'information-conscious society' and 'information society' are not synonymous. That may be true at a philosophical level, but in terms of a straightforward inquiry into literary priority it is reasonable to credit ASIS with first usage. A wide range of bibliographic database searches commissioned for the present inquiry confirmed that there was no English-language use of the term prior to 1970, at least in a document title or abstract (see Appendix 1).

The case for Japanese provenance

The alternative theory claims that 'the term "information society" was itself coined in Japan' (Morris-Suzuki 1988: 3). Two cognates are involved. 'Joho Shakai' is normally translated into English as 'information society', but has also been rendered as 'information-oriented society', 'information-conscious society', and 'information-centred society'. 'Johoka Shakai', which uses a verbal form of 'joho', has a sense analogous to 'industrialised society', and is translated variously as 'informised society', 'informatised society', 'informationised society', or sometimes simply (again) 'information society'. Osmo Wiio has disputed such translations, claiming (Wiio 1985) that the term 'communicating society' is more accurate, but his position is undercut by the fact that bilingual Japanese authors themselves translate 'joho' as 'information'. Tessa Morris-Suzuki (1988) specifies that Yujiro Hayashi did the actual coining in 1969, i.e. a year before the ASIS conference. In that year two Japanese government reports on the theme of the information society were published, on both of which Hayashi had acted as a leading advisor (Keizai 1969; Sangyo 1969): his book *Johoka*

Shakai: Hado no Shakai Kara Sofuto no Shakai e (*The Information Society: From Hard to Soft Society*), which reportedly sold 100,000 copies, appeared simultaneously.

A different, and rather more nuanced, account of Japanese literary origins can be found in the writings of Youichi Ito. Like Cawkell and others, he links the origination of the term 'information society' to 'information industries'. According to Ito, the latter term was first used by Tadao Umesao in an article entitled 'Joho sangyo ron' ('On information industries'), published in the January 1963 issue of the media periodical *Hoso Asahi* (Rising Sun Broadcasting). Ito argues that, while Umesao did not actually use the terms 'Joho Shakai' or 'Johoka Shakai', his article 'caused the "*joho shakai* (information society) boom" ' (Ito 1991a: 5). Exactly one year later, the January 1964 issue of the same periodical contained the proceedings of a discussion in which Jiro Kamishima argued that Japan was suited to become a 'Joho Sangyo Shakai' (information industrial society). The editors of *Hoso Asahi*, one of whom Ito names as Michiko Igarashi, 'apparently seized on these words and titled the article, "Sociology in information societies" '; thereafter, between November 1964 and July 1966, they ran a series of articles on the theme of the 'information society', with such titles as ' "Audience" in information societies', ' "Senders" in information societies', and 'Organizations and individuals in information societies'. As regards monographs, Ito has stated elsewhere (1981: 673) that Hayashi's 'was probably the first book in the world that used the term "informational society" or a similar term as its book title'. However, he identifies (Ito 1991a: 7) a slightly earlier usage in *Joho Shakai Nyumon* (*Introduction to an Information Society*) by Yoneji Masuda, which was published in 1968. Ito also credits Masuda with first English-language usage, again in a conference proceedings of 1970, in this case a future studies one (Masuda 1970). A final significant datum Ito supplies is that in 1971 a dictionary on information societies appeared in Japan (*Johoka Shakai Jiten*).

Discussion: the invention of 'information society'

Ito's research establishes beyond reasonable doubt that the invention of the term 'information society' occurred in Japan and not in the USA.[4] The first Japanese use of the term was in 1964, fully six years before the earliest date given by those claiming American provenance. The titles of the articles in *Hoso Asahi* demonstrate that by the mid-1960s 'information society' was already serving as a subject heading for Japanese reflection on the modern world, and the publication of a dictionary on the subject constitutes clear bibliographic proof that the term was well established by 1971. As regards first English-language usage, the American and Japanese accounts agree on the year: any applause for this achievement can therefore be shared between Masuda and the American Society for Information Science, since both employed the term 'information society' (or, in the latter's case, a *bona fide* synonym) in 1970.

However, while the *facts* provided by Ito must be admitted, his *interpretation* of some of them can be contested. Ito honours Umesao with first-ever usage, on the grounds that Umesao wrote the article on information industries which initiated the 'information society boom'. But what about Kamishima, who first used the phrase 'information industrial society', or the editors of *Hoso Asahi*, who actually printed the words 'information society'? One problem with Ito's position is that, since Umesao's article appeared in 1963, it is at least conceivable that Umesao had been influenced by Machlup, whose *The Production and Distribution of Knowledge in the United States* had been published the previous year. Questioned on this point as part of my inquiry, Ito argued that, because Umesao was an anthropologist rather than an economist it was unlikely that he knew of Machlup's work (see Appendix 2). Against this, four points can be made: first, Machlup was famous for his interdisciplinary orientation and thus may well have been read by anthropologists; second, Umesao's article was on a topic normally associated with economics rather than anthropology; third, Japanese scholars (like all serious scholars) tend to keep abreast of American literature; and fourth, an item about Machlup had appeared in the international news magazine *Time* in 1962 ('The knowledge industry'), albeit at the end of the year. Umesao is dead, however, so this issue probably cannot be conclusively proved either way. In any case, my chief objection to Ito's position is that (as was argued above) invention of the term 'information industry' cannot be regarded as automatically conferring intellectual property rights in the broader term 'information society'.

There is also a problem with attributing the invention to Kamishima.[5] It is true that he was first to use the term 'information industrial society', but the meaning of this is surely different from what is signified by 'information society'. However much they may differ regarding the exact nature of the 'information society', the majority of information society theorists believe that it is *not* the same as an industrial society: most would argue strongly that it is essentially a *post*-industrial society.[6] The juxtaposing of the words 'information' and 'industrial' is thus misleading: 'information industrial society' is as ambiguous a term as, say, 'agricultural industrial society' or 'post-industrial industrial society'. For this reason, the invention should not be attributed to Kamishima, or at least he should not be the main beneficiary.

The process of elimination leads to a perhaps surprising conclusion. It is proposed that a correct interpretation of the data at our disposal must assign to *Hoso Asahi*'s Michiko Igarashi (assuming she was the responsible member of the editorial staff) most of the glory for inventing the term 'information society'. In addition to following inexorably from a process of elimination, the proposal is based on two positive premises. First, it is grounded in the worthy socialist doctrine of the 'dignity of labour', according to which the importance of all workers in a productive process must be recognised. Ito insisted that 'the contribution of the editors of *Hoso Asahi* would not have been especially important' (Appendix 2), but he provided no justification for such a summary dismissal of the painstaking professionalism of these workers. The proposal is predicated, secondly, on a literary aesthetic which maintains that editing can transcend a mechanical process or technical skill and become a creative art. In his analysis of an Arden edition of Shakespeare's *Cymbeline*, George Steiner contends that 'the editor's task here is, in the full sense, interpretative and creative' (1975: 2). The same is true, arguably, in the present case. When Ms Igarashi extracted and recombined certain key words from the Kamishima manuscript, and finally decided to run the article under the heading 'Sociology in Information Societies', she was making a bold and significant literary departure. If we are to believe the 'information society thesis' – although that of course is still to be decided – she was doing no less than *christening the epoch*.

Recent bibliometric behaviour of the information society

First used as an English-language descriptor in 1970, as already noted, the term 'information society' increased rapidly in popularity and was soon being employed in a variety of contexts. As part of the present inquiry, online bibliometrics was employed to chart its progress with a view to ascertaining more precisely the extent of its influence. Two investigations were undertaken, a major one which explored the spread of the concept in the literatures of a wide range of academic fields, and a minor one which circumscribed the impact of the information society on two British newspapers. These will be treated in separate sections below.

Impact on academic subjects

For the first investigation the methodology comprised systematic interrogation via DIALOG of bibliographic databases representing four large subject clusters: *Information Science Abstracts* for the information sciences, *Social SciSearch* for the social sciences, *Inspec* for the engineering sciences, and *Arts & Humanities Search* for the arts and humanities. Periodical article title fields were searched using the truncated English-language phrase 'informat? (w) societ?', for the years 1984 to 1997 inclusive.[7] Reasons of specificity and precision (not to mention cost) entailed the exclusion of a large number of cognates – James Beniger (1986) lists dozens, and neologisms like 'cybersociety' (Jones 1995) have appeared since he wrote. However, truncation allowed for such synonyms as 'informational society' and 'information-centred society', as well as plurals. The search was limited to periodicals on the assumption that the article remains the primary unit for the communication of research, although admittedly this is less true in some academic fields than in others.

The results were as follows.[8] A total of 305 bibliographic references were retrieved across the databases, of which eighty-four were in *Information Science Abstracts*, ninety-two in *Social SciSearch*, 121 in *Inspec* and eight in *Arts & Humanities Search* (Figure 1.1). Several preliminary points should be made. First, the low yield in *Arts & Humanities Search* seems to indicate that the term 'information society' must make more progress before it can be said to have deeply penetrated high-brow literary culture. Second, the high yield in *Inspec* is

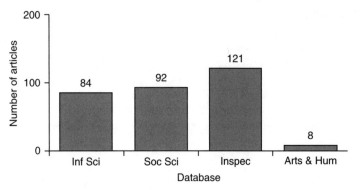

Figure 1.1   Number of 'information society' articles retrieved from a search of four databases. Inf Sci, *Information Science Abstracts*; Soc Sci, *Social SciSearch*; *Inspec* (engineering sciences); Arts & Hum, *Arts & Humanities Search*

a function of its massive coverage of periodicals (approximately twice that of the other databases), many of them far removed from what are normally considered the 'hard' sciences. Third, and more generally, the extensive coverage of these online databases meant that many of the references were duplicates. However, there were references for a total of 181 original articles, defined strictly so as to exclude not only duplications and 'false drops', but also identical papers published in more than one outlet.

A total of 112 different periodicals carried articles on the topic, a remarkable quantity. Predictably, *The Information Society: An International Journal* ran by far the largest number of relevant papers (twenty-four) over the fourteen-year time frame, and can therefore justifiably claim to be one of the 'core' journals of Information Society Studies. The *Journal of Information Science*, with twelve articles of which three-quarters were published in the last four years, has emerged as the second most important vehicle.[9] The other titles with several papers on the information society were the following:

Asian Survey (2 papers)
Aslib Proceedings (2)
Computer Networks and ISDN Systems (2)
Critique of Anthropology (3)
Digest of Japanese Industry and Technology (2)
Electronic Library (3)
Electronics and Wireless World (4)
Futures (2)
Government Publications Review (2)
IFIP Transactions A – Computer Science and Technology (3)
Information Processing and Management (2)
Information Services and Use (2)
Journal of Communication (2)
Media, Culture and Society (3)

Online and CDROM Review (2)
Special Libraries (2)
Technological Forecasting and Social Change (3)
Telecommunication Policy (2)
Telematics and Informatics (7, theme issue)
The Economic and Social Review (5, all from a theme issue)

The majority of the periodicals carried only a single relevant article. They included:

AI and Society
American Cartographer
Annals of the American Society of Political and Social Science
Cataloguing and Classification Quarterly
Educational Leadership
European Cancer News
Fujitsu Scientific and Technical Journal
Journal of Consumer Policy —
Journal of Economic Issues
Journal of Telecommunication Networks
Library Science with a Slant to Documentation
New Zealand Libraries
Optical Information Systems
Science Education
Telephony
Theory and Society
Transportation
University of Pennsylvania Law Review
World Futures

Appendix 3 contains a complete list of titles, but the foregoing selection is sufficient to demonstrate that the concept of the information society has spread across a very wide range of subjects, i.e. that it enjoys a high level of transdisciplinary 'scattering'. The periodicals varied not only in disciplinary orientation but also in level of readership, and the fact that professional and trade organs are represented alongside research journals is itself indicative of the concept's cosmopolitanism.

The diverse impact of the information society can be illuminated further by examining the organisational affiliations of authors of articles (Figure 1.2). While the majority (115 articles, or 63.5 per cent of the total) were by academic authors, a significant proportion had non-academic affiliations, including industry (14.4 per cent) and independent research institutes (7.7 per cent). Authors in governmental bodies (2.2 per cent) and libraries and information services (2.2 per cent) have also registered an interest – not surprisingly, given that the information society is believed to be transforming such institutions.

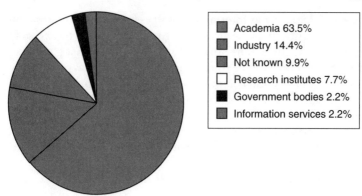

Figure 1.2 Organisational affiliation of authors of 'information society' articles

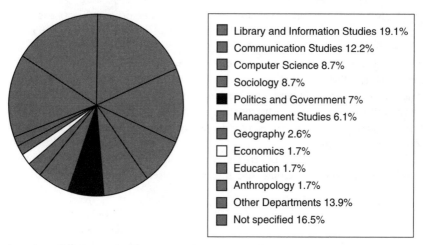

Figure 1.3 Departmental affiliation of authors of 'information society' articles

In the academic sector itself, the disciplinary profile was also varied. As can be seen from Figure 1.3, single articles originated from such unlikely sources as Hispanic and Portuguese Studies, Psychology, Community Medicine, and even – in the form of an essay on 'Excommunication in the information society' authored at Calvin College, Grand Rapids (Fortner 1995) – theology. However, the departments with the strongest interests in the information society were Library and Information Studies (twenty-two articles, or 19.1 per cent of academia's subtotal of 115 articles over the fourteen-year period), Communication Studies (12.2 per cent), Computer Science (8.7 per cent), and Sociology (8.7 per cent); none of these dominated the field, but together they accounted for almost half of the articles, perhaps more if the author affiliations in the 'Not specified' category were known. Intuitively, these are indeed the four disciplinary homes which might be expected to produce research on the information society: Library and Information Studies because the information society, however construed, must be at least partly constitutive of the *milieu* in which contemporary librarians and information scientists work;[10] Communication Studies because the transmission of information is presumably the subject matter of media and communication research; Computer Science because many computer scientists take seriously the ethical and social aspects of the information systems they create; and Sociology because the scientific study of modern social formations – their genesis, occupational makeup, technological dimensions, stratification systems, and so on – is precisely what sociology is about.

Moreover, as Figure 1.4 indicates, these fields have registered a *consistent* interest in the information society over the time frame, as opposed to a sudden and short-lived one which might be dismissed as faddishness. Thus, Library and Information Studies produced three articles in 1985, two in 1986, one per annum in 1987, 1998, and 1989, two in 1990, one in 1991 and 1992, two in 1993, three in 1995 and 1996, and two in 1997. The other subjects supplied fewer articles in total, but these too were spread relatively evenly over the whole time frame. As Figure 1.5 shows, the geographical distribution of citations was also wide, with twenty-eight countries represented, led by the USA (35.5 per cent), the UK (23 per cent), Japan (7.7 per cent), Canada (4.9 per cent), Australia (3.3 per cent), and The Netherlands (3.3 per cent). Clearly, research on the information society is no more a monopoly of one nation's thinkers than it is a 'captive market' of any single academic subject: the concept is in every sense cosmopolitan.

The general distribution of articles over the time frame should also be noted. Figure 1.6 indicates a strong and mounting interest in the mid-1980s, an

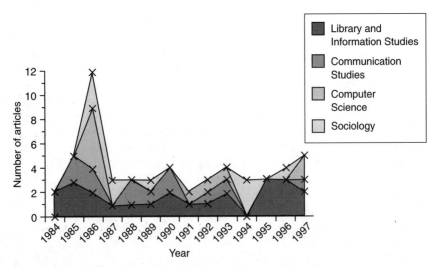

Figure 1.4 Spread of 'information society' through the four main subjects

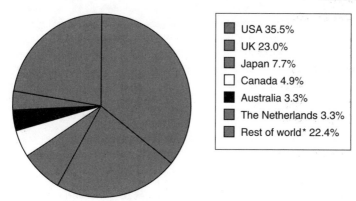

Figure 1.5 Country of provenance of 'information society' articles. *Belgium, Brazil, Bulgaria, Cyprus, Denmark, Finland, France, Germany, India, Ireland, Israel, Italy, New Zealand, Nigeria, Norway, Singapore, South Africa, Spain, Sweden, Switzerland, Taiwan, Yugoslavia

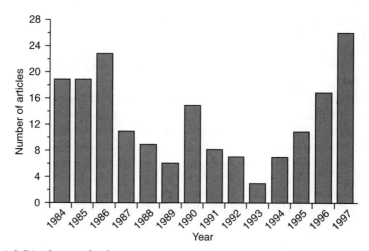

Figure 1.6 Distribution of 'information society' articles over time

abatement in the late 1980s and early 1990s (although the year 1990 somewhat contravenes this generalisation), and then a renewed surge of publication in the mid- and late 1990s. The recent interest has been spurred by some salient governmental information policy initiatives, especially in Europe and the USA. Thus, a typical article of the late 1990s discusses 'The European Union's route to the information society' or 'The information superhighway and the information society'. So long as policy-makers keep implementing their visions of the wired-up world, this high volume of annual periodical literature on the information society is likely to be maintained.

Over the time frame as a whole, the most common construction in the article titles took the form of '*x* [e.g. cartography, consumers, crime, democracy, education, governing, literacy, living, managing] in the information society'. The information society is thus used as a framework, or what might be called a conceptual template, for a strikingly diverse range of topics and issues. Moreover, contextual analysis of a sample of the full texts of papers indicated that the majority of the cited authors subscribe in some way or other to a belief in the information society:

> We are moving towards a society which attaches increasing value to information work, information services, and information tools. In this society, effectiveness and efficiency of information work and systems become the determining factors for success. They govern the competitiveness of individuals and organizations. It appears appropriate, therefore, to label this emerging society an information society.
>
> (*Journal of Information and Image Management*, 1984)

> The size and scope of the 'information society' are now familiar even in the popular literature. We can take it as read that information is the dominant resource in the United States, and coming to be so in other 'advanced' or 'developed' countries.
>
> (*Public Administration Review*, 1985)

> The interrelated issues of class and region which we discuss in this article must be seen in terms of wider and fundamental political issues relating to democracy, economic opportunity, and the quality of social and cultural life. These are the issues we raise when we ask: whose information society?
>
> (*Media, Culture and Society*, 1988)

> Beginning in 1980, another step was undertaken that established North Carolina's qualification as a distinct component of the information society.
>
> (*Society*, 1990)

> In the Industrial Era, we used to talk about the 'haves' and the 'have-nots'. Now, we must deal with the 'knows' and the 'know-nots', i.e., those who know how to use the tools required to survive in the new society and those who do not.
>
> (*Wilson Library Bulletin*, 1991)

> Finally, it becomes clear that postmodernism and network economics, mass communications and telecommunications, popular culture and management theory are talking about qualitative social change in the third stage of the information society. Since the effects and trends to which all these fields point resonate across levels of analysis – and since primary among these effects are fundamental shifts in the way we organize ourselves

as a society – cross-fertilization among these literatures seems the most likely path to follow if we seek to emerge from this turbulent period with our goals enacted and our values intact.

(Journal of Communication, 1993)

There are many issues that should be considered when developing a suite of policies for government to assist the development of the information society.

(Journal of Information Science, 1996)

Every generation believes that it is at a seminal point on the time-line of technological progress. It is either the age of iron, the age of the train, the age of flight, or in our case the information age.

(Library Review, 1997)

Theory of history (industrial era gives way to information era), economics (information as a factor of production and strategic resource), sociology (an emergent class system based on access to informational goods and services): claims often associated with the information society thesis are manifest in one form or another in these representative extracts, even where a critical stance is being developed. In other words, while some may not *like* the information society, most authors appear to be agreed as to its *reality* and *importance*. It may be too early to claim that the information society has become a new 'paradigm' in the grandiose Kuhnian sense of a way of 'seeing the world' (see Forester 1993; Yamaguchi 1990), but it can certainly be said that Michiko Igarashi's term had become, only twenty years after its invention, a powerful and versatile societal descriptor.[11]

Impact on newspapers

The findings reported above are supported by the bibliometric behaviour of the term 'information society' in the press over the past decade. This search was confined to online archives of newspapers available from DIALOG, namely *The Times* and *Sunday Times*. The high standing of these titles as monitors of educated lay opinion makes them acceptable choices for a small-scale survey of the impact of the concept of the information society on public consciousness. The search statement was again restricted to the phrase 'informat? (w) societ?'; however, given the brevity and notorious unreliability (from a retrieval standpoint) of newspaper headlines and feature article titles, search parameters were extended to the full texts.

There were 119 relevant articles over the ten-year time frame, with an extremely sharp increase after 1993 (Figure 1.7). Whereas the term 'information society' occurred in only fourteen documents between 1988 and 1993 inclusive, it was used in ten documents in 1994, thirty-two in 1995, no less than forty-three in 1996, and twenty in 1997. The upsurge was related to the appearance

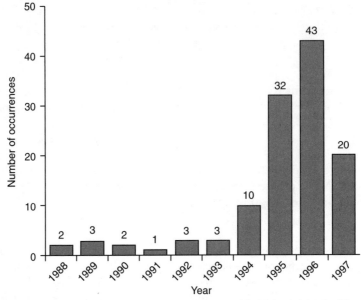

Figure 1.7 Occurrence of the term 'information society' in *The Times* and *Sunday Times*

of the World Wide Web, as well as to the European and American information society initiatives referred to earlier. The context of usage over the whole period was almost as varied as with the academic periodicals, as the following sample of document titles shows:

'Fibre optics play politics technology'
'Communism, killed by a new revolution'
'The future for Labour'
'Keeping up with today's technology'
'The White House begins to tune in: infotech electronic trading'
'Visions of the cabled future'
'Fear of economic rifts tempers the rush to cyberspace'
'Information age "will weaken the state" '
'Broadcast it to the world: digital television and radio'
'Red tape "hampers IT revolution" '
'New technology "moving too fast" '
'Even window cleaners could soon be online'
'Worldwide Web people to gather in Paris'
'MI5 appeals for power to tap digital phones'
'Cash boosts for multimedia'
'New digital awards: DTI Information Society Creative Awards'
'Gates sings Internet's praises: CBI annual conference'
'Harmonious future beckons for books and the Internet'
' "Borrowed time" at public libraries'

'Europe's plan for a higher level of IT'
'Kiosk gives the jobless a link into cyberspace'
'Some very nasty insects on the Web'
'An ominous delay: are ministers already losing their taste for openness?'

Newspaper references thus touched on substantive social issues as well as a suite of spectacular technological developments: in these examples alone, concerns are expressed regarding employment, the information poor, the viability of the public library system, political legitimacy, and the morality of online material. If it is remembered, in addition, that all of the broadsheets have felt it necessary to introduce regular 'supplements' dedicated to information technology, the public impact of the concept of the information society is surely confirmed. Evidently the man on the Clapham omnibus, who has been defined here as the educated and thus averagely sceptical layman – i.e. the typical reader of a British quality newspaper – is no stranger to at least some of the general ideas behind the information society thesis.

Overview of methodologies of the information society thesis

There is thus no gainsaying that the concept of the information society is an intellectual force to be reckoned with. However, as suggested earlier, the great question which needs to be settled is whether there are *valid grounds* for this phenomenon. Put bluntly, the prevalence of a belief in the information society does not entail that the information society actually exists in any coherent sense. This is essentially a methodological matter. To prove that the information society exists one must provide a method of verifying its existence. It must be shown how one would go about confirming the proposition that society *x* is an information society. The methodological issue is logically prior to all other issues, such as the ethical and political ones alluded to in some of the extracts cited above. As Charles Steinfield and Jerry Salvaggio explain, 'without an adequate conception of the nature of an information society, attempts to project social problems in information societies are difficult' (1989: 1). The overriding aim of the present work is the relatively modest one of arriving at an 'adequate conception' of the information society: I leave it to others to crack the social problems. My argument will centre on the proposal that the information society must be understood methodologically in three different ways, giving rise to three distinct versions of the information society thesis – four if synthetic versions are counted.[12]

First, there is the 'information sector' version, according to which modern economies are characterised by the expansion of an information sector or workforce. Its core claim is normally cast either in terms of the contribution of 'knowledge production' or 'information processing' to gross national product, or in terms of a radical reconfiguration of the workforce. The version maintains that workers in information societies are typically no longer working with *things*, as was the case in industrial societies, but with *information* in some form or other. Also known as the 'information economy' thesis, it is the oldest and most influential version of the information society thesis. In Chapter 2, I argue that the key figure in this tradition is indeed the great American economist Fritz Machlup, and the key work his *The Production and Distribution of Knowledge in the United States* (1962). The methodology contained in his book is subjected to an examination of unprecedented precision. It will be maintained here that, notwithstanding the massive influence among information society theorists of the information sector version, that version is in the end of doubtful value, and that its innate flaws may prevent it from ever providing a fully convincing account of the role of information in modern societies. In other words, it will be suggested, iconoclastically, that Information Society Studies needs to turn away from the dominant version.

In Chapter 3, the so-called 'information explosion' is discussed. This is usually understood, especially by information scientists, in terms of an allegedly exponential growth of scholarly literature, as measured by such familiar yardsticks as the number of journals in existence or the size of university library book collections. It will be argued below, however, that if the intention is to ground discourse about an information *society*, such an approach may be too narrow, i.e. that what is required for a credible equation of the form 'Information Explosion plus Society equals Information Society' is a broader conception of the information explosion embracing the information flowing across society as a totality. Chapter 3 focuses on the remarkable Joho Shakai research tradition which, although dating back to the 1960s and still active, is virtually unknown in the West. In various ways, but especially by means of their regular Information Flow Census, these Joho Shakai researchers have endeavoured to do what has been considered impossible by information scientists: to measure the total quantity of information flowing across all media in society. In what is perhaps the first major English-language appraisal of this full-blooded 'information flows' version, I will argue that Joho Shakai has much to offer Information Society Studies.

A third version of the information society thesis concerns the spread or 'diffusion' of information technology (IT). This is the popular version, in the sense of being the one which would be most familiar to the man on the Clapham omnibus. As noted above, the quality press has hailed the arrival of the information society, and what it is referring to is of course computers and the 'IT revolution'. In Chapter 4, the intellectual basis of this phenomenon is analysed. Some commentators have suggested that the 'information technology' version lacks a serious research tradition and thus a cogent methodology, but it will be argued here that such a judgement overlooks the important contribution of the British researcher, Ian Miles. So-called 'Milesianism' is presented as a systematic statement of the information technology version which can significantly enhance our understanding of perennial issues relating to the nature of the relationship between technology and society. It is suggested that the IT version may be essentially viable even if Miles himself does not fully succeed in making the case for it.

If there is any truth in two or more of these three versions of the information society thesis it follows that a synthetic or multifaceted version may also be feasible. As stated earlier, conflations and confusions are common, and it is not difficult to find a *soi-disant* information society theorist whose 'thought' is really a syncretistic mishmash of half-digested ideas borrowed from several research traditions. A genuinely synthetic theory, one which justifies each element and then skilfully fuses them into a cohesive whole, is much rarer. Chapter 5 identifies the work of the social theorist Daniel Bell as harbouring the paramount synthesis of the information society. Bell's enormous influence on information society thinking is well known, but his exact position has never before been accurately expounded, still less properly evaluated. It will be argued that his theory, while convincing in many respects, incorporates some of the weaknesses and ambiguities of the versions from which it draws, especially those of the information sector version. 'The social framework of the information society' (Bell 1980c) and other writings by Bell, understood aright, contain the strongest version of the information society thesis available, but they do not, I will suggest, completely vindicate that thesis. Chapter 5 features discussion of views recently expressed by Professor Bell in private correspondence with the present author, including Bell's puzzling claim that he is *not* an information society theorist.

Chapter 6 draws overall conclusions from what is in essence a cumulative exploration of the ideas behind the alternative versions of the information society thesis. This study in methodology begins with a *tabula rasa*, and will by the end have probed all of the key premises and inferences. It will have, as it were, 'got to the bottom of' the information society thesis, or rather information society theses. If the book is largely critical, this is because a thorough critique of methodology has been long overdue, and because to clear away foundational errors and ambiguities is surely to make a helpful contribution to any young field. By analysing information society truth-claims into their constituent elements, and also identifying the exact nature of the most convincing of the syntheses, it attempts to make Information Society Studies worthy of full admittance into the academy.

Finally, a Coda will attempt to outline the path ahead for Information Society Studies. What are the prospects for a specialism which has now been brought together as a cohesive field? How will it be positioned with respect to related disciplines and fields, both older ones such as sociology and newer ones like information science? Which media – above all, which journals – should be entrusted with its establishment and maturation as a field? And what methodological framework should guide future studies of the information society? In the light of the conclusions concerning the competing schools of thought, it ought to be possible to provide at least a rough sketch of a methodologically sound conception of the information society.

Notes

1 The man on the Clapham omnibus, the representative 'right-minded person' whose presumed intuitions are a test of morality in English jurisprudence (Devlin 1965: 15),

   will mean in the present context the educated, averagely sceptical layman: the construct
   will be further clarified as the argument unfolds.

 2 While it would be rash to claim that the term has never before been articulated, I am not
    aware of any substantive or systematic use of 'Information Society Studies'.

 3 A version of the material in this section has been published as a brief communication in
    the *Journal of Information Science* (Duff *et al.* 1996).

 4 I am grateful to Dr Gernot Wersig, of the Free University in Berlin, for referring me to
    two early German-language books on the information society, namely his own
    Informationssoziologie: Hinweise zu Einem Informationswissenschaftlichen Teilbereich (1973) and
    Karl Steinbuch's *Die Informierte Gesellschaft: Geschichte und Zukunft der Nachrichtentechnik*
    (1966). Their existence does not, of course, count against any of the claims made above.

 5 In the bibliography, Kamishima's name is listed after that of Takao Kuwahara as the
    second of three authors of the paper in question. It is a Japanese practice sometimes to
    put the main author's name in the middle.

 6 Ian Miles is a conspicuous exception to this generalisation: his theory of the information
    society as meta-industrial society is the subject of Chapter 4.

 7 A helpful citation history of the information society concept for the earlier period 1973–
    84 is reported in Paisley (1986).

 8 An earlier version of this material, covering the shorter time frame 1984–93, was published
    in the *Journal of Information Science* (Duff 1995).

 9 Other titles have from time to time tried to become the leading information society journal.
    The most recent effort is the British-based quarterly *Information, Communication and Society*
    (launched 1998). The role of core journals in the future development of Information Society
    Studies will be discussed at the close of this investigation.

10 The role of professional librarians in the information society should not be despised. On
    the contrary, Theodore Roszak, no mean social theorist, argues that information society
    issues are 'addressed more intensely and imaginatively at library conferences and in library
    journals than anywhere else' (1994: 181). I will refer to librarians at various points below.

11 In a co-citation analysis entitled 'The impact of the concept of post-industrial society and
    information society', Ming-Yueh Tsay (1995) has contributed to an understanding of the
    development of Igarashi's neologism. Tsay's methodology and parameters were different
    from mine, but he too concluded that 'the concept of [the] information society has had [a]
    profound influence on various disciplines' (1995: 329).

12 Steinfield and Salvaggio have suggested that there is a fifth distinct 'research perspective',
    which they call 'critical approaches' (1989: 3). However, while it is certainly true that
    there is an impressive body of political literature, most of it of a socialist or egalitarian
    stamp, that is sharply critical of information society thinking, it is not constitutive of a
    separate *methodology*. I have discussed ideological aspects in Duff (1990).

2 The information sector version of the information society thesis

Introduction

One of the main burdens of this investigation is to demonstrate that the information society thesis is complex in various ways, the most significant of which is that there is a plurality of distinct versions of the thesis – in a sense, there are several 'information society theses'. It is because ignorance of this truth is endemic that the task of disambiguation has become so imperative. However, it is not difficult to find a reason for the confusion: one version has been so dominant that it is hardly surprising that commentators have been misled into assuming that it is the *only* version in existence, into mistaking the part for the whole. It is this version, which is called the 'information sector' version, that is treated in the present chapter. The literature on the information sector, sometimes called the 'information economy' or 'information workforce', is already gigantic, and is being added to every day. However, it is not necessary to evaluate every item in the *corpus* in order to arrive at an understanding of the strengths and weaknesses of the version, for the simple reason that it is almost entirely derived from a single source, namely a book by Fritz Machlup entitled *The Production and Distribution of Knowledge in the United States* (1962). In a nutshell, the argument below is that this work is methodologically flawed at fundamental levels, and that the industry of like-minded studies it has spawned are as a result also flawed.

Before setting out, a hermeneutical point must be clarified. It is often claimed that Marc Porat's *The Information Economy* (1977) is the chief source of the information sector version of the information society thesis. Thus, for example, Jorge Schement writes in a respected article (1990: 449) that 'Porat's pioneering work [was the] original source of data [on] the rise of the information society'. This view is mistaken. Porat is certainly the second most important figure in the research tradition under consideration, but far from being the originator his work is actually largely an outworking of Machlup's ideas. Porat himself revealed this clearly in the main volume of his study:

> Most of the basic insights and concepts motivating this study were established in Fritz Machlup's groundbreaking book on the 'knowledge industries'. His book, analyzing the 1958 economy in detail, stands as an

enormously valuable contribution. It provides an empirical backdrop to
subsequent work by Daniel Bell, Peter Drucker, and others.

(Porat 1977, vol. 1: 44)

It is evident from such an acknowledgement that Porat was consciously following
in the footsteps of Machlup, to the extent that he regarded the latter's work as
having established the key propositions. Moreover, as will be noted below,
Machlup himself made the final judgement in a rarely cited follow-up study
(1980) that Porat's report added little of significance to the basic ideas which
he, Machlup, had originally formulated. The essential pioneer–follower
relationship cannot be denied.

What Porat did add were clearer terminology, some econometric
sophistication, and obviously – since he wrote fifteen years after his master –
extra data, including, crucially, estimates to the effect that the United States
would soon be devoting 50 per cent of its GNP to information occupations.[1]
For these contributions, especially, perhaps, the last – with half of the workforce
in information it seemed as though a mighty socio-economic Rubicon had been
crossed – the tradition has hailed Porat, but his essential position was more or
less Machlupian.[2] Thus, while there will be occasional references in the following
analysis to aspects of the Machlup–Porat axis, and Porat will also be revisited
much later in connection with Bell's adoption of his data (Chapter 5), *The
Information Economy* will not be treated in its own right.

Fritz Machlup: pioneer of the information society thesis

As early as 1960 Machlup (1962) brought to light the significance of
information industries in the national economy by formulating estimates
of the proportion of the GNP accounted for by 'knowledge production' in
the U.S.

(Arriaga 1985: 272)

The concept dates back from the late 1950s and the pioneering work of an
economist, Fritz Machlup, who first measured that sector of the U.S.
economy associated with what he called 'the production and distribution
of knowledge'.

(Beniger 1986: 21–2)

Machlup's pioneering work, *The Production and Distribution of Knowledge in
the United States*, has been seminal in establishing measures of the
information society in economic terms.

(Webster 1994: 6)

The pioneering work of Machlup attempted to document the size and
proportion of the labour force involved in the information sector.

(Melody 1996: 314)

Testimonies such as these typify the literature of Information Society Studies. Fritz Machlup, professor of economics at Princeton University and a president of the American Association of University Professors, had already secured his reputation in mainstream economics when, in 1962, he published what is regarded as the first major *apologia* for the information society.[3] *The Production and Distribution of Knowledge in the United States* is believed to contain the original proof of the startling proposition that an advanced industrial society, namely the USA, was on the way to developing a new type of economy, the 'information economy'. This proposition involved two interrelated empirical claims: first, that a significant and inexorably growing section of the gross national product of the USA can be attributed to information activities; and second, that the numerically dominant sector of the US workforce is now engaged in information-centred occupations. In the hands of Machlup's followers, these claims about an information *sector* or *economy* evolved into the information *society* thesis, as a result of the economistic assumption, implicit in the well-established terms 'agrarian society' and 'industrial society', that the nature of a society is a function of its economic setup. Whether or not the pioneer himself actually espoused that broader agenda is one of the questions this chapter will have to consider.

It will be instructive to recollect the reception that *The Production and Distribution of Knowledge in the United States* enjoyed when it was first published. T.W. Shultz, writing for the *American Economic Review* (1963: 836), opined that 'Machlup's long-standing intellectual interest in the economics of patents, inventions, and research has been an excellent training for the comprehensive task undertaken in this book'. 'At times,' he observed of Machlup's methodology, 'he inundates the reader with tables and takes some statistics at their face value'. Nevertheless, this Ivy League economist was prepared to declare the task successfully executed, and to confirm that 'Machlup's conception of knowledge and its application to the US economy clarifies greatly one of the important components of growth'. Robert Lekachman in *Political Science Quarterly* starts, with the kind of respectful gesture which was to become characteristic of the secondary literature on Machlup, by paying tribute to 'Professor Machlup's high reputation as an economic theorist' (1963: 467). Finding nothing to fault in Machlup's methodological platform, he concludes his eulogy with the words, 'seldom has a pioneering investigation of so complex a topic as a freshly defined industry received so elegant and so fascinating an initial treatment'.

However, the tribute which gave Machlup the greatest pleasure came from the eminent economist Kenneth Boulding, who felt compelled to 'underline the great importance and the pioneering nature of this study' (1963: 38). While noting that the statistics-based approach of *The Production and Distribution of Knowledge in the United States* 'could easily be mistaken for a simple exercise in national-income arithmetic', Boulding argued that this 'should not blind the reader to its revolutionary potential'. Indeed, he regarded the book as capable of completely refashioning economic thought: 'the very concept of a knowledge industry,' he claimed, 'contains enough dynamite to blast traditional economics into orbit'. Machlup himself was later to recall, with unconcealed satisfaction, that 'the most widely used attribute reviewers bestowed on my work was "pioneering" ' (1980: xxi). From the beginning, then, *The Production and Distribution of Knowledge in the United States* was hailed as a work of ambitious parameters, of outstanding originality, and of mould-breaking power – in short, it was seen as a classic.

Given such a warm matrix, it is perhaps not surprising that 'Machlup 1962' is regarded today by exponents of the information society thesis as being a source of almost unassailable authority, as what information scientists call a 'benchmark text', or, in the argot of modern literary criticism, a 'canonical work'. However, in spite of Machlup's evidently axial role in the information society thesis there have been very few detailed critiques of his position. To be sure, many books and articles on the information sector have been written, especially since Porat revived the Machlupian tradition in 1977, but they characteristically deal with the pioneer in a merely perfunctory or genuflectory, or at least generally affirmative, way, *presupposing* his ideas as opposed to *exposing* them to scrutiny. Even those offerings which seem to promise disciplined analyses, such as Frederick Williams's *Measuring the Information Society* (1988) and Raul Katz's *The Information Society: An International Perspective* (1988), are prone to disappoint in this respect. The former turns out to be a case study of the information sector in Texas. Katz's is of wider geographic reach, but it too does not question any of the basic propositions laid down by Machlup, instead assuming from the beginning that 'the research literature [had] provided substantial evidence [of] the emergence of a sizeable information-intensive sector' (1988: 3). All the rest, really, is exegesis: these authors, and many others like them, may argue over taxonomic minutiae, and debate whether industry *x* or occupation *y* should count as informational, but they are essentially tinkering with the model rather than testing it.[4]

Research papers which actually name Machlup in their titles also somehow fail to gauge his position, as two examples from the Library and Information Studies field will illustrate.[5] In 'Machlup's categories of knowledge as a framework for viewing library and information science history', Francis Miksa (1985) makes no attempt to ascertain the validity of Machlupian categories, proceeding instead to *apply* them in a conceptualisation of twentieth-century librarianship and the information revolution. Similarly, in 'Machlup and the information age' (1987), Richard Johnson, celebrating the twenty-fifth anniversary of the publication of *The Production and Distribution of Knowledge in the United States*, salutes it as a 'seminal work' in which evidence had been adduced to 'show the increasing importance of the knowledge industries'. Although Johnson refers to Machlup's arguments as 'tortuous' and 'excessively' detailed, this is the sum total of his criticism – if, indeed, to call a work of scholarship too detailed qualifies as serious criticism. He concludes that Machlup was a great pioneer who left an abidingly valuable legacy of tools and concepts for the 'information age' (Johnson 1987: 274–5).

The same pattern can be observed even in the most rigorous and critical medium of the 'info sphere', doctoral dissertations. Surprisingly, before 1980 not one PhD had addressed any aspect of Machlup's thought. That year saw the appearance of 'Trading in the marketplace of ideas: a contribution to the theory of production of knowledge' by Charles Sigismund. Using a case study methodology, Sigismund faithfully applied Machlup's theory to an analysis of how the invention and sale of a technique for synthesising musical tones might contribute to the American economy. Ten years later, Dong Yeong's dissertation on 'A sectoral analysis of the information sector in the information economy' (1990a) also assumed much, as can be plainly seen from the opening words of the research paper he published simultaneously:

> Recent empirical studies of advanced economies *indicate that* the information sector is the main source of national income, employment, and structural transformation. For example, in the United States it has been *demonstrated that* the information sector generates approximately half of the national income and employment.
>
> (Yeong 1990b: 230, my italic)

'Indicate that' and 'demonstrate that' are the coinage not of inquiry but of *fait accompli*: whatever refinements Yeong will go on to introduce, it is guaranteed that they will be largely predicated on Machlup's premises. Much the same can be said of other theses. A PhD on 'Knowledge and information occupations in Singapore: a country case study' (Valencia 1986), or an EdD on 'Perceptions of the impact of the information society on the poor' (Danjczek 1987), or even a DMin on 'Cogent preaching: effective ministry in an information society' from the prestigious Fuller Theological Seminary (McAnlis 1986), will, as their titles suggest, *utilise* Machlup-inspired concepts of the knowledge industry or information society as spring-boards for favoured theories and projects – they will not *scrutinise*. In short, Sigismund, Yeong, Valencia, and the others, like Porat (whose work also began life as a doctoral thesis), are *Machlupians*.[6]

The aim now is to remedy this state of affairs by devoting the bulk of Chapter 2 to an in-depth analysis of *The Production and Distribution of Knowledge in the United States*. I will look at what the pioneer actually said, rather than relay myths about what people think he said. How much does this text really supply in the way of evidence for what has become known as the information society thesis? What are the characteristic forms of Machlupian argumentation, and are they cogent or otherwise? Whose ideas does Machlup himself build upon, if anyone's? Such questions still need to be answered, and they can be answered only by a fresh examination of the primary source. The analysis offered below amounts more or less to a *commentary*, and so the treatment will be linear rather than thematic. There are admittedly disadvantages with this approach, especially where Machlup's own sequencing is less than lucid or logical; but they are outweighed, I trust, by the benefits which will accrue from a thorough textual analysis. For the time has come for Information Society Studies to move away from genuflections, generalisations, and applications, and instead to revisit the methodological and epistemological basics. It should be stressed that my critique is directed at one line – what was really only a side-line – of Machlup's thought: it does not have any bearing at all upon this eminent thinker's many contributions to mainstream economics.

Analysis of *The Production and Distribution of Knowledge in the United States*

Methodological and epistemological preliminaries

As the striking, almost shocking, title suggests, *The Production and Distribution of Knowledge in the United States* is a full-scale effort (400 pages in total) to evaluate knowledge-related activities from an economic point of view, to *valorise* them. It is credited, as we saw in the reviews, as the first such attempt, and it is largely the originality, the sheer boldness of the project, that has led to its canonisation. Machlup was well aware of the mould-breaking nature of his thesis, and in the opening chapters of his book does his best to set the stage for the counter-intuitive scenario of an economic treatment, not of monopolies or mergers or the automobile industry, but of *knowledge*. In the present section the key methodological and epistemological premises are scrutinised. While the examination is lengthy and at times highly detailed, it should be borne in mind that if the foundations of any intellectual edifice are not well laid, that edifice will, or should, eventually fall.

> Anything that goes under the name of 'production and distribution' sounds as if it clearly fell into the economist's domain. An analysis of 'knowledge', on the other hand, seems to be the philosopher's task, though some aspects of it are claimed by the sociologist …When I tried out the title of this study on representatives of various disciplines, many were rather surprised that an economist would find himself qualified to undertake this kind of research … If these things have to be explained, 'Let George do it.' George is always someone in another discipline.

This cheerful disclosure on the first page of *The Production and Distribution of Knowledge in the United States* reveals that the information society thesis, at least in the prototypical form in which it is here being advanced, is rooted in an interdisciplinary no-man's-land. Now what conclusions should be drawn? Interdisciplinarity is in some respects a great strength. For example, it enables the project to draw from multiple knowledge bases, from those Machlup has identified, namely economics, philosophy, and sociology, and from others unmentioned, such as librarianship, information science, and communication studies. However, interdisciplinarity can also be seen as *extra-territorialism*, as intellectual statelessness, which brings with it a risk that the information society thesis will not be subjected to academic standards comparable in rigour to those applied to truth-claims within mature 'stand-alone' disciplines. Specialists will be able to criticise particular aspects, but only a polymath could verify or falsify the thesis as a whole, and polymaths – of any disciplinary configuration – are rare. The point here is not to condemn *a priori* a new line of research, but simply to be realistic at the outset regarding the implications of its ambiguous academic basis. Machlup himself will adopt the role of 'George', and it would be irresponsible not to draw attention to the size of his self-appointed task and the inherent dangers.

Another matter which needs to be clarified as soon as possible is the meaning and scope of the term 'knowledge'. As noted above, the received wisdom holds that Machlup's book is the primary source of the information society thesis, but the book's title mentions *knowledge* rather than *information*. Something evidently needs to be said about why a text on one subject should inspire a school of thought apparently interested in a different subject. The quickest route from the one to the other would be straightforwardly to equate the terms in question, and this is indeed the path Machlup takes:

> I propose that we get rid of the duplication 'knowledge and information.' There are those who insist on distinguishing 'information' from 'knowledge,' for example, by having 'information' refer to the act or process by which knowledge (or a signal, a message) is transmitted. But even if the word is not used for the act of communicating but for the contents of the communication, one may want 'information' to refer to disconnected events or facts, and 'knowledge' to refer to an interrelated system (though others want to confer upon 'systematic' or 'ordered' knowledge the nobler title, 'science'). One author [the economist, Anthony Downs], for example, proposes to contrast 'knowledge,' or 'contextual knowledge,' which 'illuminates the basic causal structure of some field of operations' with 'information,' which 'provides current data on the variables in that field.' The specialist in 'information theory' [Warren Weaver] uses the word, as he frankly admits, in a 'rather strange way,' in 'a special sense which ... must not be confused at all with meaning.' To him, 'information is a measure of your freedom of choice when you select a message ... Thus greater freedom of choice, greater uncertainty and greater information all go hand in hand.' This concept serves a significant purpose in an important field, but it is not what is commonly meant by 'information.' Perhaps the fact that the special use of the word is becoming increasingly current should make it more desirable to use, whenever possible, the word 'knowledge' for the ordinary meaning of 'information.' *Webster's Dictionary* defines 'information' as 'knowledge communicated by others or obtained by personal study and investigation,' or alternatively as 'knowledge of a special event, situation or the like.' Hence, in these ordinary uses of the word, all information is knowledge.
>
> (Machlup 1962: 8, citing Downs 1957 and Weaver 1955)

This passage is quoted at length because it displays weaknesses which are characteristic of Machlupian argumentation. The critique can start by drawing attention to the brisk, no-nonsense tone. The pioneer was clearly under the impression that the matter of establishing the relations between knowledge and information could be sorted with a few strokes of his pen. He seems not to appreciate that such relations are exactly the kind of issue which has taxed partisans of one of the most profound philosophical specialisms, epistemology, for several millennia. Announcing a few pages on that he has effected a departure from his own discipline of economics, he asserts that he intends to 'linger with particular pleasure in some outlying fields', and implores 'the representatives of these fields of learning [to be] hospitable to the ingressions of a friendly outsider'. However, hospitality, even in its regular mundane context, is conditional upon a suitably humble deportment, and there is little in Machlup's approach to suggest this.

The truth is that professional epistemologists would be likely to eject the author of the foregoing quotation from their territory, and not without justification. For even if we excuse the tone, almost every sentence in the passage can be contested. Machlup begins by distancing himself from those who, in their endeavour to distinguish knowledge from information, 'insist' that information refers to the act or process of communicating knowledge. This makes 'information' into a process noun, like 'impartation' or, in one of its several senses, 'instruction' (as in 'the instruction of the young is a sacred duty of any society'). 'Knowledge' thus becomes the object of the act of 'information'. But this is surely an archaic and most unusual usage of the word 'information', and one which obviously makes information and knowledge incommensurable. The issue is not whether we should 'get rid of the duplication' of knowledge and information *qua* act or process, but whether we should get rid of the distinction between knowledge and information, both *qua* objects of communication. To suggest otherwise is to set up an easily demolished straw-man, a common rhetorical tactic, but one which does little to advance the cause of genuine inquiry.

Machlup's next target is those – he cites the economist Anthony Downs as an example – who equate information with 'disconnected events or facts' and knowledge with 'an interrelated system'. However, they do so quite justifiably, so what exactly is Machlup insinuating against these people? Taking his own example, the terms in which Downs's distinction is drawn seem to be eminently plausible. A scientist will typically discover and process a great deal of information – facts, figures, statistics – but his ultimate aim is surely 'knowledge', the placing of all of his or her findings and data into a context of theory and explanation. In ordinary parlance we do place knowledge 'above' information, and we see science as a special case of knowledge. We say that universities impart knowledge, and would look askance at any university which claimed only to communicate information. (The latter might, on the other hand, be the aim of a short training session, or of a particular lecture handout.) To suggest otherwise is to fly in the face of ordinary language – a very dangerous move which always needs a full defence.

Regarding the strangeness of Weaver's non-semantic definition of information

Machlup is correct. Ordinary language invariably associates information with meaning, and it is certainly to be regretted that the miscalled field of information theory has propagated a non-semantic rendition of the term. In fact, this rendition has become even more prevalent in the years since Machlup wrote, notably in the computing community: nowadays it is not uncommon to find someone referring to anything which can be converted into bits and bytes as 'information' – whether it be bibliographic references, Milton's prose, pornography, gobbledygook, lying propaganda, or any other kind of text or image. On such a view, somewhat absurdly, misinformation is as much 'information' as are factual truths. It is indeed the case that this is 'not what is commonly meant by "information"', not what the man on the Clapham omnibus would mean by it either in 1962 or today.

However, while Machlup is thus right to reject Weaver, the next sentences in the quoted passage contain, unfortunately, a robust *non sequitur*. From the fact that information theory has robbed 'information' of its semantic content, it does not at all follow that it is 'more desirable to use, whenever possible, the word "knowledge" for the ordinary meaning of "information"'. Whatever *Webster's Dictionary* may say, the fact is that speakers of ordinary English do *not* use these two terms synonymously. Rather than treat them as synonyms or even co-ordinates, ordinary language assumes, as I have just suggested, a firm conceptual hierarchy in which information is *subordinated* to knowledge. Data and wisdom can also be fitted naturally into this framework, as follows, in descending order of epistemic rank:

Wisdom
Knowledge (including Science)
Information
Data.

To use astronomy as an illustration, *data* might be the raw results of various space probes, *information* the reports in which such data are collated and packaged, *knowledge* the theoretical frameworks and equations into which the reports are absorbed, and *wisdom* the sensitive and timely use of the enhanced understanding of physical reality afforded by this new knowledge.

Anyway, Machlup goes on to stipulate that, for the purposes of his book, knowledge should incorporate not only 'that which is known' but also 'the state of knowing'. He readily concedes that, given this terminology, such everyday activities as talking, listening, and reading, which involve a 'state of knowing', are as much a part of the process of knowledge production and distribution as the record of scientific discovery and invention. Indeed, he explicitly resists any restriction to 'socially new knowledge' (Machlup 1962: 7), a term he accommodates inside what look very much like 'sneer quotes'. Even his admiring contemporary reviewers adverted to the stunningly wide parameters of Machlupian knowledge (e.g. Hunt 1965: 311); but none dared to criticise him, and one even praised him for his 'unacademic and unsnobbish' approach (Lekachman 1963: 467).[7] Should they not rather have asked whether the broad road might ultimately lead to destruction, or at least to obfuscation? The definition is so alien to ordinary language and common-sense intuitions that one of the main planks in Machlup's methodological platform must be regarded as *prima facie* shaky. We would surely have expected a much narrower definition, not necessarily one restricted to new empirical or scientific knowledge, but at least one which is not quite so epistemologically overpopulated. In short, by misappropriating the term 'knowledge', Machlup's bold 'terminological proposals' (1962: 7–8) could only make matters much worse than information theory had already made them.[8]

Having established, at least to his own satisfaction, an ecumenical epistemology, Machlup proceeds, in the first of an almost endless number of taxonomic manoeuvres, to split knowledge into five distinct types, namely: (1) 'practical knowledge', such as 'professional knowledge', 'business knowledge', 'workman's knowledge', and 'household knowledge'; (2) 'intellectual knowledge', including all of the arts and sciences; (3) 'small-talk and pastime knowledge', including light entertainment, jokes, and games; (4) 'spiritual knowledge'; and (5) 'unwanted knowledge', that is, knowledge 'acquired accidentally', such as television commercials and newspaper advertisements. Machlup contends that all of these are legitimate and computable components of knowledge production and distribution. However, even if they are reclassified in line with ordinary intuitions as, in many cases, species of information rather than knowledge, there will be misgivings about their suitability for treatment in any kind of thesis about economic or societal development. Two examples show this. Apropos of type (1), if household knowledge, i.e. knowledge of cooking and so on, is included, then, since most female labour in pre-industrial societies is devoted to household knowledge, many pre-industrial societies would appear to qualify as information societies. It does not help to say that post-industrial societies are unique in that their household knowledge alone is based on scientific principles, since, even if this is true (which is debatable), the problem with Machlup's position is precisely that it does not restrict the term knowledge to scientific knowledge or to applications of hard information.

A similar difficulty arises with regard to type (3). If all oral communications are allowed – if, for example, jokes and anecdotes are subsumed in information/ knowledge – it could easily follow that there is little that is distinctive from an informational point of view about modern societies. After all, do not most pre-modern societies spend much of their time talking and telling stories? This is certainly true, to take just one random example, of village life in contemporary Cameroon, so is Cameroon a society devoted to knowledge production – an information society? Indeed, on Machlup's premises, have we not had 'five thousand years of the information society' (Traue 1990)?

Thus, the problem is that if one sets out on ecumenical premises, many pre-modern societies would appear to stand a very good chance of qualifying as information societies, an outcome which is contrary to the trajectory of social development (agrarian–industrial–post-industrial) espoused by information society theorists. Of course, Machlup might reply that he has not said anything about post-industrialism, that the developmental trajectory was part of an additional set of claims which was overlaid upon his own by Daniel Bell and other co-opters of the knowledge industry thesis. There is certainly some truth in Johnson's assertion that 'Machlup did not describe changes in American society. His desire was more modest: to investigate the production of knowledge' (1987: 271). Nevertheless, it remains the case that if the Machlupian position is worth defending it must be saying something new and important about the modern world, and it is this which is *prima facie* undermined by the inclusion of age-old skills such as knowing how to cook dinner or to tell stories.

As its title indicates, the emphasis of the primary source is not knowledge *per se* but the *production* and *distribution* of knowledge. Machlup proceeds to invoke the economist's dogma that production is production if and only if ' "valuable input" is allocated to the bringing forth of "valuable output" ' (Machlup 1962: 36); and, as in traditional national-income accounting, he insists that an input 'counts' only if it has had at least an opportunity cost, and an output only if someone is willing to pay for it. This major definitional swerve has far-reaching implications, ruling out at a stroke many areas of human activity. For example, cooking must now be left out of 'knowledge production' unless it takes place within a commercial organisation. However, leaving to one side the *ethics* of dismissing summarily the bulk of human labour (female, unreported, unpaid), the pioneer's sudden appeal to the canons of accounting rectitude raises as many questions as it answers. If traditional economics in general, and national-income accounting conventions in particular, are to furnish the tools with which the knowledge sector is measured, it must be asked whether they are capable of fulfilling a function for which they were never designed.

Again, it might be objected that to impugn Machlup's methodology in this way is unreasonable: he was, after all, a pioneer who, before anyone else, 'discovered the information economy' (Nass 1987: 698). But I am questioning not his right to *innovate*, only his possibly over-hasty choice of *instrument*. The attempt to abstract a previously hidden item – knowledge/information – from the official statistics is not necessarily doomed to failure, but it is necessarily Procrustean. Perhaps – it is only a suggestion here – Machlup would have been wiser to develop entirely new measures of knowledge production, to begin not with the national accounts but with a *tabula rasa*? At the very least, we are entitled henceforth to look upon his chosen methodology as more akin to an original interpretation of a well-thumbed ancient text than to an experimental investigation.

It is clear, anyway, that the methodological approach of *The Production and Distribution of Knowledge in the United States* is basically statistical, in the sense of involving novel interpretations of economic data. It is salutary, therefore, to discover that this was virgin territory for Machlup. Many years later, while recounting the book's origins, he states that he 'had never before in [his] past work engaged in statistical investigations' (1980: xvii). But why was this not revealed in the book's preface, or anywhere else? Since 'statistical investigations' are not just important to but *constitutive of* the information sector version of the information society thesis, this belated admission is rather disconcerting. A majority of subsequent information society theorists have cited 'Machlup 1962' as their benchmark text and adopted, either entirely or largely, its methodology. Now it turns out that the pioneer was new not only to his subject matter – knowledge production – but also to the whole methodology by which he approached it. From one point of view, certainly, this adventurousness is laudable: the mainstream scholar leaves behind the security of his familiar fields to hazard all for the advancement of learning. However, given this highly irregular background, a question mark must hang over the *ex cathedra* mode in which the information society thesis is typically delivered.[9]

It is time now to condescend to particulars and examine closely the various industries regarded by Machlup as making up the information sector. As has already been said, there has hitherto been far too much generalising and summarising and assuming in Information Society Studies. It is not until we have isolated what a theorist actually counts as a concrete item of evidence for his (the leading information society theorists have indeed all so far been male) thesis that we will be able to judge whether or not his overall case is convincing, and this is *a fortiori* true of the primary source. The programme of analysis will follow Machlup's own classification of what he keeps insisting on calling the 'knowledge industries': education, research and development, communication media, information machines, and information services.

Education

'Perhaps the finest portion of this volume,' Lekachman enthused (1963: 468), 'is the long *virtuosic* chapter on education which displays the talents of interpretation and advocacy for which the author is equally famous among his fellows'. A more dispassionate spectator might, to the contrary, be rather disappointed that the first of Machlup's knowledge industries, and the one, moreover, which will account for the lion's share of total knowledge production, is the prosaic and all-too-familiar world of education. However, Lekachman's observation regarding the pioneer's 'unusual gift for taxonomy' cannot be disputed. Education is divided into no fewer than eight types: (1) education at home; (2) education in school; (3) training on the job; (4) instruction in church; (5) training in the armed forces; (6) educational television; (7) self-education; and (8) learning from experience. But then, in a characteristic sudden reverse manoeuvre, Machlup eliminates types (7) and (8), on the grounds that they do not necessitate a teacher or instructor. While he concedes the obvious point that his parameters are still much wider than those employed in 'most discussions of education', which are of course confined to education in school, he nevertheless argues that all of the remaining categories involve 'resource allocation', and must therefore be included (Machlup 1962: 52). Let us begin, however, with school education.

School education

Machlup maintains that the cost of formal education cannot simply be a matter of totalling the official figures for primary, secondary, and tertiary institutions, but must also, as with education in the home, include the implicit opportunity costs, in this case earnings foregone by students (which in US parlance subsumes older school children), cost of tax exemptions, and so on. As can be seen in Table 2.1, school education accounted for a huge proportion of the total education bill, causing the other education types to pale into insignificance. Thus, while education in the home and in the army cost $4,432 million and $3,410 million respectively in 1958, the figure for higher education alone in the same year was $12,757 million, and for total school education, $46,831 million. Education as a whole, including earnings foregone by mothers and students, represented 11.8 per cent of US GNP in 1956 and 12.9 per cent in 1958.

Now while schooling at all levels is obviously an economic and social function of importance in mature societies, we should perhaps make an effort to narrow the focus to the *kind* of schooling which is particularly significant in such societies. This really means higher education, for whereas all societies have rudimentary educational systems for children, it is only the more advanced ones that formally educate adults – as opposed to just training them for war or trade. Perhaps sensing this, Machlup marshals statistical evidence to the effect that higher education in the USA had been expanding for many decades. Table 2.2 demonstrates the dramatic increase in the proportion of young people enrolled in higher education institutions in the USA, which had gone from 1.7 per cent of 18–21-year-olds in 1870 to 33.5 per cent in 1960. We are told that expenditure on higher education multiplied 135 times between 1900 and 1960, while GNP increased a mere twenty-nine times. Machlup also supplies data to the effect that the intellectual level within higher education was escalating: in 1870 only one doctorate was awarded in the whole of the United States, representing a minuscule 0.01 per cent of bachelor's degrees, while in 1960, 9,700 were awarded, making up 2.4 per cent of bachelor's degrees. Leaving aside all the tendentious imputations concerning 'earnings foregone by students', it seems that we are now being provided with the right calibre of ammunition for an information society thesis.

Non-school education

One of the most surprising inclusions in the pioneer's scheme is home education. Machlup notes that this is normally omitted from national accounts on the grounds that it has no costs, that is, no payments are made for it; but he argues that it cannot be dismissed because, although *monetary* payments are not involved, there is an *opportunity* cost:

Table 2.1 Summary of total cost of education, 1956 and 1958 (in millions of dollars) (from Machlup 1962: 104–5)

	1956	1958
Education in the home		
Income foregone by mothers educating pre-school children	4,341	4,432
Training on the job		
Formal training programmes operated by firms	800	1,000
Production loss and cost of training newly hired workers	1,940	2,054
Total	2,740	3,054
Education in the church		
Current congregational expenses	1,400	1,588
New construction of churches and synagogues	775	879
Total	2,175	2,467
Education in the armed forces		
Total	3,410	3,410
Elementary and secondary education		
Current expenditures	9,863	12,358
Plant expansion	2,748	3,290
Implicit rent	2,200	2,744
Cost of tax exemptions	920	1,022
Earnings foregone by high-school students	11,211	13,519
Transportation, supplies, and clothing	336	406
Total	27,278	33,339
Higher education		
Current expenditures	2,283	2,900
Plant expansion	686	1,122
Implicit rent	712	808
Cost of tax exemptions	302	317
Earnings foregone by college and university students	6,283	7,189
Transportation, supplies, and clothing	368	421
Total	10,634	12,757
Commercial vocational and residential schools		
Total	219	253
Federal funds for education		
Funds not elsewhere included (various training programmes, etc.)	241	342
Public libraries		
Operating expenses	122	140
Capital outlays	12	n.a.
Total	134	140
Grand total	51,172	60,194

Source: Not given by Machlup, but the data presumably derived from US Office of Education, *Biennial Survey of Education*, and similar titles

n.a., not available

Table 2.2 Enrolment in institutions of higher education, compared with total population, 1870–1960 (from Machlup 1962: 78)

| Year | Population (resident) | | | Enrolment in institutions of higher education | | | | | |
| | Total | Age 18–21 | | Total | | Public | | Non-public | |
	(thousands) (1)	(thousands) (2)	% of (1) (3)	(thousands) (4)	% of (2) (5)	(thousands) (6)	% of (2) (7)	(thousands) (8)	% of (2) (9)
1870	39,905	3,116	7.8	52	1.7	n.a.	—	n.a.	—
1880	50,262	4,253	8.5	116	2.7	n.a.	—	n.a.	—
1890	63,056	5,160	8.2	157	3.0	n.a.	—	n.a.	—
1900	76,094	6,131	7.9	238	3.9	91	1.5	147	2.4
1910	92,407	7,254	7.9	355	4.9	167	2.3	189	2.6
1920	106,466	7,869	7.0	598	7.6	315	4.0	282	3.6
1930	123,077	9,369	7.3	1,101	11.8	533	5.7	568	6.1
1940	131,954	9,845	7.4	1,494	15.2	797	8.1	698	7.1
1950	151,234	8,439	5.8	2,297	27.2	1,154	13.7	1,142	13.5
1952	155,761	8,728	5.2	2,148	24.6	1,113	12.8	1,035	11.9
1954	161,191	9,002	5.0	2,500	27.8	1,395	15.5	1,105	12.3
1956	167,259	9,536	5.0	2,947	30.9	1,682	17.6	1,265	13.3
1958	173,260	10,629	5.1	3,259	30.7	1,912	18.0	1,346	12.7
1960	180,126	11,204	5.3	3,750	33.5	2,210	19.7	1,540	12.9

Source: US Bureau of the Census, *Current Population Reports* and US Office of Education, *Biennial Survey of Education*

n.a., not available

> The mothers who stay at home to 'bring up' their children have to forego the income they could earn otherwise. The sacrifice of this alternative use of their time is the cost, social as well as private, of education in the home.
>
> (Machlup 1962: 53)

He then duly proceeds to try to estimate the income foregone by child-rearing mothers, arriving at the enormous figure of $4,432 million for 1958. Unfortunately, there are very serious methodological problems with this chain of reasoning.

First, an apparent inconsistency should be identified. If Machlup wants to include the opportunity costs of education in the home, we must call into question his prior dismissal of self-education as a candidate for quantification: self-education surely involves extensive opportunity costs since many of those who engage in it either choose, or are forced, to forego productive labour, at least for part of their time. Second, and taking up a point I made earlier, there are disturbing ramifications for the information society thesis in general: if opportunity costs are to be accommodated in the analysis of modernity they must also – if they are not to give rise to a charge of special pleading – be accounted for in pre-modern societies. Finally, it is debatable whether opportunity costing should in principle be a weapon in the armoury of an innovative economic or socio-economic thesis, even given a consistent application and a disregard for any knock-on effects for the theory of social development. It simply seems too nebulous, too counterfactual, to support the kind of weight being placed upon it. What a pioneering thesis surely requires is as solid a foundation of data as can be acquired, rather than a heavy reliance on dubious hypotheticals. Put bluntly, this particular manoeuvre looks too much like a clutching at straws, and it is worth noting that Porat, despite his loyalty to Machlup's 'basic insights and concepts', recognised that the argument from opportunity costs should be foregone (1977: 44–5).

Training on the job is less amorphous than education in the home, but it too suffers from a conspicuous lack of hard statistics. *Faute de mieux*, Machlup is constrained to argue from the estimates of various unrelated research reports. Since inductive reasoning of this kind is common in his writings (and that of his followers), it may be helpful to quote another fairly extensive excerpt:

> Mincer [one of Machlup's sources] seems inclined to rely on a survey in New Jersey, according to which approximately 5 per cent of all employees participated in formal training ... Applying the New Jersey percentages to the entire country, Mincer believes that the formal training programs by US business firms may have cost between $2,000 and $3,000 million in 1958. I doubt that the New Jersey findings are representative, chiefly because the types of industries located in New Jersey are too dissimilar from the national pattern ... My first estimate of the 1958 cost of formal training programs by US businesses was only $335 million. This may have been an underestimate, which I am now prepared to correct, but I cannot

persuade myself that the cost was more than $1,000 million in 1958. To indicate my judgment that there is a rising trend in this sort of undertaking, I make my 1956 estimate of the cost of formal training programs in business firms $800 million.

(Machlup 1962: 60)

The pervasiveness in this transcript of the language of impression and estimation is unsettling. It could be rewritten thus:

Mincer was wrong to generalise from his one-off survey of New Jersey, and his 1958 figure for the USA, namely $2,000 to $3,000 million, is therefore much too high. However, seeing his figure makes me suspect that my own initial estimate of $335 million was much too low. So let's more or less split the difference, and call it $1,000 million.

Now what value can such argumentation have in an academic treatise – some, much, or none? It would be draconian to proscribe it completely, even where the author, by his own admission, 'had never before engaged in statistical investigations'. The answer is perhaps that, while guesses and generalisations may legitimately play *some* role in a pioneering work, this particular pioneer gives every indication of a propensity to *overuse* them, and to be much too cavalier in the way that he goes about it. Machlup did later make a considerable effort to improve some of his estimates, for example in the three volumes of a research-based work entitled *Information through the Printed Word: The Dissemination of Scholarly, Scientific, and Intellectual Knowledge* (Machlup *et al.* 1978). However, in terms of the development of the information society thesis, these and other later works were of little significance: it is to *The Production and Distribution of Knowledge in the United States* alone that canonical status has been given, and it is essential therefore to ascertain whether the arguments presented in that book can stand up by themselves to criticism.

That the pioneer of the information society thesis was happy to boldly venture where statistically minded angels might fear to tread is also evident in his treatment of church education. Machlup notes that despite the American constitution's separation of church and state, many state schools have religious foundations, making it difficult to determine what exactly is to count as church instruction. Nevertheless, he affirms that, 'having declared that a distinction can hardly be made, we shall of course proceed to make one' (Machlup 1962: 65). Let us pause again for a moment and ask, was that poetic licence? If it is, what is it doing in a supposedly scientific volume, and if it is not, why is Machlup proceeding with the impossible? After this unpropitious start, his next move plunges the argument into further murkiness. 'We shall not,' he informs us, 'attempt to distinguish religious instruction in a narrow sense of the word from religious activities in general'. What he actually means by this is that *all monies spent on churches and church activities will be counted as educational outlays*. It is again highly revealing to watch some of the reasoning:

Some perfectionists might contend that sermons are educational while prayers and hymns are not. But apart from the fact that it would be hard to split the cost of religious services between sermons and other phases of worship and liturgical proceedings, it would be narrowmindedness to accept singing in the school [Machlup includes this under school education] but reject singing in the church as part of the educational process.

(Machlup 1962: 65)

However, as this critique has already been at pains to show, scientific rigour, which is what Machlup really means here by perfectionism, is precisely what the information sector version of the information society thesis has always needed; and scientific rigour would surely not count hymn singing – in either school or church – as educational in any tolerably relevant sense. Put more formally, Machlup's argument is that if we accept p (singing in school), we must accept q (singing in church); now p certainly entails q; however, p should be rejected.

Alongside the doubts that must be engendered by the recklessness with which Machlupian argumentation advances, another strong objection materialises at this point, one whose structure has already been encountered in the references to various household activities as candidates for knowledge production. Machlup is in the process of providing grounds for the claim that the economic role of education is increasing in modern societies, a claim which will be adopted *mutatis mutandis* by most subsequent information society theorists. But if religious education – and religious activities as a whole – are included then many pre-industrial societies will surely count as information societies. In most ancient societies life was built around the temple, so does this entail that Solomonic Israel, say, was an information society? The same question can of course be posed on behalf of the radical Islamic societies of today. To raise such questions is again to suggest that some of the weapons taken up by Machlup will turn out to be double-edged. A broad definition of key words like education or knowledge may indeed help to advance the thesis that the USA has a knowledge-centred economy or that it is an information society, but only at the conceptually (and politically?) unacceptable cost of conferring information society status on many other social species. We might end up not with *technocracy* but with *theocracy*, an unpalatable result, one would imagine, for the prophets of a new epoch.

Educational television (ETV), however, seems much more conducive to cogent information society thesis-making. Machlup postpones his discussion of ETV until his chapter on communication media, and there we find him enthusiastically detailing a wide range of initiatives in 'in-school TV', 'community TV', and so on. He is clearly most impressed by the scale of this activity, for example by the fact that a course in physics, telecast over 157 stations at 6.30 a.m., was supposedly watched by no fewer than 400,000 people, including at least half of the country's science teachers. If such successes continue, he forecasts, 'the present emphasis of commercial TV on producing pastime knowledge in the form of popular entertainment may eventually give way to a distribution of broadcasting time that gives a better chance to the production of intellectual knowledge' (Machlup 1962: 264). However, this is practically all he says about ETV, and it is by no means enough. The forecast was of course wrong: 'intellectual' television has been in constant retreat and is now virtually non-existent in the USA. But that is merely a regrettable historical contingency, and the deeper conceptual point which Machlup seemed to be missing is that ETV is precisely the type of activity which could fuel a thesis about knowledge production in the world's most technologically advanced economy near the end of the second millennium. Instead of clutching at methodological straws like the 'opportunity costs' of mothers bringing up children or the singing of hymns in church or school, the pioneer ought, arguably, to have wielded this robust weapon to the full. Not for the last time, he seems to let go of a golden opportunity.

Research and development

In the Machlupian taxonomy, research and development (R&D) is the second branch of knowledge production. Here, in the primary source, disparate quantitative data relating to R&D are collated for the first time under the rubric 'knowledge industry'. Although Machlup had conflated *production* and *distribution* in order to 'save words' (1962: 7), in this context, at least, they are best kept apart. For unlike primary and secondary education and, indeed, much of what goes on in tertiary education, and unlike most of the other branches yet to be discussed, R&D is specially concerned with creation, with the *production* of knowledge. The pioneer admits that his definitional parameters are here markedly less bloated than those with which his project started: they encompass, as he puts it, only 'knowledge-production in the narrow sense', that is, the production of 'socially new knowledge' – specifically, 'new knowledge about how things are, or how things could be made' (1962: 145). It has been claimed recently (Schement and Curtis 1995: 72) that Machlup 'experienced difficulty in defining the production of "new knowledge" ', but there is no evidence of this in the text, nor is his conception of knowledge in the narrow sense *intrinsically* problematic. On the contrary, it is, as has already been argued, the broader Machlupian way that is counter-intuitive, and an instinctive reaction to this epistemological retreat in the direction of ordinary language is therefore likely to be sympathetic.

Following established practice, Machlup divides R&D into the three main categories of basic research, applied research, and development. He then proves that he knew the work of at least one of the other thinkers now considered to have been a pioneer of information science, by quoting Vannevar Bush's definition of basic research as that which 'results in general knowledge and an understanding of nature by its laws' (Machlup 1962: 146, citing Bush 1945). As can be seen from Table 2.3, this accounted in 1958 for 6 per cent of the total 'conduct' of US R&D expenditure (i.e. expenditures excluding costs of

Table 2.3 Federal government obligations for research and development, by character of work, 1958–60 (from Machlup 1962: 155)

Character of work	1958 Expenditure (million dollars)	% of expenditure on 'total conduct'	1959 Expenditure (million dollars)	% of expenditure on 'total conduct'	1960 Expenditure (million dollars)	% of expenditure on 'total conduct'
Basic research	331	6.0	488	6.7	494	6.4
Applied research	703	12.7	956	13.2	1,109	14.4
Development	4,320	78.0	5,592	77.3	5,903	76.7
Military personnel[a]	188	3.4	197	2.7	195	2.5
Total conduct of R&D	5,542	100.0	7,233	100.0	7,701	100.0
Expansion of R&D plant	336	6.1	662	9.2	447	5.8
Total obligations for R&D	5,878	106.1	7,895	109.2	8,148	105.8

Source: National Science Foundation, Federal Funds for Science

[a] The pay and allowances of military personnel engaged in research and development are not broken down by the character of work

plant expansion), a proportion which went up to 6.7 per cent in 1959 and then fell back slightly to 6.4 per cent in 1960. In the same year, 14.4 per cent of R&D expenditure went on applied research, defined as research concerned with 'results which promise to be of ultimate use in practice'. But by far the greatest part of the R&D budget, at 76.7 per cent in 1960, was spent at the practical 'development' end of the research process, much of it in high-technology industries like aircraft and chemicals. As regards the magnitude of the combined sums involved, Machlup quotes figures going back to 1920: in that year $80 million was spent, representing 0.09 per cent of GNP; this increased to $377 million in 1940, or 0.37 per cent of GNP; and to $14,000 million in 1960, amounting to 2.68 per cent of US GNP.

Machlup himself acknowledges the crudity of the calculations with which figures for R&D expenditure are derived, and indeed feels compelled to issue a particularly strong caveat that 'the user should never forget the questionable origin of the data' (1962: 156). Similar qualifications also permeate his ensuing discussion of the growth of the research scientist community. Thus, a single paragraph from page 160 contains all of the following locutions: 'probably', 'forgetting all caution', 'do not seem', 'cannot have', 'probably' (again), 'admittedly', 'must have been' (which of course usually means that an adventurous inference is being attempted), 'may possibly', 'not likely', 'can happen', 'sometimes', 'it *may* happen'. However, let us assume for the sake of argument that the R&D totals are credible. I wish now to suggest that the pioneer's way of interpreting them – his gloss – is curiously ineffective.

Machlup speaks enthusiastically of 'the enormous growth of R&D, from "early times" – twenty or thirty years ago – to the present', of growth which 'has certainly been phenomenal' (1962: 151, 155). However, apart from a throwaway suggestion that such increases may be evidence of a 'new research-mindedness' in the United States, he actually has very little to say about the societal significance of R&D, and his chapter on this branch of knowledge production is shorter than the rest. His underlying difficulty, of course, is that the figures for R&D, even the most recent, are more or less negligible from the point of view of their percentage share of total knowledge production, and, *a fortiori*, of total US GNP – only 2.68 per cent in 1960, for example. Indeed, R&D amounted, in quantitative terms, to considerably less than one-fifth of the value of the education branch, and basic research on its own to less than half that of church education.

Thus, in order to support statements about a knowledge economy, or even just tentative suggestions about a budding research consciousness, a quite different approach is required. The counting-house methodology has to give way. The focus needs to move from quantity to quality, so that the *intrinsic* importance of R&D can be exploited. Indeed, would one not *prima facie* have expected a book with the title *The Production and Distribution of Knowledge in the United States*, published in the early 1960s, to be *entirely* about R&D? This does not mean that one would have expected such a book to claim that every modern American is a scientist or a technician; one would have expected it, rather, to try to argue that research in its various phases had become something like the *essence* or the *engine* of the US economy. Michael Young, in his brilliant fantasy *The Rise of the Meritocracy* (1958), had foreseen a 'Technicians' Party' coming to prominence. Machlup seems to miss the point, for instead of lingering over his figures for R&D, he rushes on to talk about his next, bigger (and therefore better?), 'branch' of 'knowledge production'. One cannot help feeling that, as with ETV, he squandered a golden opportunity to say something interesting about the modern world.

It is instructive briefly to contrast Machlup's treatment of R&D with Daniel Bell's. Bell will (as detailed in Chapter 5) make a great deal of the significance of these bald statistics. Rather than simply tabulating and totalling figures, he will venture to elicit their *meaning* for modern societies, and will emphasise in particular the epochal importance of pure research, or what he will call 'theoretical knowledge'. Whereas Machlup merely notes the increase in the number of research workers in America, Bell, going to the opposite extreme, will use similar data as a cue for speaking of the scientific community as 'the most crucial group in the knowledge society', as 'the chief resource of the post-industrial society', and even as having a 'messianic role'. Now it is not being suggested that all of Bell's interpretations are accurate. On the contrary, I will argue that some of them are demonstrably unsustainable, as any reference to messianic roles should immediately indicate. Nevertheless, a focus on the social role of research is surely correct, in the sense that the theory of advanced societies must allocate to *this* type of knowledge production a privileged place. If a thinker is going to say anything important about the second half of the twentieth century he or she will have to emphasise 'R&D' – both 'R' on its own and how 'R' has been systematically utilised in 'D' and in the technologies and machines that have changed our lives. Webster points out that 'the enthusiasm of the information economists to put a price tag on everything has the unfortunate consequence of failing to let us know the really valuable dimensions of the information sector' (1995: 13). Indeed – but perhaps it was inevitable that, in the matter of discerning the signs of the times as opposed to merely plotting them, the economist had to hand over to the sociologist?

Communication media

If, as was argued above, whole swathes of what Machlup includes under education have to be discounted, and if R&D, even on his own estimates, counts for so little, his thesis about a knowledge sector clearly still has a long way to go. The next branch of knowledge production is communication media. Defining communication as 'the conveying of knowledge' (1962: 207), Machlup immediately concedes that this is another very broad term which could overlap with education (the communication of knowledge for a particular purpose) and other aspects of his knowledge sector: 'indeed,' he opines, 'almost the entire book' is about communication. Now this too is problematic. If 'Machlup's view of information does not distinguish it from communication' (Schement and Curtis 1995: 3), we seem to have further confirmation that the underlying concept of information is far too nebulous. While it is perfectly in order to explore the links between information and communication (e.g. Martin 1995), it is surely a mistake to use the term 'communicative society' as a synonym for 'information society' (e.g. Stonier 1985). Information is clearly distinguishable from communication, information being the *object* and communication the *vehicle*, *process* or *channel* through which information passes from one subject to another. No matter how we wish to define knowledge or information – whether as socially new R&D, as in analyses of research communication by information scientists (e.g. Meadows 1998), or, as with Machlup and his school, very much more widely, or perhaps as a half-way house between these poles – the fundamental distinction between node and channel must hold. The running together of the two is thus yet another 'terminological proposal' which is unlikely to inspire confidence in those who care to read Machlup's book closely. Let us see, however, which media he has in mind. These he divides into print and non-print. Since a large number of items are included in each category, the following comments will have to be very selective.

Print media

We may begin with books, as the best-known print medium. From the point of view of later information society thinking, we would expect Machlup to have adduced startling and compelling evidence of massive growth in this area of the economy. Instead, we face a great hermeneutical upset, for, far from emerging as a reporter of the information explosion, the first fact that Machlup discloses is that 'the number of books published was greater in 1914 than in any year thereafter until 1953', and that, even as late as 1959, the number was 'not more than 24 per cent above that of 1914 (whereas population had increased by 78 per cent and GNP by 988 per cent)' (Machlup 1962: 208). In other words, there has been no information explosion in the USA. This is upsetting in two ways. First, the doctrine of the information explosion, while logically distinct from that of the information sector, is, as a matter of contingent fact, usually bound up with it. Hence it is very surprising to read of a society which was simultaneously undergoing an expansion of the information or knowledge sector and a contraction of the publishing industry. Second, it is especially surprising that the USA was the subject of these countervailing trends. Of course, America is not nowadays considered to be the only information society, and book production in the UK, France, and other European countries was, as Machlup himself points out, much higher (as it still is today). Nevertheless, there is a problem for the information society thesis, for according to the standard, and at least partly Machlup-inspired, exposition of that thesis, the USA was the first country to become an information society, and is, either by implication or by explicit argument, a model of the emerging global socio-economic order. The awkward question is thus: does it make sense to call a country which apparently cannot even produce as many books as nations a quarter of its size a 'knowledge society' or 'information society'?

Moreover, it is not as though the figures on book production are portrayed as being atypical. Machlup seems to go out of his way to kill off all notions of an information explosion. Thus, addressing the oft-repeated claim that 'knowledge doubles every ten years', he evinced a scathing scepticism:

> I suppose that what the author of this statement meant when he said 'knowledge' was the number of books accumulated in the libraries. This would be a very misleading index of knowledge, or even of book knowledge. The same subject matter is covered in many books with only slight variations in exposition; it is repeated over and over again in varied form for different audiences. And when what was first printed is later found to be false or inaccurate, new propositions replace the old ones – which are removed from the accepted body of knowledge – but the books in which the new propositions are published are added to those which contain the old ones. We do not destroy old books, fortunately; but to include them in a count of the 'stock of knowledge' is highly misleading.
>
> (Machlup 1962: 122)

One line of defence against this attack would be to argue that it is not in books but in some other medium that the information explosion is to be found, two likely candidates being patents and journals; but Machlup gives no comfort there either. In his discussion of R&D, he had made a point of demonstrating that there had been a *decline* in patenting in America since the 1920s, relative to total R&D expenditures and other relevant magnitudes (1962: 170–4). Similarly, and almost incredibly – research papers in scholarly journals are cited as the main evidence in most arguments for the information explosion (e.g. Lancaster 1978; Goffman and Warren 1980) – he pours cold water on the widely held belief in a journal explosion. Table 2.4, culled from sources like the *Annual Report of the Librarian of Congress*, is presented in order to give the lie to notions of 'exponential' growth. Indeed, Machlup states unequivocally that the number of periodicals had declined in recent decades, and concludes that 'all in all, the growth in the distribution of periodicals, though better than for books, has been poor compared with that of some other products of knowledge industries' (1962: 220).

Now it is probable that, notwithstanding his impeccable sources, Machlup was underestimating the quantitative dimensions of serial information. The prevalence of 'n.a.' (not available) in Table 2.4 is an indication that at the time of writing *The Production and Distribution of Knowledge in the United States* he had not really researched this phenomenon very thoroughly. Moreover, as noted above, he later greatly improved some of his estimates, especially in the areas normally associated with the information explosion: volumes 1–3 of the collaborative work with Kenneth Leeson and others (1978), devoted, respectively, to book publishing, journal publishing, and library holdings, are among the most detailed and comprehensive surveys of their subjects in existence. However, my crucial point remains that in the *primary source* of the

Table 2.4 Periodicals: numbers of titles, issues, and copies distributed, and receipts from sales, subscriptions, and advertising, 1910–59 (from Machlup 1962: 219)

			Circulation (millions)		Receipts (millions of dollars)		
Year	No. of periodicals published (1)	No. of issues copyrighted (2)	Sum of averages per issue (3)	Average circulation × no. of issues per year (4)	Total (5)	Sales and subscriptions (6)	Advertising (7)
1910	n.a.	21,608	n.a.	n.a.	n.a.	n.a.	n.a.
1914	n.a.	24,134	n.a.	n.a.	136	64	72
1919	4,796	25,083	n.a.	n.a.	240	85	155
1929	5,157	44,161	202	4,196	507	185	323
1939	4,985	38,307	240	5,865	409	185	224
1947	4,610	58,340	385	6,848	1,019	407	612
1950	n.a.	55,436	n.a.	n.a.	1,119	470	648
1954	3,427	60,667	449	7,767	1,413	531	882
1956	n.a.	58,576	n.a.	n.a.	n.a.	n.a.	n.a.
1958	n.a.	60,691	n.a.	n.a.	1,588	557	1,031
1959	n.a.	62,246	n.a.	n.a.	n.a.	n.a.	n.a.

Source: US Department of Commerce, *US Census of Manufactures*; Library of Congress, *Annual Report of the Librarian of Congress* and *Annual Report of the Register of Copyrights*

n.a., not available

information sector version the information explosion is denied. Whether or not there is additional evidence against his statements is irrelevant to this investigation: what is being underlined here is the uncomfortable fact that *the information explosion is not only not cited as part of the case for the information sector, it is rejected outright.* The moral seems to be not only that there is a plurality of strands of information society thinking, but also that these strands, once disentangled, do not necessarily pull in the same direction.

Non-print media

Machlup also attempts to quantify trends in many non-print media, ranging from theatre to telephony. He collates enough information regarding expenditure on theatre to be able to opine that it 'is not a well-developed branch of knowledge production in the United States', again especially when compared with some European countries (Machlup 1962: 243). This is worth quoting to remind us of how odd, how radical, Machlup's way of speaking is. Our ordinary intuitions, it is suggested, are more or less as follows. We do see the stage as a *bona fide* communication medium, but to see it as *knowledge production* is to see it in a truly different light. Yet we do not, upon reflection, feel constrained to reject this interpretation, probably because we do regard many plays and operas as at least minimally educational. However, when the pioneer moves on to include figures for spectator sports, i.e. baseball, boxing and so on, as equally aspects of communication *qua* knowledge production, we feel that he has definitely parted company with our intuitions. 'It would be ridiculous,' Machlup writes, 'to exclude from our survey a ball game seen in attendance, but to include it when it is seen on television or read about in newspapers'. But the answer to this argument is, of course, that newspaper and television reporting of the ball game should never have been counted in the first place, not because they do not constitute communication, but because they do not amount to knowledge. In formal logic we are, as with singing in church, facing the argument 'if p then q' – and again we must reject p.

Not surprisingly, those dominant twentieth-century mass media, radio and television, are reported as having witnessed 'some of the largest growth rates encountered in this study' (Machlup 1962: 251). The statistics do not need to be rehearsed, but one remark is in order. The blurring of the lines between information and mass communication poses a particular problem for the information society thesis. For a long time, these media have been the subject of academic fields like Communication Studies (sometimes called Communication Science) and Media Studies – and now also Cultural Studies. If information society theorists wish to talk about radio and television, in what way are they going to be saying anything different from the scholars of these neighbouring fields? It would be wrong here to lay any serious charges at Machlup's door. He was neither a professional information scientist nor a communication scholar, but rather an economist of above-average adventurousness. As the founder of what later came to be called the information society thesis, he could not have been expected to pre-empt all subsequent demarcation disputes. Nevertheless, it is worth registering that the parameters of the information sector laid down in *The Production and Distribution of Knowledge in the United States* were so wide and so elastic that they were bound to bequeath disciplinary squabbles.

Machlup also makes much of telephony as a modern communication medium. *The Production and Distribution of Knowledge in the United States* pre-dated, and failed to predict, the development of telematics, but its author's perceptions of the socio-economic status of telephones – even today we 'don't really know very much about the social uses of the telephone' (Schement and Curtis 1995: 50) – are still worth recording. Machlup was pleased to be able to say that in this branch of knowledge production, at least, his country was the world leader:

> So far as the number of telephones is concerned, the United States is ahead not only of every single country in the world but also of all of them taken together ... In 1958 the numbers were 67 million in the United States (including Alaska and Hawaii) and 58 million in the rest of the world.
>
> (Machlup 1962: 277)

However, can even a macro-economist seriously believe that the USA's deficit in books and plays can in any sense be compensated for by a surplus in telephone calls? It is not as if American calls were likely to be transmitting vast quantities of intellectual knowledge. On the contrary, Machlup himself estimates that they mainly involve practical and pastime knowledge, but comments that the high proportion of telephonic trivia 'does not "depreciate" the role of the telephone in our lives; indeed, it is part of the high standard of living of the American people – male as well as female'. Again, we are moved to ask, chorus-like, what significance the communication of chit-chat can have for an economics of knowledge production and distribution, and *a fortiori* for a more far-reaching information society thesis? And again, if *that* is what Machlup's book is about, how would telecommunications distinguish the contemporary USA from the talkative Red Indian culture it brutally displaced?

Finally, some comments will be made on Machlup's inclusion of conferences, or what he calls 'conventions', as a species of non-print communication media. Like their famous predilection for telephoning one another, Americans' well-known propensity to associate would be likely to contribute comparative statistics of a type conducive to Machlupian goals. Still, we cannot but be disconcerted by the manner in which he came upon the idea of including conventions:

> I am indebted to Robert W. Michie, Vice-President of the Chesapeake and Potomac Telephone Companies, for suggesting the inclusion of this topic in the survey of the production of knowledge. Mr Michie also kindly sent me a copy of *Conventions: An American Institution*, which is the source of the quantitative information in this section.
>
> (Machlup 1962: 291)

This attribution is more than a little instructive in what it discloses about the haphazardness of the methodological foundations of the information sector version, one might almost say their *arbitrariness*. Is it the way of sound science to act on the casual suggestions of telephone company vice-presidents? Even if this kind of serendipity is permissible, it is at any rate not unreasonable to expect an empirical scientist to calibrate and corroborate the 'quantitative information' contained in a monograph which someone happens to have posted to him, and moreover one with a faintly propagandistic title; but Machlup does no such thing. Can we allow even a *pioneer* such licence? Perhaps he should have called his work something along the lines of *Notes Towards an Economics of Knowledge* (or, ideally, *of Information*). Had he done so, 'Machlup 1962' would probably not have come to be regarded as a sacred text, and we would have been spared some of the unthinking obeisance in which the information society literature today abounds.

This is not to imply that all conference activity should be banished from the knowledge sector. On the contrary, the conferences of learned associations are a forum which has always been of interest both to information scientists and to sociologists of knowledge. As is his wont, however, Machlup spoils the picture by incorporating not merely learned conferences but the convocations of all other types of organisation as well, ranging from the American Medical Association to the Masons, and from the American Association of University Professors to the Camp Fire Girls: the purpose of all of these can, he assures us, be 'characterized as the dissemination and exchange of knowledge'. Citing the book lent to him by Michie, he states that in 1957, 20,000 conferences were attended in the USA, by a total of 10 million persons, and that the total expenditure incurred was around $1,600 million (Machlup 1962: 292–3, citing Turner 1958). This is certainly an impressive figure, even if it does include food, drink, and travel expenses, but it should be pointed out that a thesis predicated on the homogeneity of, on the one hand, a national convention of university professors and, on the other, a chapter meeting of the Masons (and Ku Klux Klan?) is a thesis vulnerable not just to refutation but perhaps also to mockery. And whatever adroit semantic or definitional manoeuvres may have been taking place in the background, the common-sense intuitions of the man on the Clapham omnibus are going to be offended by a theory which classifies a gathering of the Camp Fire Girls as a species of knowledge production.

Information machines

Had this book been written a few years earlier there would hardly have been enough material for an entire chapter on 'information machines.' The recent development of the electronic-computer industry, however, provides a story that must not be missed, and which easily fills a chapter, in a book on knowledge-production.

(Machlup 1962: 295)

The role of the computer in the information society thesis is one of the most misunderstood areas of Information Society Studies. Many contemporary theorists focus exclusively on the economic, social, and political impact of information technology (IT): 'information society', in such mouths, simply means a society in which IT is pervasive. Logically, this entails that, had IT in general and the electronic computer in particular not gained ascendancy, then there would be no information society. However, if this corollary is accepted then the information technology version of the information society thesis (discussed in Chapter 4) must be completely separate from the information sector version. For the quotation above, at the start of Machlup's treatment of what he calls 'information machines', shows that, so far as the pioneer himself was concerned, knowledge production can flourish in the absence of computers. The recent development of the computer industry, or what would now be called, with hindsight, the beginnings of the 'information revolution', provided for Machlup an additional chapter, but was far from being constitutive of the whole story. No doubt, the information revolution rekindled interest in the general concept of the information society, but it remains the case that the information society thesis cannot be interpreted as an intellectual response to exclusively *technological* developments.[10]

Machlup's category of information machines includes not just electronic computers, but also all other types of instruments, machines, or devices which produce knowledge in his sense: thermometers, compasses, watches, typewriters, and microscopes, to name a few. The legitimacy of this particular piece of terminological tolerance can be defended. It cannot be denied that such devices as compasses and thermometers have an informational role when used in conjunction with the human mind, and if so perhaps the term 'information technology' is today used in too narrow a sense. After all, it is not as though in the pre-computer world there were no technological aids in the production, dissemination, organisation and storage of information: only, it might be argued, an arrogance or ignorance under the spell of the modern 'cult' of information technology could contest this fact. On the other hand, there is also no doubt that the average person understands 'IT' to mean computing, and perhaps also now electronic telecommunications where these are connected to computer systems.

The semantic plot thickens, however, when Machlup proceeds to argue for the inclusion of automatic control devices, such as environmental control systems for the household. Ironically, this would be uncontroversial from the point of view of contemporary understandings of IT, which tend to include what Ian Miles was later to christen 'home informatics'. However, as Machlup himself points out, strict adherence to his own definition of knowledge production would not permit the proposed extension, 'since the creation of an impression upon a human mind was required' (1962: 299). Nevertheless, in spite of their violating his own core criterion of a change of epistemic state, he duly includes them! Once again, we are given the impression of an advocate engaged in special pleading, an impression reinforced when it is noted that Machlup wants to count such unlikely candidates as musical instruments and even watch-cases. If such tolerance is permitted is it any wonder that the predominance of the information sector can be 'proved'? But does such a 'proof' amount to anything more than a Pyrrhic victory? (The difficulties involved in defining IT are pursued in more detail in Chapter 4.)

Although the computer was, in Machlup's taxonomy, only one species of the genus 'information machine', it was regarded as by far the most *promising* species. A little stage-setting may be helpful here. Machlup was writing in the infancy of the information revolution. ENIAC,[11] that 'fickle monster' (Bell 1980b: 36), had been manufactured less than two decades before the publication of *The Production and Distribution of Knowledge in the United States*. The so-called 'first generation' of computing (1951–8), based on valves and vacuum tubes, had given way to the 'second generation' of transistors and semiconductors, but integrated circuits were still unknown, Silicon Valley still largely the habitation of farmers, and personal computing for the masses the material only of dreams. Machlup himself notes that as late as 1956 the value of computers was under half that of typewriters. However, by the turn of the decade they had already begun to show great economic potential and, equally importantly, had already acquired what can only be described as a mystique or even glamour. Even then, long before the microelectronics revolution, they were seen as the information machine of the future, the information machine of information machines. Thus Machlup could already write that they had enjoyed a 'phenomenal career' and provided a 'story that must not be missed'.

Contemporary rhetoric of the information revolution is notorious for hyperbole, but some of its seeds can evidently be found in the journalese of this supposedly 'high-brow' primary source of the information society thesis. There is surely 'optimism' (Burton 1992), and even a hint of 'technological utopianism' (Kling 1994), where Machlup alludes lyrically to the 'ascent' and 'mysteries' of 'this amazing machine' (1962: 306–7). Indeed, despite his chronologically disadvantaged position on the time-line of IT, he would appear to have been a hard-core cyberphile. He even devotes several pages to describing the workings of analogue and digital computers, and why would a treatise on the information sector suddenly become a technical manual unless its author were suffering from something like awe? Even when Machlup eventually returns to his proper theme of statistics, and produces estimates for computer sales, his lack of objectivity is manifest. Total sales, we are told, went from $10.3 million 'pre-1954' – it is not clear what 'pre-1954' is supposed to mean, if not simply prehistoric – to $462.1 million in 1959, according to data obtained from 'one of the leading firms in the industry'. This figure, even if reliable, is minuscule compared with the total information sector, but Machlup nevertheless closes his discussion in an almost euphoric frame of mind concerning the 'beneficial economic effects of the new development' (1962: 322). Is it any wonder then that later information revolutionaries were mistakenly to believe that 'Machlup 1962' was the foundation of their own theories of socio-technical change?

Information services

The fifth and final branch of knowledge production is information services. Machlup starts his chapter on them in an exceptionally defensive tone. For while he believes, or at least professes to believe, that education, R&D, communication media, and information machines would be 'recognizable by most as eligible for inclusion in a study of the production and distribution of knowledge' (1962: 323), he knows that he must admit that this alleged majority may not hold for what he intends to include under the rubric of information services. It is indeed the case that the main area of controversy concerning the argument for an information sector is the recategorisation of certain occupations as information services, as sociologists Rhona and Julian Newman made vividly clear:

> Cavalier use of terms in this field [studies of the information sector] dates back to Fritz Machlup, who was so keen to establish the importance of knowledge in the economy that he counted even strip-tease dancers as knowledge workers.
>
> (Newman and Newman 1985: 498)[12]

Again, however, there has been a lack of understanding of what the pioneer himself actually said about information services, about his conceptual frameworks and his candidates for inclusion and exclusion; and, in particular, there has been confusion about how much he owed his successor Marc Porat in respect of a 'hidden' information workforce.

The problem with the information services as a component of the knowledge sector, Machlup argues, does not pertain to those industries which are *wholly* engaged in selling information or advice, because, according to the definition of knowledge production on which his book is premised, 'the activity of *telling anybody anything*, by word of mouth or in writing, is knowledge-production': 'problems arise', rather, 'where this complete specialization is not achieved and information services are produced together with other goods and services' (1962: 323, my italic). The Machlupian agenda, we know, was to incorporate as large a proportion of the economy as possible in the knowledge sector, but the reasoning he here employs is of a type not encountered so far, namely a straightforward argument from precedent: R&D statistics standardly include figures for the R&D activities of organisations even where R&D is not the *sole* activity of these organisations, and even where the organisation does not have a separate R&D department; *ergo*, it is also possible, both conceptually and practically, to separate the information-producing aspects of an organisation from the non-information-producing aspects. While, as usual, Machlup astutely concedes that this is a 'matter of judgment' and that 'some of the decisions are likely to be subject to charges of inconsistency or arbitrariness', he proceeds in full confidence that the exercise will be statistically meaningful.

It is vital to register here a basic fact which is widely overlooked in the information sector tradition. *Machlup's information sector includes not only industries whose final product is exclusively information; it also includes intermediate services and activities.* As has already been mentioned, Porat is commonly lauded for having 'discovered' what he christened the 'secondary information sector', a sector which, in contradistinction to the 'primary information sector', covers the information-related activities of non-information industries. But here in *The Production and Distribution of Knowledge in the United States*, a decade and a half before Porat's work was published, we find Machlup contemplating the 'hidden' information economy right at the beginning of his chapter on information services – albeit using different nomenclature. It is really rather worrying that almost the entire information sector secondary literature makes the mistake of thinking the pioneer was too blind to see this very obvious point. Porat did indeed aid the cause of clarification by giving these hidden activities a proper name, i.e. 'secondary information sector', but that is all. A fresh examination of the primary source can at least set the record straight on this one matter.

While Machlup highlights the informational content of a wide range of professions and trades, he does not attempt to include all submerged information activities:

> Almost every industry produces some information. Most firms must inform prospective customers what they have to offer, at what prices, qualities, etc.; they must inform buyers that the orders have been received and executed, that the bill amounts to so and so much, that payments are due, etc.; sometimes they must give their clients directions for the use of the product. All these pieces of information are integral parts of the business in which the firms are engaged, and no one will suggest that these 'information services' be listed among the firm's products, and that the firms be listed as members of knowledge-producing industries.
>
> (Machlup 1962: 323)

However, this throws up another hermeneutical problem of consistency within the pioneer's work. Is he justified in excluding the general class of activities referred to in the quotation? To do so seems *un-Machlupian*, for surely 'no one will suggest' is the kind of verbal tool which, applied to himself, would have prevented *The Production and Distribution of Knowledge in the United States* from going ahead at all? Machlup does go on to say that where the aforementioned information services comprise a 'very large' part of a firm's activities, their value should be counted as knowledge production, but this compromise is unsatisfactory. If knowledge production is defined as he has insisted that it be defined, i.e. in terms of any change of epistemic state, then why not include the price information activities of all firms? Such activities may not amount to much for any individual firm but the *aggregate* for the economy as a whole is bound to be colossal. If we wish to count all the leaves in a forest we do not limit ourselves to the tall trees with conspicuously copious coverings: to arrive at a tolerably accurate estimate we must look at the small trees and the bushes as well. Thus the information sector methodology appears to be flexible enough to be bent in any direction Machlup chooses, even backwards – a quality which hardly inspires confidence in its underlying probity.

So much for the exclusions: which activities are included as *bona fide* information services? Machlup begins with the 'professional' services which 'specialize in producing and selling information and advice, namely legal, engineering, accounting, and medical services' (1962: 326). However, in spite of saying that these specialise in information he argues that not *everything* done by such professionals is truly informational. There is, he thinks, no difficulty with lawyers in this respect, but with doctors only *half* of what they do is informational, i.e. such activities as patient examinations, the making of case notes, the formulating of diagnoses, and the writing of prescriptions. It is not at all clear where Machlup gets his 50 per cent figure from, because he certainly does not quote any sociology of medicine. More importantly, a raw intuition needs to be loudly heard: we are simply not inclined to think of doctors of the medical kind as even partly knowledge or information workers. Even the most intellectual and 'hands-off' physician is involved not – so goes the intuition and, indeed, the etymology – in information work but in *physical* work, repairing broken bodies as a mechanic repairs cars. To include doctors *at all* is one of Machlup's most bizarre proposals, and one which should not be passed over lightly.

However, if half of doctoring must be classed as information work, there are certain knock-on effects for the information society thesis. The text soon reveals that Machlup does not see fit to include any other category of health professional. 'Payments to dentists,' he writes tendentiously, 'should be regarded entirely as purchases of physical work, rather than purchases of knowledge' (1962: 326–7). Dentists might be surprised to discover that they do not routinely engage in such activities as health education, advice giving, note taking, form filling, and so on. There may be quantifiable differences between an average dentist and an average physician in this respect, just as there are surely quantifiable differences between the average physician and the average surgeon, but what is manifestly invidious is a simplistic 'either/or' approach. Much the same can be said regarding a host of other allied health occupations which Machlup does not even mention. One more example, statistically of great potential weight, is nursing. He excludes all variants of nurse from his knowledge kingdom, but why? If he is including bedside advice and note taking for doctors, why does he not do so for nurses? We are just not told.[13]

It is not being insinuated that Machlup was demeaning health workers by failing to see that what they do is knowledge-based. He perhaps did suffer from a hierarchical view about who is and who is not an 'intellectual' or a 'professional', but here the point is that he abuses his own distinction between physical and knowledge-producing activities. If he accepts (some) doctoring into his knowledge sector, then he must accept (some) nursing, and (some) speech therapising, and so on. Where one draws the line is, frankly, anybody's guess. As Leon Goldstein points out, for Machlup 'the determination of criteria for inclusion or exclusion is grounded *not* in the veridical apprehension of what things are but in *decisions* determined by the investigator's sense of what his problems are and how they are to be dealt with given the limitations of his procedures' (1981: 1064). However, the problem is not just that *The Production and Distribution of Knowledge in the United States* is by and large based on truth-by-decision rather than truth-by-discovery, but also that the truths-by-decision seem in many cases to be inconsistent with one another.

Parallel arguments apply to Machlup's decision to include all engineers, while excluding mechanics and other 'artisans', but once these hurdles are surmounted the rest of his catalogue of 'knowledge occupations' is relatively uncontroversial: bankers, brokers, financial services staff, estate agents, management consultants, auctioneers, government administrators, and the like. The only other major issue is with certain types of information service hiding in the small print of a miscellaneous class called 'general government'. 'Protective services and alien control' (Machlup 1962: 345) really does mean that policemen are to count as information workers. That is curious enough, but Machlup then astonishes by the sheer capriciousness of his decision about *which* policemen to include: the FBI is informational because it is mainly an 'investigative' force, whereas state and local police forces are non-informational, and this despite the fact that 'some FBI tasks require physical force, e.g., when the G-men "shoot it out" with gangsters'. 'It is assumed here,' he writes hopefully, 'that the proportions between investigative and protective services are sufficiently different to justify putting the FBI and state and local police into different boxes' (1962: 346).

The man on the Clapham omnibus, and probably also the woman on the New York subway, would be quick to point out that, at least as regards local forces, much of what the average policeman does is just as informational as the activities of an FBI agent, an engineer, or a doctor. However, by now we are inured to such inconsistencies. To borrow Machlup's own jocular but also self-revealing phrase, the 'marginal arbitrariness' (1962: 347) of this final inclusion can make little difference to the overall arbitrariness of his taxonomy. If the gatherings of the Camp Fire Girls are counted as knowledge production why should not FBI–Mafiosi shootouts also be counted as knowledge production? And if we allow Machlup all of this, how can we deny him the additional idiosyncrasy of excluding the *bona fide* knowledge-communicating activities of the 'local bobby'? However, will we not then conclude that Machlup and his like are engaged in a fundamentally fatuous exercise?

The information sector as a totality

It will be recalled that Machlup's interest *qua* macro-economist is the makeup of the US GNP, and his burden throughout this iconoclastic volume has been to highlight the role of knowledge (or what most people would call information) in the national product. In the penultimate chapter of *The Production and Distribution of Knowledge in the United States*, he duly proceeds to form his long-awaited aggregation of the various branches or industries of the knowledge sector. As can be seen from Table 2.5, the total for knowledge production in 1958 was $136,436 million. The Machlupian methods of justification have already been examined for many of the figures featured in this table, but it may be helpful to repeat one or two salient points. The 'all education' figure, at $60,194 million, is by far the largest of the totals for the five branches, and amounts, in fact, to almost half of the information sector. Now sixty billion dollars is an impressive figure, even for a large country, but let us remember that nearly four and a half (4.432) billion, accounting for more than basic research, postal services, and public libraries put together, derives from the highly dubious concept of the 'opportunity cost' of education in the home. Similarly, elementary and secondary schools, at approximately thirty-three billion, constitute by far the biggest single 'industry' in this or any other branch of knowledge production, but of this figure over half is not a proper monetary outlay at all but a shadowy 'implicit' cost; and for higher education the shadowy element is almost twice the size of the substantial element. Many other figures have been disputed, but if only the aforementioned items are discounted, the education budget, as it were, is slashed by almost exactly 50 per cent, and the 'grand total' for the information sector suddenly shrinks in size from $136,436 million to $106,405 million. Such differences are, by any standards, dramatic.

Machlup is aware, however, that the dollar value of knowledge production means little except in comparison with total national product. The really important statistic is the ratio of the information sector to the gross national product, since what the information society thesis is celebrated for is its promotion of the idea of an historic sectoral shift in the context of the economy as a whole. The 1958 US GNP, adjusted to allow for all the statistically unorthodox costs subsumed in education and elsewhere, was $478,300 million. As noted, the total for the information sector for this year was $136,436 million, and so it follows that the information sector or knowledge economy accounted for 'almost 29 per cent' (Machlup 1962: 362) – actually, it is more like 28.5 per cent – of adjusted GNP. For the sake of argument, then, knowledge production accounted for nearly a third of US GNP at the end of the 1950s. Machlup clearly has much confidence in this figure, as the following exultant paragraph shows:

> The 'exact' ratio of knowledge-production to GNP matters little. There are probably some items the inclusion of which will be questioned, particularly among the information services. A few items, on the other hand, were omitted simply because we found it too difficult to estimate their value. But even if questionable items were stricken out, or omitted items included, the total would not be substantially affected; the ratio would not be much different from the 29 per cent calculated on the basis of our figures.
>
> (Machlup 1962: 362)

Table 2.5 Knowledge production, by industry or branch, source of funds, and character of output, 1958 (millions of dollars) (from Machlup 1962: 354–7)

Industry or branch of knowledge production	Year	Total value	Paid for by			Intermediate product		Final product (consumption or investment)	
			Government	Business	Consumers	Though treated as final product in official statistics	Recognised in official statistics as cost of current production of other goods and services	Though treated as cost of current production or entirely omitted in official statistics	Recognised in official statistics as final product
Education									
Education in the home	1958	4,432	—	—	4,432	—	—	4,432	—
Training on the job	1958	3,054	—	3,054	—	—	3,054	—	—
Education in the church	1958	2,467	—	—	2,467	—	—	—	2,467
Education in the armed forces	1958	3,410	3,410	—	—	—	—	—	3,410
Elementary and secondary schools									
Monetary expenditures	1957–8	16,054	13,569	—	2,485	—	—	—	16,054
Implicit costs	1957–8	17,285	3,414	—	13,871	—	1,022	16,263	—
Colleges and universities									
Monetary expenditures	1957–8	4,443	2,423	—	2,020	—	—	—	4,443
Implicit costs	1957–8	8,314	781	—	7,533	—	317	7,997	—
Commercial, vocational, and residential schools	1958	253	—	—	253	—	—	—	253
Federal programmes, n.e.c.	1957–8	342	342	—	—	—	—	—	342
Public libraries	1958	140	140	—	—	—	—	—	140
All education		60,194	24,079	3,054	33,061	—	4,393	28,692	27,109
Research and development									
Basic research	1958–9	1,016	615	275	126	—	—	275	741
Applied R&D	1958–9	9,974	6,515	3,385	74	—	—	3,385	6,589
All R&D		10,990	7,130	3,660	200	—	—	3,660	7,330

Communication media

	Year	Total							
Printing and publishing									
Books and pamphlets	1958	1,595	347	43	1,205	—	43	—	1,552
Periodicals	1958	1,811	—	1,031	780	—	—	1,031	780
Newspapers	1958	3,956	—	2,503	1,453	—	—	2,503	1,453
Stationery and office supplies	1958	1,852	180	720	952	180	720	—	952
Commercial printing	1958	2,879	570	2,280	29	570	2,280	—	29
Photography	1958	1,600	—	—	1,600	—	—	—	1,600
Phonography	1958	1,035	—	—	1,035	—	—	—	1,035
Stage, podium, and screen									
Theatre and concerts	1958	313	—	—	313	—	—	—	313
Spectator sports	1958	255	—	—	255	—	—	—	255
Motion pictures	1958	1,172	—	—	1,172	—	—	—	1,172
Radio and television									
Radio stations revenue	1958	523	—	523	—	—	—	523	—
Television stations revenue	1958	1,030	—	1,030	—	—	—	1,030	—
Radio and TV sets and repairs	1958	1,982	—	—	1,982	—	—	—	1,982
Radio and TV investment	1957	806	—	806	—	—	—	—	806
Other advertising	1958	5,000	—	5,000	—	—	—	5,000	—
Telecommunications media									
Telephone	1958	7,642	1,529	2,813	3,300	1,529	2,813	—	3,300
Telegraph	1958	318	64	117	137	64	117	—	137
Postal services	1958	3,000	52	2,048	900	52	2,048	—	900
Conventions	1957	1,600	—	800	800	—	800	—	800
All media		38,369	2,742	19,714	15,913	2,395	8,821	10,087	17,066

Information machines

	Year	Total							
Printing trades machinery	1958	350	—	350	—	—	—	—	350
Musical instruments	1958	190	—	—	190	—	—	—	190
Motion picture apparatus	1958	147	—	147	—	—	—	—	147
Telephones and telegraph apparatus	1958	1,200	—	1,200	—	—	—	—	1,200
Signalling devices	1958	200	—	200	—	—	—	—	200
Measuring and control devices	1958	4,968	—	4,400	568	—	—	—	4,968
Typewriters	1958	272	—	272	—	—	—	—	272
Electronic computers	1958	332	43	289	—	—	—	—	332
Other office machines and parts	1958	1,263	—	1,263	—	—	—	—	1,263
All information machines		8,922	43	8,121	758	—	—	—	8,922

Table 2.5 (continued)

Information services

Legal	1958	3,025	—	1,518	1,507	—	1,518	—	1,507
Engineering and architecture	1958	1,978	—	1,978	—	—	1,978	—	—
Accounting and auditing	1957	1,138	—	1,138	—	—	1,138	—	—
Medical (excl. surgical)	1958	2,083	—	—	2,083	—	—	—	2,083
Securities brokers, etc.	1958	647	—	72	575	—	72	—	575
Insurance agents	1958	2,173	—	—	2,173	—	—	—	2,173
Other business services	Various	2,943	—	2,943	—	—	2,943	—	—
Government	1958	3,974	3,974	—	—	3,974	—	—	—
All information services		17,961	3,974	7,649	6,338	3,974	7,649	—	6,338
Grand total		136,436	37,968	42,198	56,270	6,369	20,863	42,439	66,765

n.e.c., not elsewhere covered

This was the first momentous statistical disclosure concerning the information economy and the rock upon which the information society thesis (or at least its dominant version) was to be built. It was also, to switch metaphor, a baton which other eager researchers took it upon themselves to carry. In particular, as already noted, Porat was to expend enormous effort – *The Information Economy* (1977) was published in nine volumes – in seeking to demonstrate that the share of the information sector in US GNP would soon pass the magical 50 per cent mark: once that took place, allegedly around 1980, the information society thesis seemed impregnable. The fact that not just 'a few items' (in Machlup's relaxed terminology) among the information services, but also – if my criticisms have been on target – *great swathes* of all of the other categories in Machlup's information sector were intrinsically suspect, has been downplayed or simply ignored.

Finally, what is needed for a convincing story is not so much a one-off figure as a diachronic account over as long a period as possible. The information society thesis, even in its unreconstructed Machlupian form, had to be, if not a theory of social *progress*, then at least a set of claims about societal *change*. It is thus no surprise that the paragraph cementing the alleged '29 per cent' revelation is immediately followed by this statement:

> We strongly suspect that the share of knowledge-production in GNP has been increasing over the years. Indeed we can show that in recent years knowledge-production has been growing faster than GNP, and this implies that its share in GNP has increased.
>
> (Machlup 1962: 362)

Obviously, the growth of the information sector, particularly relative to total GNP, is something that Machlup *wanted* to be able to demonstrate. If the ratio were found to have been 45 per cent in 1925 and 35 per cent in 1945 – if the 'knowledge industries' were in *decline* – then *The Production and Distribution of Knowledge in the United States* would probably not have been such a resounding success. Princeton University Press, Machlup's publishers, might have had to retitle it along the lines of *Twilight of the Knowledge Industries: The American Economy in Intellectual Decline*. Economists, like information scientists and sociologists, wish to discover positive trends and correlations, and especially to be the first to document the embryonic – and thus to enjoy the kudos of the prophet. However, in order to achieve an epistemic status more robust than that of an 'historical blip', they must take a long view. Machlup himself specifically states that 'a rate of increase observed over a short period *does not* warrant an assumption that this increase will be "sustained" over a longer period' (1962: 367, my italic). Does he, then, produce sufficient evidence for an information sector thesis *qua* thesis concerning a novel kind of *evolution*?

Regrettably, the short answer to this question is 'No'. He presents detailed figures regarding the rates of increase for knowledge-producing industries only between 1947 and 1958 (Machlup 1962: 370–3). The period 1954–8 is classed as the 'most recent period' and 1947–58 as the 'longer period'. On average, the knowledge sector increased at an annual rate of 8.8 per cent for the former and 10.6 per cent for the latter, compared with 5.1 per cent and 5.9 per cent, respectively, for US GNP. The figures are – how could they be otherwise? – 'even more impressive' if the rates of increase for the knowledge industries are contrasted with the rates of increase for the non-knowledge industries, which were only 3.7 per cent and 4.1 per cent respectively. Machlup makes out that there have been considerable rates of increase for almost all aspects of knowledge production over both periods, but he fails to mention the obvious fact that if the rate of increase was 10.6 per cent for 1947–58 and only 8.8 per cent for 1954–8 then the rate of increase of the putative knowledge economy was slowing down. This does not in itself negate his overall thesis, but it does suggest that a countervailing current may have been at work in the late 1950s.

As a matter of fact, when Rubin and Huber measured the US knowledge industry using a strict Machlupian methodology (1986: 19), they found that it accounted in 1980 for no more than 34.3 per cent of GNP – up less than 6 per cent on the 1958 figure. In any case, even Machlup's twelve-year 'longer period' is far too short to justify serious claims about growth or evolution. If one wishes to make or imply statements about epochal change, one must paint on a very much wider historical canvas, as, for example, does John Feather in *The Information Society: A Study of Continuity and Change* (1998). Given the *scale* of the evidence vouchsafed in Machlup's text, should the dogmatism of information society rhetoric – a rhetoric, essentially, of the race, and more particularly of the sprint – not have been in some degree tempered?

The occupations approach

One would expect Machlup's case to rest after his dramatic 'grand totals' had at last been revealed. In fact, this is not what happens, and he instead tries in his last chapter to reinforce his argument by approaching the information sector from a different angle. His doctrine of the information sector version of the information society thesis thus appears in two variants. The first, which he calls the 'industry approach', refers to the share of the putative knowledge industries in the gross national product, and this is what has been expounded, and for the most part criticised, in the preceding pages. The second variant, which Machlup calls the 'occupations approach', denotes not the industries which produce or communicate knowledge but rather the occupations in which people engage: it disaggregates to a more individual level by looking at what kind of work is actually done by the knowledge or information workers. As Machlup writes at the start of the tenth chapter of *The Production and Distribution of Knowledge in the United States*, 'the focus will now be on the worker, his activity and occupation, rather than the industry in which he is employed' (1962: 377).

The fact that the pioneer had devoted the bulk of his book to the industry variant shows how strongly enamoured he was with that approach, but we are entitled to question whether he had struck a sensible balance. No doubt

Machlup, like most macro-economists, found it natural to think in terms of whole industries, and no doubt he was also to some extent hemmed in by the industrial classifications used by most of the official statistical series of his day. Nevertheless, it could be argued that in many respects his occupations approach is intrinsically more interesting and more promising than the other one, and that he ought therefore to have given it considerably more attention. To be able to say that the *archetypal worker* of the near future is neither a farm hand nor a factory employee but rather a producer of knowledge is to make an arresting and sociologically significant statement. Such a statement would deliver us from the 'counting-house': it would be non-trivial, important, the kind of discovery that is worthy of a treatise rather than a brief communication in an econometrics journal. It is no surprise, therefore, that much of the Machlup-inspired information sector tradition has in practice emphasised the 'occupations approach', especially after Bell superimposed his sociology of work on Machlup's and Porat's data (see Chapter 5).

In order to ground the information society in this complementary way, the argumentation for a new kind of occupational structure must of course be cogent. I wish now to finish the critique by exposing some of the weaknesses in the forms of argument employed in this final Machlupian boost. The pioneer acknowledged, as indeed he had to, that 'the operator tending certain machines or apparatuses may have to watch measuring instruments and react by quick manipulations to the information they convey' (Machlup 1962: 40), i.e. that most human labour is based to some degree on knowledge. Now he states that, in spite of the fact that manual labour involves mental activity and that, conversely, mental labour frequently involves some muscular activity, the distinction between mental and manual work – or between 'white-collar' and 'blue-collar' workers – is valid. Armed with this basic assumption, he proceeds with great despatch to reclassify the occupational statistics of the US Census. By the conventions of the time, workers were divided into eleven major occupation groups, namely: (1) professional, technical, and kindred; (2) farmers; (3) managers and officials; (4) clerical; (5) sales; (6) craftsmen; (7) operatives; (8) domestic; (9) other service; (10) farm labourers; (11) non-farm labourers. Machlup quickly reorganises these into three meta-classes: (A) white-collar workers, consisting of (1), (3), (4), and (5); (B) manual and service workers, consisting of (6), (7), (8), (9), and (11); and (C) agricultural workers, consisting of (2) and (10).

Table 2.6, which combines these categories with census figures from 1900 to 1959, indicates that the quota of white-collar workers saw the most spectacular development, increasing from 5 million in 1900 to 27 million in 1959; over the same period the number of manual and service workers also increased, although much less markedly, while the ranks of farm workers were depleted. Table 2.7 then translates these figures into percentages. In terms of relative shares of the economy, class (A) increased from 17.6 per cent in 1900 to 42.1 per cent in 1959, (B) increased from 44.9 per cent to 48 per cent, and (C) decreased from 37.5 per cent to 9.9 per cent. Thus, on the white-collar/

Table 2.6 Labour force, or economically active civilian population, by broad occupation categories, 1900–59 (millions of persons) (from Machlup 1962: 381)

Category	1900	1910	1920	1930	1940	1950	1959
White-collar	5	8	11	14	16	22	27
Manual and service	13	18	20	24	27	30	31
Farm	11	12	11	10	9	7	6
Total	29	37	42	49	52	59	65

Source: US Bureau of the Census, *Occupational Trends in the United States, 1900–1950* and *Current Population Reports*

Note

Because of rounding, figures do not always add up to total

Table 2.7 Labour force, percentage distribution over broad occupation categories, 1900–59 (from Machlup 1962: 382)

Category	1900	1910	1920	1930	1940	1950	1959
White-collar	17.6	21.3	24.9	29.4	31.1	36.6	42.1
Manual and service	44.9	47.7	48.1	49.4	51.5	51.6	48.0
Farm	37.5	30.9	27.0	21.2	17.4	11.8	9.9

Source: US Bureau of the Census, *Occupational Trends in the United States, 1900–1950* and *Current Population Reports*

blue-collar axis, total white-collar labour increased from 17.6 per cent to 42.1 per cent over the time frame, while blue-collar labour decreased from 84.3 per cent to 57.9 per cent. 'This trend, uninterrupted for 60 years and probably longer,' Machlup writes using his favourite epithet, 'is *most impressive*' (1962: 382, my italic).

Unfortunately, it is established far too easily to be convincing. It takes up less than two pages of text. Moreover, it is not as if these encapsulate or extrapolate from a sustained piece of argument or evidence: on the contrary, all of the previous 380 pages of argument and statistics are left aside and a completely new set of statistics is suddenly brought on to centre-stage. The inevitable impression, indeed, is that the occupations chapter is a rushed sequel to the main story. No attempt is made to explicate properly these new data, and, except for the note under Table 2.6 about figures not quite adding up, the customary caveats and qualifications are conspicuously absent. It is as though Machlup had at last tired himself out and was feeling that his thesis was in danger of dying the death of a thousand qualifications. But no clemency can be shown now. It is disappointing, but must be frankly stated, that the argument for the second variant of the pioneer's information sector version of the information society thesis consists simply in dividing the eleven occupational groups of the US Census into two or three broader categories which appear to have been suddenly created *ex nihilo*.

More must be said about these innocuous-looking tables. They have had a very particular significance for information society research in that, while Machlup himself did not try to promote them as proof of 'post-industrialism', they pointed for the first time to a tripartite economy composed not of agricultural, industrial, and service workers, but rather of agricultural, industrial, and knowledge or information workers. This feat was based on two clever manoeuvres, namely the inclusion of both manual and service workers under the heading 'industrial', and the equation of knowledge workers and white-collar workers. Now there are major problems with both moves. How is it, we are compelled to ask, that manual and service workers are all of a sudden fused into a single category of 'industrial workers', a category which is normally *distinguished* from that of service workers? Machlup achieves this simply by classifying both manual and service workers as 'physical workers', and then replacing the word 'physical' by 'industrial'. He does it in the space of *two sentences* – hardly long enough for a rigorous argument. Ironically, had he taken the more natural route of positing a four-part workforce, i.e. agricultural workers, manual or industrial workers, service workers, and white-collar or knowledge workers, he would thereby have not only created a less Procrustean taxonomy but also anticipated an invention attributed to his successors in the information sector tradition: the 'quaternary sector', in this sense of the term, had to wait many more years before being identified.

As regards the equation (the second manoeuvre), Machlup does concede that the proposition 'all white-collar workers are knowledge workers' might actually stand in need of some demonstration. As we have seen, US Census occupational groups (1), (3), (4), and (5) are constitutive of his white-collar class. In order to prove that all white-collar workers are knowledge workers we would expect him to try to prove that all of these groups are made up entirely of knowledge workers. When we look closely at his argument, however, we find that he essays a rather different route. He divides all occupations into three more new classes, Class I covering occupations which are either wholly or partly knowledge-producing, Class II covering occupations which are not knowledge-producing, and Class III comprising students (including school children old enough to work). As can be seen from Table 2.8, some but not all of the occupations making up the white-collar groups are placed in Class I, while others have been relegated to Class II. The relegations include, of (1) (professional, technical, and kindred workers), dentists, funeral directors, all nurses, pharmacists, 50 per cent of doctors and surgeons, and all hospital technicians. Similarly, of (3) (managers and officials), shop and garage managers are demoted on the grounds that they 'participate in the physical work carried on in their shops'; and, of (5) (sales workers), hucksters and peddlers are kept out because 'they are less specialised in "sales talk" than in handling the merchandise sold' (1962: 383).

Now obviously if Machlup wants his sums to add up he has to find some more knowledge-producing occupations for Class I, and he does this simply by including what he regards as the more intellectual sections of the working class, namely printers, compositors, and some other craftsmen and foremen. Finally, the figures for students are factored in as a wholly knowledge-producing occupation. The net result of these taxonomic twists and turns is that, over the time frame covered, i.e. 1900–59, there had been a demonstrable 'steady increase' in knowledge-producing occupations running concurrently with a 'steady decline' in non-knowledge-producing occupations (1962: 386) – *quod erat demonstrandum*.

Further analysis of such modes of argumentation is unnecessary. Suffice to say that a few more arbitrary assumptions and persuasive definitions and counter-intuitive recategorisations, and a prepossessing table or two, were deemed sufficient – in the pioneer's eyes, and those of his faithful followers – to establish the 'occupations approach' to the information society thesis, thereby corroborating the 'industry approach'. The proof of the increasing role of the knowledge or information sector, i.e. of what would later be called 'informatisation' or 'informationisation' (no one, mercifully, has ever suggested 'knowledgisation'), was now, supposedly, doubly certain. But if ever an intellectual case has deserved that mordant phrase from Aristotle about someone 'defending a thesis at all costs', this surely was it.

Perhaps we can finish with an extremely revealing extract from the very last page of *The Production and Distribution of Knowledge in the United States*:

> The reliability of the data with which we worked must not be overestimated, and the legitimacy of several of the uses we made of them may be questioned. Indeed some of the statistical procedures were accepted only

Table 2.8   Occupations of the economically active population, by participation in knowledge-producing activities, 1900–59 (from Machlup 1962: 384–5)

	1900 (thousands)	%	1959 (thousands)	%
Class I				
(1) Professional, technical, and kindred workers	1,234	—	7,264	—
Not knowledge-producing workers of this group	177	—	1,447	—
Knowledge-producing workers of this group	1,057	3.64	5,787	8.42
(3) Managers, officials, and proprietors	1,697	—	7,025	—
Not knowledge-producing workers of this group	973	—	2,929	—
Knowledge-producing workers of this group	724	2.49	4,096	5.96
(4) Clerical and kindred workers (all knowledge-producing)	877	3.02	9,671	14.06
(5) Sales workers	1,307	—	4,557	—
Not knowledge-producing workers of this group	1,007	—	2,674	—
Knowledge-producing workers of this group	300	1.03	1,883	2.74
+ Knowledge-producing craftsmen, foremen, etc.	139	0.48	317	0.46
All knowledge-producing occupations	**3,097**	**10.7**	**21,754**	**31.6**
Class II				
Not knowledge-producing craftsmen, foremen, etc.	2,923	—	8,698	—
Operatives, etc.	3,720	—	12,759	—
Private household workers	1,579	—	2,302	—
Other service workers	1,047	—	6,217	—
Labourers, except farm and mine	3,620	—	4,207	—
Farmers and farm managers	5,763	—	3,028	—
Farm labourers and foremen	5,125	—	2,694	—
Occupations excluded from Class I (nurses, etc.)	2,157	—	7,080	—
All not knowledge-producing occupations	**25,934**	**89.3**	**46,985**	**68.4**
Total civilian labour force	29,029	100	68,739	100
Class III				
Full-time students in grade 9 and higher	937	3.2	13,340	19.4
A. Potential civilian labour force	29,966	—	82,079	—
B. Potential civilian labour force in knowledge-producing occupations (Groups I and III)	4,034	—	35,094	—
B as a percentage of A	**—**	**13.5**	**—**	**42.8**

Source: *Historical Statistics of the United States*; Bureau of Labor Statistics, *Special Labor Force Report No. 4*; US Office of Education, *Advance Release*

as makeshifts and in the hope that others may improve upon our most imperfect effort ... [But] our attitude of caution regarding the accuracy of statistical data and the reliability of ratios between them should not be misread to imply serious reservations concerning the validity of the generalisations developed in this book. Many things can be said about general trends and interrelated developments even if the illustrative or supporting data are less than accurate. What has been said about changes in occupational structure remains valid even if the basic statistics are off the mark ... While statistical tables have crowded the pages of this book, concern about their adequacy should not crowd out the message it conveys.

(Machlup 1962: 400)

The place for Machlup to stop would have been, of course, at the words 'imperfect effort'. That would have been a fittingly modest finale to a suggestive but inherently controversial essay in left-wing statistical hermeneutics, and it would have sounded a strong note of caution for the whole information sector tradition. Unfortunately, the pioneer, as is plainly seen here, could not leave it at that. He moves on immediately to cancel the effects of his own caveats, and ends in a highly self-assured and evangelical mode. Dogmatism finally triumphs over doubt – and it has triumphed ever since.

Postscript: Machlup's unfinished sequel

The Production and Distribution of Knowledge in the United States is the primary source of the information sector version of the information society thesis, if not of the information society thesis as a whole, and for that reason it was subjected above to scrutiny of forensic precision. It would be incorrect, however, to suggest that this was the only book which Machlup wrote that is germane to the information society thesis. In fact, the remarkable success of his 1962 monograph eventually caused him to conceive a much more ambitious, multidisciplinary and multi-authored sequel in which knowledge was supposedly to be afforded its first ever comprehensive treatment. The project was intended to run to eight volumes, under the general heading *Knowledge: Its Creation, Distribution, and Economic Significance* (Machlup 1980: 13);[14] there was even talk of ten volumes (Rich 1982: 331). 'The project as a whole,' enthused a fellow economist at the University of Chicago, 'is quite breathtaking in its scope and recalls scholarship of another era ... who else could have undertaken such a task?' (Rosen 1986: 141).

In the event, however, Machlup's death in 1983 cut short the programme and only four volumes appeared, two of them posthumously, under the following titles: vol. I, *Knowledge and Knowledge Production* (1980); vol. II, *The Branches of Learning* (1982); vol. III, *The Economics of Information and Human Capital* (1983); vol. IV, *The Study of Information: Interdisciplinary Messages* (1983).[15] Of these, *Knowledge and Knowledge Production* is by far the most relevant to the information society thesis, and it will be the subject of this postscript. My remarks here will be relatively brief, for three reasons. First, the project as a whole was, as just noted, unfinished. Second, the mature thoughts Machlup managed to leave with us actually add very little to what he had already said, as will be seen. Third, the role of this later work in the evolution of the information society thesis has not been crucial: it is cited only infrequently, and many scholars seem to be unaware of its existence. In fact, it is safe to surmise that had *Knowledge and Knowledge Production* and the other volumes not been written, the information sector version of the information society thesis would still be flourishing today.

As with the prototype, it is illuminating to place the sequel in some historical context by showing the critical reception it encountered. *Knowledge and Knowledge Production* was reviewed in a wide range of fields. Beginning with Machlup's disciplinary home of economics, a notice by A.W. Coats opened with the now-familiar tribute: 'Fritz Machlup,' it states, 'has long been one of the world's most widely known, eminent, and prolific economists', and is, moreover, an author whose 'unflagging energy' we 'cannot fail to marvel at' (Coats 1982: 210). Clearly, with such an introduction, there was never likely to be much in the way of cool analysis, so it comes as no surprise that at the end of the review Coats endorses Kenneth Boulding's rather fatuous statement (made in connection with the 1962 work) about the concept of a knowledge industry containing 'enough dynamite to blast traditional economics into orbit'. P. Mandi, another economist, laments Machlup's death and then goes on to say that, while the project as a whole could not yet be evaluated, 'it is already clear that a basic work has been started in this interdisciplinary subject, which must not be ignored' (Mandi 1983: 152). This is less deferential but still weak. The 'basic work' had surely been 'started' nearly twenty years before, in *The Production and Distribution of Knowledge in the United States*, and the time was already well overdue for a fundamental methodological critique. The kinds of allowances we make for pioneering ideas and new intellectual fields – their period of grace, as it were – should not have to be made a second time. Why, then, was Machlup still meeting such indulgence from members of his own discipline?

Outside of economics, *Knowledge and Knowledge Production* also enjoyed a good press. Sociologist Burkart Holzner hailed its publication as 'a major event for social science' (1982: 296). He notes that an economic treatment of knowledge is unusual, because 'there has not been an economics of knowledge, as there has been a distinguished tradition of the sociology of knowledge'; nevertheless, he affirms that sociologists 'stand to benefit greatly from Machlup's present efforts, as they already have benefited from his earlier publications, especially *The Production and Distribution of Knowledge in the United States*'. As regards the reception from the queen of the sciences (as Aristotle called philosophy), Mark Blaug likewise paid tribute to Machlup's 'pioneering study' of 1962 (1982: 323). This kind of routine citation counts for little, but Blaug was also prepared to state publicly that 'philosophers of science will find that Machlup is well versed in their subject'. However, while Machlup's ideas might have been acceptable to a few philosophers of science, the evidence shows that he had no standing in the philosophical community as a whole: not one specialist journal of epistemology and not one generalist philosophy journal noticed *Knowledge and Knowledge Production*. Blaug goes on to quote, apropos of Machlup's attempt to valorise knowledge, Franz Werfel's aphorism on arguments for the existence of God:

For those who believe, no words are necessary, and for those who do not, no words will suffice.

In its original context, this was a wildly irrationalist view, one which would kill off entire disciplines like natural theology. It is equally out of place here, except perhaps in so far as it brings sharply to mind the issue of whether the information sector might be, at least partly, a matter of faith rather than pure reason.[16]

Machlup's later work was thus received with respect bordering on reverence both inside and outside his own field, and no doubt increased the general enthusiasm for the thesis he had pioneered. But in spite of all the positive citations, the sober truth is that *Knowledge and Knowledge Production* added little of substance to the Machlupian case for an information society. The text will now be negotiated briefly, with the following highly focused question uppermost: to what extent does it revise *The Production and Distribution of Knowledge in the United States*; or, put more candidly, to what extent does the later work avoid the errors and ambiguities which have been uncovered in the prototype? As will soon be seen, the answer to this question is that the passage of eighteen years between the two works appears, unfortunately, to have had practically no beneficial effects upon Machlup's thinking.

The follow-up project was arguably misconceived right from the start. Machlup states that his research team amounted to around sixty personnel, overwhelmingly research students, including 'economists, anthropologists, psychologists, historians, educationists, engineers, literature majors, information scientists, computer scientists, and other specialists' (1980: preface). Perhaps we can leave aside the delicate issue of whether it is legitimate to call research students – intellectual apprentices, presumably – 'economists' or 'historians' or whatever; but the fact that there was not a single epistemologist, i.e. theorist of knowledge, in a team devoted to an analysis of knowledge cannot pass without comment. Why did Machlup not want an expert in this core field aboard? Did he perhaps exclude the most fundamentally necessary 'angle' on his project because he sensed that, with a tough-minded epistemologist nearby, its parameters might have had to be drastically curtailed? In the original work, Machlup had confidently adopted the role of 'George', the multidisciplinary polymath, so we are not surprised to read in the sequel of his intention to express opinions on 'problems of language philosophy [he means linguistic philosophy], epistemology, intellectual history, political philosophy, ethics, aesthetics, and what not' (1980: 21). Such disdain for intellectual parochialism is in some ways admirable, but there can be no doubt that, even with the assistance of researchers, the new project was overextended. Even if we confine ourselves to the fields in this particular list, most of which are philosophical specialisms, it can with certainty be said that no one in the twentieth century has made non-negligible contributions to all of them. However, if the task was beyond a Robert Nozick, a Peter Strawson, or even a Ludwig Wittgenstein – who, while being the founder of linguistic philosophy and one of the finest thinkers of the modern age, made comments on, say, political philosophy which are regarded by specialists as banal – is it likely that macro-economist Fritz Machlup (or Machlup-plus-postgraduate-private-army) could succeed?

For the first thing that a professional epistemologist would have done is insist that the concept of knowledge on which the project was predicated is too broad:

> One point should be clarified right now: my concepts of knowing and knowledge are unusually wide. I do not confine myself to scientific or technological or verified or practical or intellectual knowledge. Anything that people think they know I include in the universe of knowledge.
>
> (Machlup 1980: preface)

This was the pioneer's major preliminary mistake in 1962, and clearly it was destined to vitiate the sequel too. However, now Machlup is guilty not only of sowing wild epistemological oats but also of obduracy. Coats suggests (1982: 210) that the definition of knowledge in *Knowledge and Knowledge Production* was 'even broader than in the earlier study', since it incorporated discussions of topics not covered in 1962, such as pornography and other species of what Machlup calls 'forbidden knowledge'. In fact, while the *explication* of knowledge became wider the underlying *definition* did not change; but the point remains that Machlup held fast to his eccentric definition for twenty years, despite its intrinsic implausibility and despite the criticisms that appeared from time to time in the secondary literature. Moreover, by the time *Knowledge and Knowledge Production* was published, the terminology – which it is agreed must be credited to Porat – of *information* economy and *information* society was well established, and yet Machlup was still insisting on using the word 'knowledge': indeed, his last projected volume was to be entitled not the 'information society' but the 'knowledgeable society'. It was a case of Machlup *contra mundum*.

If knowledge is still 'anything that is known by somebody' and knowledge production 'any activity by which someone learns of something *he* or *she* has not known before, even if others have' (Machlup 1980: 7), and if 'all information is knowledge', then epistemic (if not gender) hierarchies have been overturned. Machlup is still blind to the following:

Wisdom
Knowledge (including Science)
Information
Data.

Indeed, he goes beyond *The Production and Distribution of Knowledge in the United States* in the vehemence of his rejection of tighter semantic parameters, berating contemporary philosophers as 'justified true belief zealots' and 'JTB fanatics' (Machlup 1980: 37–8). It obviously meant nothing to this self-assured economist that the characterisation of knowledge as justified true belief, far from being the programme of extremists, was, and still is, the quintessence of mainstream Anglo-American epistemology.

Machlup's treatment of Porat is of a piece with the intransigent attitude we have been noticing. As has already been pointed out, *The Information Economy* was published in 1977 and was quickly absorbed into the information society canon. But Machlup was distinctly unimpressed with it, and what he says is confined to a few terse words in the preface and introductory chapter of *Knowledge and Knowledge Production*. Acknowledging that Porat's work covered more industries than his own, he attributes this partly to the wider range of statistical data available to Porat, and partly to the fact that 'Porat included among the "quasi-information industries" in his "secondary sector" some industries to which I had not given this status', and which, he continues, 'I still prefer to exclude' (Machlup 1980: 19). Indeed, Machlup viewed Porat's statistics as 'a partial merger' – one senses that only courtesy prevented him from using the word 'conflation' – of his own 'industry' and 'occupations' approaches.

Porat's emphasis on the secondary information sector also leaves the pioneer cold. Machlup concedes that the clear separation of the primary and secondary sectors in the information economy was regarded by others as a 'major procedural innovation', but thinks that Porat's concepts and hence figures were incommensurable with his own, and that his own methodology is still better (Machlup 1980: xxviii). Machlup's final allusion, in a section in which he tries again to defend his own forays into other fields, can be read as an attack on Porat's narrower intellectual range:

> The admirable nine-volume work on *The Information Economy* by Marc Porat is sufficient proof that one may confine oneself to economic statistics.
>
> (Machlup 1980: 21)

In other words, the master has no time for putative methodological innovations issuing from lesser scholars.

The rest of the sequel tells the same story. After some perfunctory lip-service to difficulties associated with the measurability of the knowledge industries, Machlup proceeds, with no further ado, to measure them. The industry approach is still preferred to the occupations approach, and the very same industries are charted, the only difference being the nominal one that artistic creation and communication are treated separately from the communication media (Machlup 1980: 232–3). It becomes clear that Machlup in the new volume is holding *completely* to the methodology of *The Production and Distribution of Knowledge in the United States*, and so it follows inevitably that the 1980 work is vulnerable to all of the criticisms which have been applied to the 1962 work. There is surely, therefore, no need to say any more about it. Schement and Curtis decided that Machlup's 'conceptualization of knowledge production continues to be awkward' (1995: 72). If the foregoing commentary has been accurate, it is necessary to go further and say that his conceptualisation of the knowledge or information sector has always been inherently dubious. The information sector version is thus built upon unstable methodological foundations.

Notes

1 It should also be mentioned that Porat adhered rather more faithfully to official statistical categories than did Machlup. However, Machlup himself did not regard this as in any way an improvement upon his own methodology.

2 A.E. Cawkell's recent statement that Machlup 'concluded that 50% of the US labour force was engaged in information processing operations' is another confusion which appears from time to time in the information sector literature (Cawkell 1998: 57).

3 Fritz Machlup (1902–83) was one of many subsequently influential thinkers who were nurtured in the Vienna of the 1920s and 1930s, studying with such luminaries as Ludwig von Mises, Felix Kaufmann, and Alfred Shultz. The Nazi terror, of course, foreclosed this brilliant chapter in intellectual history, and Machlup was among those fortunate enough to escape to a teaching position in the USA. According to *Time* magazine (1962), his name should be pronounced *mock-loop*. Some fascinating biographical material can be found in Dreyer (1978).

4 I will not give a formal breakdown of the growth of the Machlupian school, but representative texts include, in chronological order, Organization for Economic Cooperation and Development (1981), Cooper (1983), Robinson (1986), Nass (1988), and Poirier (1990).

5 Although librarians today acclaim *The Production and Distribution of Knowledge in the United States*, they failed to see its significance when it first appeared. Machlup later (1980: xxv) claimed that his book was reviewed in what he calls the 'magazines and newsletters' of 'librarians' and 'information scientists', but I could find no trace of reviews, listings, or citations in the major professional organs of the day, namely *Library Association Record*, *Journal of Documentation*, *Aslib Proceedings*, *American Documentation*, and *Library Quarterly*.

6 The adjective *Machlupian*, much employed in Chapter 2, is not a neologism of the present work. It was used in Michael Rubin and Mary Huber's *The Knowledge Industry in the United States 1960–1980* (1986: e.g. 3), a painstaking piece of scholarship with which Machlup himself had been closely associated before his death.

7 Of course, this is not to imply that no one else has criticised him. 'Machlup's definition of knowledge seems to be excessively broad, as Bell argues', writes Manuel Castells in *The Rise of the Network Society* (1996: 17). Bell's highly ambivalent criticisms are discussed in Chapter 5.

8 I would actually go much further than Machlup here, and argue that information theory should be forced to relinquish totally the term 'information' in favour of 'signal' or 'transmission'. This would kill two birds with one stone. It would present information science with the option of renaming itself 'information theory', and it would allow computer science to have the coveted term 'information science'. Regrettably, this matter cannot be pursued here.

9 It is perhaps also significant that in Machlup's compilation of essays published as *Methodology of Economics and Other Social Sciences* (1978) there is no mention at all of the methodology he had espoused to measure knowledge and its contribution to US GNP. It would seem that he compartmentalised his thinking, keeping the economics of knowledge separate from mainstream economics. It is even possible that, in certain moods, he did not see the former as a genuine branch of social science.

10 When Machlup mused nearly two decades later about what had influenced him to write *The Production and Distribution of Knowledge in the United States*, he stressed that the 'well-nigh spectacular growth in the 1950s' of the information machine industry, growth which was 'led by the development of the computer and electronic data processing', was a factor in convincing him of 'the need for a quantitative study that would show the share of each knowledge industry in the gross national product of the United States' (1980: xvi–xvii); but psychological causation is not the same thing as logical necessity.

11 Electronic Numerical Integrator and Automatic Calculator.

12 To be fair to Machlup, Newman and Newman were being slightly mischievous. 'Strip-tease' is never mentioned in *The Production and Distribution of Knowledge in the United States*. However, Machlup does include dancers and performers as knowledge workers, and if 'strippers' in the USA of his day were part of the formal economy they would presumably have been subsumed in his totals. It is perhaps a mark of the immaturity of Information Society Studies that even a leading commentator like David Lyon (1988: 52) can quote Newman and Newman without having checked their colourful claims against the primary source.

13 By contrast, Porat did include half of all nurses, thereby significantly augmenting his information services totals. René Poirier's long list of 'occupations with ambiguous informational status' (1990: 271–2) shows how little agreement exists among partisans of what he calls the 'information economy approach'. More recently, Paschal Preston has offered another typology of information services, designed specifically with the Irish information economy in mind: divided Porat-style into 'primary' and 'secondary' sectors, it claims to build on 'earlier models advanced by Fritz Machlup, Marc Porat, the OECD and other sources' (Preston 1997: 193).

14 The proposed volumes tallied closely with the chapter sequence of *The Production and Distribution of Knowledge in the United States*: vol. 1, *Knowledge and Knowledge Production*; vol. II, *The Branches of Learning, Information Sciences, and Human Capital*; vol. III, *Education*; vol. IV, *Research and New Knowledge, Cognitive and Artistic*; vol. V, *Media of Communication*; vol. VI, *Information Services and Information Machines*; vol. VII, *Knowledge Production: Its Size and Growth*; vol. VIII, *Knowledge Occupations and the Knowledgeable Society*.

15 Rubin and Huber's *The Knowledge Industry in the United States 1960–1980* (1986) was considered by its authors to be, in some respects, the equivalent of volumes V–VIII.

16 The legitimacy of casting doubt on Blaug's judgement receives some support from the unlikely direction of *The Accounting Review*. For Orace Johnson, *Knowledge and Knowledge Production* contains 'philosophical inconsistency', notably in its decisions concerning what to include and exclude as knowledge production, alongside the 'true gems of insight' (Johnson 1982: 224). Moreover, Johnson was prepared to make the challenging statement that had Machlup's hypothesis concerning the knowledge sector been cast in the form of a doctoral dissertation it might well have been rejected by the examiners. 'Critics,' he explains, 'may regard the hypothesis as imprecise, the design too loose, and the problematic results too subject to error in doing the project'. The detail of these criticisms is not the point now: what is important, rather, is to observe how an independent thinker, even in what is often regarded as a largely 'vocational' field (i.e. accountancy), can outline a critique which strikes at the foundations of the Machlupian programme.

3 The information flows version of the information society thesis

Introduction

Although Machlup and his school have dominated English-speaking information society research, it is a mistake – of worryingly high incidence – to think that their 'information sector' version constitutes the only available methodology. There is actually more than one route by which theorists have tried to move from point A, industrial society (or more generally, non-information society), to point B, information society. The present chapter expounds and evaluates what will be referred to as the 'information flows' version of the information society thesis. The fruit of a cluster of innovative Japanese research programmes collectively dubbed Joho Shakai (information society) or Johoka Shakai (informationised society), this version attempts to measure the amount of information cascading across the communication channels of society.[1] Methodologically distinct from the information sector approach, it quantifies not the *production* or *distribution* of information, but rather its *consumption*. The analysis proceeds below with one main question to the fore: has the information flows version had more success than the information sector version in securely grounding the information society thesis?

It is important at the outset to realise that 'information flows' in the present context goes well beyond its traditional meaning in information science. Beginning with Derek de Solla Price's *Little Science, Big Science* (1963), bibliometricians have done much valuable work in charting the growth of scholarly documentation – the proliferation of journals, patents, and technical reports, the physical expansion of research library buildings, and so on. The drawback from the point of view of the information society thesis, however, is that such phenomena cannot easily support grandiose statements about a new society or epoch: they deal, by definition, with only a small, albeit important, fraction of total information flows. Joho Shakai, by contrast, offers a *macrolevel* account of information flows. Like information scientists, Joho Shakai theorists ask the question, *Is Information Exploding?* (Ministry of Posts and Telecommunications 1972), but their reply is formulated in terms of the measurement of *all* information flows – without privileging science or any other particular kind of information or knowledge. That is to say, they set out with the assumption that the so-called 'confetti culture' (Klapp 1986) – streams of information flowing at all times and in all directions – impinges not only on professional elites but also on the man on the Clapham omnibus, and indeed on the whole populace. Using this full-blooded construal of the information explosion, Joho Shakai is *prima facie* much better placed to sustain any thesis concerning socio-economic change.

While the Japanese origins of the descriptor 'information society' have already been explored (Chapter 1), one or two further details must now be given concerning the historical relationship between the information sector version and the information flows version. In the preface of the first of his update volumes, Machlup stated that a Japanese translation of *The Production and Distribution of Knowledge in the United States* had been published in 1969 under the title *Chishiki Sangyo*, which literally means 'knowledge industry' (Takahashi and Kida 1969), and that this phrase had 'caught on in Japanese discussion' (Machlup 1980: xxv). He goes on to suggest that as a result of large sales of his book, 'interest in the growth of knowledge production has remained intense', and says that a 'research institution', which he does not name, had published another book (title unspecified) measuring knowledge production in Japan. Machlup may have been referring to *An Analysis of the Information Economy in Japan from 1960 to 1980* (Komatsuzaki *et al*. n.d.), published by the Research Institute of Telecommunications and Economics (RITE) some time in the 1970s, or to an earlier draft thereof: Rubin and Huber describe this as a work 'following Machlup's intellectual framework' (1986: 6). If not, he might have had in mind one of the other RITE research efforts described below, although these do *not* follow his framework. Either way, Machlup seemed to be under the impression that all information society research in Japan was of the 'information sector' variety which he had pioneered. If this is the case, he was mistaken. While there has certainly been Machlup-type research activity in Japan, and while most Western commentators on the Japanese information society still seem to be aware only of that type (e.g. McLean 1985; Morris-Suzuki 1988), the Joho Shakai work discussed below is entirely *sui generis*.

This claim is supported by considering its disciplinary orientation. Joho Shakai has been led neither by economists nor by information scientists, but by researchers whose angle of interest in information has been specifically its *communication*, more particularly its telecommunication. Tetsuro Tomita, the first author to report Joho Shakai in an English-language medium, enjoyed the intriguing job title of 'Counsellor of Telecommunications' in Japan's Ministry of Posts and Telecommunications: his ground-breaking article appeared in an issue of the *Telecommunication Journal* (Tomita 1975). Furthermore, the scholar who has done more than anyone else to promote Joho Shakai, Professor Youichi Ito of Keio University, is known as 'Japan's most internationally prominent media researcher' (Splichal *et al*. 1994: 17): his key writings are found in leading journals of communication (e.g. Ito 1981, 1991a, 1991b). Finally, Sheldon Harsel, one of the few Americans to have shown any interest in this Japanese school, explicitly situates Joho Shakai within the academic tradition of Communication Studies, noting that 'even the earliest Japanese works on

Information Society development drew on a century of concern with the personal, societal, and cultural functions of mass communication' (Harsel 1981: 712). Thus, it is *not* the case that 'the term Jahoka [sic] Shakai or Information Society represents a synthesis of work by both Japanese and American scholars' (Bowes 1981: 699). Joho Shakai is an original effort which blazed its own trail independently of studies of the information sector. Moreover, far from comprising a mature synthesis of Japanese and American work, it is still – in spite of now being over thirty years old – virtually unknown in the West. The burden of exposition and critique rests very heavily.

Primitive Joho Shakai efforts: the Information Ratio and the Johoka Index

It will be argued below that Joho Shakai's major contribution to Information Society Studies is the Information Flow Census. Before examining this, however, brief attention should be paid to two primitive research exercises. Neither of these was particularly convincing, but they are believed on good authority (Ito 1981) to have played a non-negligible role in the early development of Joho Shakai. In a small way, they helped to make possible the Herculean task of quantifying the 'informationisation' of Japanese society as a totality.[2]

The first significant attempt to measure the information explosion, described in RITE reports of 1968 and 1970, was called Joho Keisu. Translated 'Information Ratio', this was a straightforward index of the ratio of expenditure on 'information-related' activities to total expenditure. RITE's research investigated, and duly confirmed, the eminently plausible hypothesis that people will spend money on telephones and books once their fundamental needs for food, clothes, and shelter have been satisfied; or, put more formulaically, that as societies advance economically the proportion of national income spent on information and communications will increase. The Information Ratio had obvious structural similarities with the well-established correlation known as Engel's law, according to which the proportion of family expenditure on food varies *inversely* with family income.

Perhaps RITE's most interesting demonstration was that the Information Ratio varies significantly by country. Figure 3.1, from their 1968 report, shows the Information Ratio along the y-axis against per capita income along the x-axis. Citizens of the USA enjoyed the highest ratio, allocating, even as far back as the 1960s, about 40 per cent of their income to information-related goods and services. But the graph also indicates – and this was no doubt gratifying for the staff at RITE – that the Information Ratio was also very high in Japan, especially when set against its modest average income level. With a per capita income six or seven times less than that of the USA, the Japanese were spending, over thirty years ago, approximately a third of their income on information. Ito makes the fascinating suggestion – which I must refrain from pursuing – that cultural factors are at work here, i.e. that, just as it is known that Latin peoples are more likely than Anglo-Saxons to spend spare money on luxurious

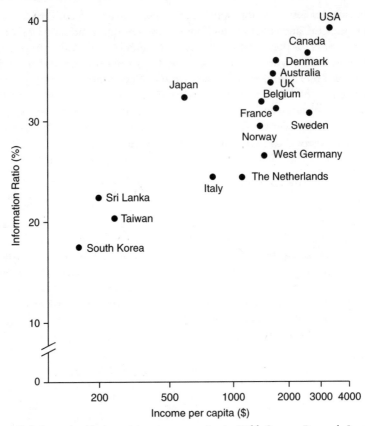

Figure 3.1 Information Ratio and income per capita in 1966. Source: Research Institute of Telecommunications and Economics 1968

meals, so 'the propensity to spend money on information-related activities appears to be stronger in some countries or cultures than in others' (Ito 1981: 674). On the whole, the RITE rankings were congruent with those of theorists subscribing to the information sector version of the information society thesis: America leads the way in informationisation, with Western Europe and the East Asian 'tigers' in, respectively, slow and swift pursuit. The methodology, however, was very crude. RITE did not try to identify the informational elements in the family budget, assuming instead that every expenditure which was not on something overtly non-informational like victuals or transport should be treated as information-related. While it neatly circumvents the vexed question of how to define information, this negative approach also entails that the Information Ratio ended up as little more than a measure of the ratio of *miscellaneous* expenditures to total domestic consumption (Tanaka 1978: 196).

RITE also pioneered a rather more sophisticated formula which they called the Johoka Index. As already mentioned, 'Johoka' is a verbal form of 'joho' and is often used in conjunction with 'Shakai' (society) to form 'informationised society'. 'Johoka' can also exist on its own, where it means 'informationisation': this enables Japanese authors to speak of degrees or phases of informationisation, much as we do with the word 'industrialisation'. The Johoka Index incorporated the Information Ratio alongside a range of other factors supposedly indicative of a nation's level of informationisation. These were organised as follows (after RITE 1970):

A Information Ratio
1 Information expenditure as a proportion of total expenditure

B Quality of information activities
1 Proportion of service workers in total labour population
2 Proportion of students in total appropriate age group

C Amount of information
1 Telephone calls per person per year
2 Newspaper circulation per 100 people
3 Books published per 1,000 people
4 Population density (a measure of interpersonal communication)

D Distribution of communication media
1 Telephone receivers per 100 people
2 Radio sets per 100 households
3 Television sets per 100 households

The Johoka Index can be broken down into three strands. B relates to the production sector and has something in common with Machlup's methodology. Categories A and C are measures of information flows within society, i.e. of information consumption. D is also *sui generis*: measures of the 'distribution of communication media' are not measures of information *flows* or of the information *sector* but of something else, of what would today be called 'technological infrastructure' or 'IT diffusion'. The three elements tally to some degree with the 'versions' of the information society thesis discussed in this book.

Table 3.1 shows the Johoka Index of Japan and some other countries typically included in Japan's political reference group. Figures representing each of the categories are provided, with the overall Johoka Index calculated as their mean value. Thus, in 1953 Japan had an Information Ratio worth 73, Quality of information activities valued at 85, an Amount of information figure of 93, and enough telephones, radios, and televisions to earn it a rating of 49 for the Distribution of communication media. When added together and divided by four, these numbers yield a Johoka Index of 75. Ten years later, in 1963, the index had risen to 193, a leap which owed much to increases in the diffusion of media; and RITE estimated that by 1975 it would have nearly doubled to 379. The USA, of course, emerges as the most advanced nation, with a Johoka Index of 272 in 1953, 370 in 1963, and 648 (projected) in 1975. However,

Table 3.1 Johoka Indices of Japan and other nations (see text for explanation)

	Japan			USA			UK			West Germany			France		
	1953	1963	1975*	1953	1963	1975*	1953	1963	1975*	1953	1963	1975*	1953	1963	1975*
Johoka Index	75	193	379	272	370	648	133	231	312	76	160	292	88	136	249
Information Ratio	73	126	184	141	159	171	120	132	146	87	105	124	118	121	157
Quality of information activities	85	113	185	203	294	374	65	112	163	65	87	112	82	108	120
Amount of information	93	108	152	96	142	232	104	118	151	59	103	119	53	54	105
Distribution of communication media	49	426	996	647	992	1815	243	560	815	92	344	828	101	261	615

Source: Research Institute of Telecommunications and Economics 1970

*Estimated

what is again striking about the figures is that Japan, having started as the least informationised of the five nations, had by the early 1960s moved into third place, after the USA and the UK. Moreover, RITE, in 1970, was estimating that Japan would shortly overtake the UK to become 'the second most "informationalized" society in the world' (Ito 1981: 676).

The Johoka Index pointed in the right direction for a more rounded account of the informational dimensions of socio-economic development. However, as with Joho Keisu, it was too simplistic. It aspired to be an 'information society index' (Tateno 1978: 9), but it could not work as such precisely because it omitted a sociological rationale, an account of how the various putative empirical criteria of informationisation fuse in a theory of society. For example, when RITE stated that 'a post-industrial society is a society with a per capita income of more than \$4000, a service sector which exceeds 50% of total labour force, a student population of more than 50% of the relevant age cohort, and an Information Ratio of over 50%' (reported in Ito 1981: 676), the stipulation looked wholly arbitrary. It begged too many questions. Why is \$4,000 the economic cut-off point? Why should the student population have to be so high? What relevance does services employment have to informationisation? I will argue later that Information Society Studies does indeed need to turn towards a *synthetic* approach to the measurement of informationisation. However, this cannot be simply a matter of seizing a set of *prima facie* loosely related criteria and then announcing that if society x satisfies a mean value of all of them, society x must be an information society.

Joho Shakai's grand experiment: the Information Flow Census

Joho Shakai's greatest contribution so far to information society methodology has been an ambitious Information Flow Census regularly conducted by the Ministry of Posts and Telecommunications (MPT) in Tokyo. Now the point of the Information Flow Census is essentially very straightforward: it is an empirical survey of the *volume* and *vehicles* of information in circulation in a society. In much the same way that population censuses show how many people there are in a society, and into what categories (occupational, residential, and so on) they fall, the goal of the Information Flow Census was and is to be able to say that there is a 10^n amount of information in society, and that this information is shared among such-and-such media in such-and-such proportions. The idea can be traced back to a report published in 1969 by the Information Study Group of the Association for Economic Planning, entitled *Johoka Shakai no Keisei (The Formation of an Informationised Society)*: appearing shortly after the Information Ratio and the Johoka Index were launched, this document contained the first-ever attempt to 'express the amount of information flow in different media by a common unit' (Ito 1981: 680). In the event, the Information Study Group's programme was not followed through, but some of its ideas were adopted by the much better-resourced MPT, which in 1975 produced the first truly comprehensive census of Japanese information flows. The work has been maintained ever since, with the results published by the MPT's General Planning and Policy Division in their annual *White Paper on Communications*.

MPT methodology

The MPT officially defined information very broadly as any symbol, signal, or image having a meaning for either the sender or the receiver. In practice, a semantics-free information theory approach has been followed: if a sender speaks gibberish down a telephone line to a receiver then this 'flow' enters the census as information. The census also makes no distinction between old and new information, embracing every message flowing through the whole range of communication channels. Only three conditions have been applied: (a) there must be a transfer of information from one point to another, thereby excluding transfers inside a single communication system, such as a standalone computer; (b) the flow must be intentional: unwilled messages such as those allegedly transmitted by 'body language' are excluded; (c) both the sender and the receiver must be either human or a machine working directly to a human will, ruling out animal communications. Flows have been measured across an extraordinarily wide range of media. They cover both personal ('point-to-point') and mass media, and both print and electronic media, and include the following: public telephones (i.e. call boxes); mobile telephones (which have been used by the Japanese business community for a generation); private telephones; wire broadcast and telephone (a specialised system used in local networks); public telegraph; private telegraph; radio; television; wire broadcast; cable television; mail; direct mail; newspapers; books; magazines; advertising literature; phonograph records; music tapes; lectures; education; entertainment; outdoor advertising (billboards, etc.); and even, in the early censuses, face-to-face conversations ('outside the home', but not further defined).

Since the main objective of the Information Flow Census was, and is, to compare and aggregate transmissions of information across different media, the MPT researchers were faced with the problem of finding a viable common denominator for their data. This led them to the construction of 'conversion rates' stipulating how much information was being carried by a particular medium over a specified time. Initially, they chose binary digits as the unit of measurement. However, they soon discovered that the bit rate varies with the form of transmission of a message: sending a character by telegraphy or computers, for example, involved between five and eight bits, whereas its transmission by facsimile required (after translation into pixels) hundreds. For this reason they transferred to words after the first census. Table 3.2 shows some typical MPT conversion rates. As can be seen, a minute of speech was deemed to use up on average 120 words, while a picture on a page was worth eighty. A minute of television or cinema or of a lecture in the classroom was worth 1,320 words, because such minutes characteristically comprise a rapid sequence of pictures as well as words. Although the details of some of the conversion rates might be disputed, this attempt to work out the informativeness

Table 3.2 Conversion rates for various information media

Medium	Form of expression	Normal unit of measurement	Conversion rate (words per unit)
Telephone	Voice	minute	120
Telegraph	Characters	character	0.3
Data communication	Characters	character	0.3
Facsimile	Still pictures	page	80
Radio broadcasting	Voice	minute	120
TV broadcasting	Voice + Moving pictures	minute	1,320
Mail (postcard)	Characters	character	0.4
Newspaper	Characters	character	0.4
Book	Characters	character	0.4
Music record and tape	Music and/or Voice	minute	120
Conversation (outside home)	Voice + Images in motion	minute	1,320
School education	Voice + Images in motion	minute	1,320
Social education	Voice + Images in motion	minute	1,320
Cinema	Voice + Images in motion	minute	1,320

Source: Ministry of Posts and Telecommunications 1978

of non-verbal media has been one of Joho Shakai's most engaging contributions to methodology.

The volume of information in society

Table 3.3 contains some of the raw data for the first census in 1975. It will be noticed immediately that there is no single column headed 'Volume of information', the reason being that the MPT made a fundamental distinction between *supply* and *consumption* of information. Column 4 (Supply A) refers to the information transmitted by the sender regardless of whether or not the information is read or otherwise consumed at the other end, while column 5 denotes the amount of information actually consumed. In some cases, especially with point-to-point media, the figures are the same. For example, it was estimated that in 1960, 3.034×10^9 pages of private mail were sent; since private letters are usually read in their entirety, the assumption was made that 3.034×10^9 pages of private mail were also consumed. Private telephone calls too normally exact the full attention of the receiver, so if 8.616×10^9 minutes of calls were documented in 1972 then 8.616×10^9 minutes of information flow were both supplied and consumed. On the other hand, direct mail, i.e. what is today called junk mail, does not typically command the attention of all who are subjected to it, so the supply figures are considerably higher than the consumption figures.

The MPT took the view that in order to reflect their nature as mass media, the supply of radio and television programmes should be measured at the receiver end, and thus count as multiple information transfers (although they of course

Table 3.3   Volume of information flow classified by type of media (from Tomita 1975: 340–3)

Medium	Year	Unit	Supply A	Consumption B	Standard supply $A \times \alpha$ (bits)	Effective consumption $B \times \beta$ (bits)
Public telephone	1960	min	Same as at right	2.557×10^{10} min	1.5726×10^{15}	0.5870×10^{14}
	1965			4.287	2.6365	0.9003
	1970			7.497	4.8628	1.6605
	1972			10.903	6.4530	2.2035
Private telephone	1960	min	Same as at right	0.613×10^{9} min	0.3776×10^{14}	1.2894×10^{12}
	1965			1.702	1.0467	3.5742
	1970			5.256	3.2324	11.0376
	1972			8.616	5.2988	18.0936
Private data transmission	1960	min	Same as at right			
	1965			0.0108×10^{9} min	0.0200×10^{13}	0.0256×10^{12}
	1970			0.2257	0.4182	0.0341
	1972			0.8790	38.6846	40.4080
Facsimile	1960	copy	Same as at right	1.6597×10^{7} copy	1.2610×10^{12}	1.3809×10^{11}
	1965			2.8220	2.3140	2.3479
	1970			5.1035	4.1849	4.2461
	1972			8.6397	7.0846	7.1882
Radio	1960	min	1.87×10^{14} min	2.61×10^{12} min	3.4595×10^{19}	9.3177×10^{15}
	1965		2.16	0.77	3.9960	2.7489
	1970		2.48	0.86	4.5880	3.0702
	1972		2.61	1.59	4.8285	5.6763
Television	1960	min	0.53×10^{14} min	1.91×10^{12} min	3.1005×10^{19}	1.5471×10^{16}
	1965		1.29	5.95	7.5465	4.8195
	1970		1.72	6.60	13.3300	6.5736
Mail	1960	copy	Same as at right	3.034×10^{9} copy	3.7318×10^{14}	3.7925×10^{13}
	1965			4.276	5.2595	5.3450
	1970			5.232	6.4354	6.5400
	1972			5.834	7.1758	7.2925
Direct mail	1960	copy	1.77×10^{9} min	6.266×10^{8} copy	2.0355×10^{13}	3.9163×10^{12}
	1965		2.26	8.000	2.5990	5.000
	1970		2.82	9.983	3.2430	6.2394
	1972		2.92	10.328	3.3553	6.4550
Books	1960	unit/ min	1.460×10^{8} unit	0.931×10^{11} min	0.6716×10^{16}	3.8730×10^{14}
	1965		2.833	1.383	1.3032	5.7533
	1970		4.690	1.831	2.1574	7.6170
	1972		4.684	1.956	2.1546	8.1370
Advertising literature	1960	sheet	3.489×10^{9} sheet	4.761×10^{8} sheet	2.8610×10^{14}	3.9612×10^{12}
	1965		3.788	5.170	3.1062	4.3014
	1970		6.367	8.689	5.2209	7.2292
	1972		6.630	9.048	5.4366	7.5280

Source: Ministry of Posts and Telecommunications

α = standard volume of information; β = effective volume of information

Average flow distance L (km)	Standard supply distance $A \times \alpha \times L$ (bit-km)	Effective consumption distance $B \times \beta \times L$ (bit-km)	Annual circulation cost C (yen)	Standard supply unit cost (yen) $C/(A \times \alpha \times L)$	Effective consumption unit cost (yen) $C/(B \times \beta \times L)$
5.1	0.8020×10^{16}	0.2744×10^{15}	2.19×10^{11}	2.7306×10^{-5}	7.981×10^{-4}
9.7	2.5574	0.8742	4.22	1.6501	4.942
15.4	7.4887	3.0155	9.86	1.3166	3.270
23.9	15.4227	5.2561	12.47	0.8085	2.372
34.2	1.2914×10^{15}	0.4410×10^{14}	2.224×10^{10}	1.722×10^{-6}	5.043×10^{-4}
30.0	3.1402	1.0723	3.491	1.112	3.256
25.9	8.3720	2.8587	6.982	0.798	2.337
24.2	12.8231	4.3787	9.340	0.728	2.133
21.4	0.0428×10^{14}	0.0548×10^{13}	0.124×10^{9}	2.897×10^{-5}	2.263×10^{-4}
19.5	0.8155	1.5902	0.490	0.601	0.308
13.8	53.8847	55.7630	59.499	1.115	1.067
9.2	1.2521×10^{13}	1.2704×10^{12}	2.09×10^{8}	1.669×10^{-5}	1.645×10^{-4}
15.0	3.4710	3.5219	2.55	0.735	0.724
17.4	7.2817	7.3882	3.07	0.422	0.416
9.0	6.3761	6.4694	4.35	0.682	0.672
61.1	2.1138×10^{21}	5.6931×10^{17}	1.12×10^{10}	5.299×10^{-13}	1.967×10^{-8}
64.4	2.5734	1.7708	1.00	3.886	5.649
56.0	2.5693	1.7193	1.86	7.239	10.818
54.3	2.6219	3.0822	2.06	7.857	6.684
57.5	1.7828×10^{21}	0.8896×10^{18}	2.80×10^{10}	1.571×10^{-11}	3.147×10^{-8}
50.5	3.810	2.4338	6.85	1.797	2.815
51.5	6.8650	3.3854	8.94	1.302	2.641
163.8	0.6113×10^{17}	0.6238×10^{16}	0.378×10^{10}	0.6183×10^{-7}	0.608×10^{-6}
159.9	0.8410	0.8549	0.691	0.8216	0.808
156.0	1.0039	1.0202	1.260	1.2551	1.235
154.5	1.1087	1.1264	1.608	1.4503	1.428
163.8	3.3341×10^{15}	6.4166×10^{14}	1.23×10^{10}	0.3689×10^{-5}	1.917×10^{-5}
159.9	4.1558	7.9973	2.21	0.5317	2.763
156.0	5.0591	9.7335	4.12	0.8143	4.233
154.5	5.1839	9.9701	5.36	1.0339	5.376
40.6	2.7267×10^{17}	1.5724×10^{16}	0.935×10^{10}	3.429×10^{-8}	0.595×10^{-6}
40.6	5.2910	2.3358	2.659	5.026	1.138
40.6	8.7590	3.0925	5.714	6.524	1.848
40.6	8.7483	3.3036	6.937	7.930	2.100
2.14	0.6128×10^{15}	0.8477×10^{13}	1.998×10^{9}	3.268×10^{-6}	2.357×10^{-4}
2.14	0.6647	0.9205	2.895	4.355	3.145
2.14	1.1178	1.5470	6.514	5.830	4.211
2.14	1.1634	1.6110	7.610	6.541	4.724

usually issue from a single studio): the supply figures for electronic mass media were thus arrived at by multiplying the message by the size of the potential audience, as given, for example, by the number of radios or television sets in society. The difference between the volume supplied and the volume consumed can be colossal: for example, of 1.89×10^{14} minutes of TV supplied in 1972 only 6.40×10^{12} were watched, and the mismatch had grown over the whole time frame. However, while the supply of mass media, so defined, will always be greater than its consumption, with other media the converse is sometimes true. Books, for example, had to be measured not only in 'units', i.e. copies, but also in 'minutes', because they are often read by more than one person. In other words, by 'consumption' the MPT really means perception rather than purchase – a significant departure from conventional economics.

Table 3.3 indicates that the volume of information flowing through most of the media was increasing. For example, information supplied by means of books increased from 1.460×10^8 units in 1960 to 4.684×10^8 in 1972, having peaked at 4.690×10^8 in 1970, while the volume of information supplied in the form of advertising literature nearly doubled over the time frame. As for electronic media, public telephone calls increased from 2.557×10^{10} in 1960 to 10.903×10^{10} in 1972, facsimile increased from 1.6597×10^7 in 1960 to 8.6397×10^7 in 1972, and private data transmission, which seemingly did not exist in recordable form in Japan in 1960, went from 0.0108×10^9 in 1965 to 0.8790×10^9 in 1972. These data indeed demonstrate an 'informationisation' of Japanese society. The figures were both huge as absolute totals and indicative of rapid rates of increase, and they placed researchers, arguably for the first time in history, in a position where they could assert on solid empirical grounds that a society had indeed undergone a generalised – as opposed to scientific or STM – information explosion.

Bunshu Shakai: breakdown of the census figures

The MPT investigated not only the volume but also the distance and cost of information flows in Japan. By 'distance' they meant the total physical space covered by the transmission of messages from sender to receiver. This was measured in 'bit-kilometre' (or, later, 'word-kilometre'), on the analogy of 'ton-km' and 'person-km' in transportation statistics. The bit-km was derived by multiplying the quantity of information consumed by the number of kilometres between senders and receivers; for example, the bit-km of a transmission which travels 100 km is 100 times that of the same message travelling 1 km. Column 8 of Table 3.3 indicates that the average flow distance of a public telephone call increased from 5.1 km in 1960 to 23.9 km in 1972, while the bit-km went from 0.8020×10^{14} to 15.4227×10^{14}. By contrast, the distance of the average private call decreased from 34.2 km to 24.2 km. No doubt such figures are commonplace in telecommunications surveys, but the Information Flow Census broke new ground by working out equivalents for television, radio, books, and many other media. For example, the average TV broadcast travelled

57.5 km in 1960 and 51.9 km twelve years later, while the average book was sent 40.6 km over the whole time frame. Overall, it was demonstrated that Japan was becoming more 'telecommunicative', in the sense of being inclined to communicate over progressively longer distances.

The practical utility of the bit-kilometre figures becomes more obvious when they are combined with calculations of the comparative costs of information flows. 'Information flow cost per unit' was defined as the cost of sending one unit of information by a particular medium over one unit of distance, and was derived by dividing the information flow cost by the information flow amount-distance (i.e. consumption × distance). Figures 3.2 and 3.3 delineate the comparative cost of transmitting messages between 1960 and 1972, for personal and mass media respectively. Upward movement in these diagrams indicates an expansion in the circulation of information in society, and vice versa. Leftward movement indicates a reduction in information flow cost per unit, and vice versa. Hence, an upward-leftward curve suggests that a medium is prospering, while a downward-rightward movement is a sign of declension. Of the personal

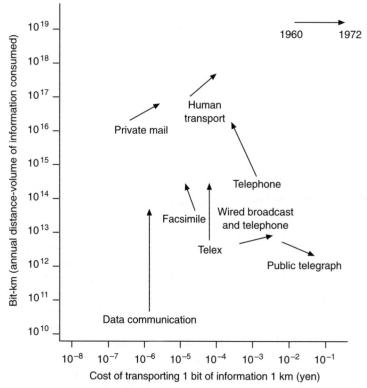

Figure 3.2 Distance-volume of effective consumption of information and unit cost: personal communication media (from Tomita 1975: 347). Source: Ministry of Posts and Telecommunications

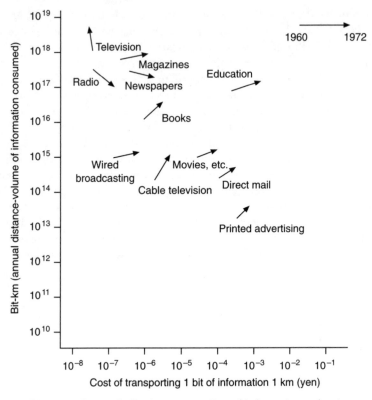

Figure 3.3 Distance-volume of effective consumption of information and unit cost: mass communication media (from Tomita 1975: 348). Source: Ministry of Posts and Telecommunications

media, telephony, facsimile, and data communication were expanding their share at the expense, notably, of telegraphy. At the same time, while human transport (presumably couriers) and mail were not yet losing ground, their increasing unit costs seemed to bode ill for the future. As regards mass media, television, including cable TV, was clearly in the ascendancy in Japan during this period, while newspapers and the cinema were going into decline. In reporting these figures, Tomita argued that only those media possessing an in-built mechanism for lowering their own unit costs had a long-term future, and was convinced that electronics alone could supply such a mechanism. This led him to recommend that 'the first approach to any information media policy preparatory to the next age should be to consider how electronics can be applied to all other media': for those which cannot be thus modified, he concluded ominously, information policy would involve a consideration of 'how they should be treated in their final stage' (Tomita 1975: 349).

Whether or not this kind of obituary-writing was warranted, the inexorable substitution of electronic for non-electronic media was one of the MPT's salient findings. However, not all electronic media were safe, as the rightward-downward curve for radio shows. Naoyuki Okada, ruminating on the same data set, suggested that, although radio and TV still accounted for 96 per cent of total mass media flows, this 'does not necessarily mean that the broadcast media will be the nucleus of an Information Society'; he predicted that point-to-point data communication was destined to play the leading role (Okada 1978: 156). The 1978 *White Paper on Communications* made this momentous prognosis official:

> The demand for information provided by mass media, which are one-way communication, has become stagnant, and the demand for information provided by personal telecommunication media, which are characterized by two-way communication, has drastically increased. This means that our society is moving toward a new stage of Johoka Shakai in which more priority is placed on segmented, more detailed information to meet individual needs instead of conventional mass-reproduced conformed information.
>
> (MPT 1978, cited in Ito 1981: 688)

Ito designates the emergent social formation 'Bunshu Shakai', meaning 'segmented information society' (1991b: 41–2). The information environment of Bunshu Shakai is to be characterised not by propaganda, advertisements, and other staples of the mass media, but by 'extracted' information, i.e. information which the individual him or herself derives from their environment through direct observation, active information gathering, and research. Ito cited the searching of online databases as a model of extracted information; since he wrote, of course, the growth of the Internet has done much to vindicate Bunshu Shakai. Thus the Information Flow Census seems to supply an empirical basis not just for an undifferentiated theory of the information society, but also for a more nuanced theory of *stages* of informationisation. I postpone a fuller evaluation until later.

The Japan–USA comparative census

Despite an impressive track record of a quarter of a century of assiduous research and publication, the MPT Information Flow Census has been almost entirely ignored by Western information society theorists. However, its early reports did inspire one bilateral conference in 1977 hosted by the University of Washington. Speakers included the chief figures in Joho Shakai, notably Tetsuro Tomita and Youichi Ito, and, adding considerable academic respectability, the distinguished American communication scholar Ithiel de Sola Pool. (Marc Porat, partisan of the Machlupian version, was also discreetly in attendance.) The mood of the delegates was confident, with Ito predicting that they would be responsible for 'formally and systematically' introducing the Joho Shakai 'paradigm' into the United States (Ito 1978: 253).[3]

That certainly did not happen – the information sector version has retained any paradigmatic status on offer – but the conference did result in one significant piece of collaborative research under Pool's leadership (Pool *et al.* 1984). As with the MPT's pioneering work, *Communications Flows: A Census in the United States and Japan* construed the measurement of information flows as a matrix for a broader claim about the nature of information societies:

> The understanding of an information explosion based upon quantitative evaluation seems to be crucial for the United States and Japan, which are information suppliers and consumers in the world. Such studies may also influence other countries to conduct similar research, and through a concerted global effort the Information Flow Census may be recognized as an important social indicator for information-oriented societies.
>
> (Pool *et al.* 1984: preface)

Pool *et al.* also strongly believed, as have most information society theorists whatever their methodological pedigree, that the information society transcends national differences and represents in some degree a standard post-industrial social formation: the concurrent trends documented for Japan and the United States 'reflect,' they opined, 'the course of modern information societies, not just coincidences in two countries' (1984: 36).

The 'improved methodology'

Pool *et al.* claim in their preface that, while their research built upon the earlier work by the MPT, it employed an 'improved methodology'. The similarities, however, are quickly revealed to be much more extensive than any dissimilarities. The same common unit, namely words, is used: notwithstanding the linguistic niceties involved in normalising the denotation of 'word' across two very different languages, Pool *et al.* made sure that they did not repeat the MPT's early error of trying to operate with binary digits. They also employed a very similar, only shorter, list of media: television; cable television; records and tapes (USA only); cinema; school education; newspapers; magazines; books; telephone books (Japan only; classed with other books in the US data); direct mail; first class mail; telephone; telex; telegrams; mailgrams (a service started in 1972 combining post and telegraphy; USA only); facsimile; and data communication. Indeed, it transpires that for the Japanese data sets in this comparative survey, the researchers relied entirely upon the early MPT census figures discussed above. This is disappointing, since the Japanese collaborators on a project whose findings were published in the mid-1980s might have been expected to draw upon later censuses. Moreover, the US data went up to 1980, which entails that the two data sets are partly incommensurable.

The improvement in methodology consisted simply in a hard-headed decision to abandon the attempt to convert pictures and other non-verbal information into verbal equivalents. 'We felt,' Pool *et al.* write (1984: 4), 'such conversions to be beyond the state of the art; indeed it strains the limits of audacity to throw all explicit words together'. While acknowledging that much is lost in excluding non-verbal communications, they claim that they 'do not know how to include them in a meaningful way'. Audio-visual media are still on their list, but Pool *et al.* ignored all imagery and music and counted only the actual words transmitted during programmes. It is a moot point whether this was really an improvement. Certainly, the MPT conversion rates are problematic, but it may still be the case that even a crude attempt at converting non-verbal media into words is preferable to ignoring major dimensions of the information explosion: if one thing is clear about post-industrialism and the information society it is surely that the 'hegemony' of text is being eroded.

It would be wrong, however, to imply that Pool *et al.* thought that their informetric techniques were unimpeachable. On the contrary, like Machlup, they confessed their methodological shortcomings almost with alacrity, acknowledging that there were 'data problems for every single medium' – from books, where reading research was far too patchy, to data communication, where, in the early 1980s, 'adequate reporting of traffic [did] not yet exist' (Pool *et al.* 1984: 10). They cheerfully state that their project was based largely on 'secondary analyses', on data 'that were collected and published for other purposes' (1984: 40). Pool *et al.* also freely admit that they had a special problem with the delineation of comparative trends, due to the incommensurability of sources and surveys conducted in different countries: divergent definitions of data, divergent conceptions of a word, divergent levels of experience in the research teams, divergent operating procedures among data compilers, and divergent lists of media (see above) were among the factors which, it was acknowledged, militated against the face value of comparative statistics. Nevertheless, they were confident, again very like Machlup, that in the end any biases and errors would cancel each other out: the basic trends could not, they thought, be denied. As for absolute totals, Pool *et al.* solve the problem to their own satisfaction by encouraging the reader to assume a margin of error:

> Perhaps the cautious reader of this report who happens to be interested in absolute levels of media use, rather than trends, should discount the figures he finds by 10% or even by 20%.
>
> (Pool *et al.* 1984: 12)

This blasé caveat would have been entirely at home in *The Production and Distribution of Knowledge in the United States*. In short, the fundamental logic of Pool *et al.*'s case is akin to that of the exponents of the information sector version of the information society thesis: *there may be such-and-such methodological problems, but the overall conclusions are definitely valid.*

Salient findings

Pool *et al.*'s conclusions, like their methodological premises, echoed those of the Joho Shakai pioneers:

> We find in both [countries] an information explosion, a growing overload
> of messages for humans to absorb, and an evolution of traffic that is largely
> shaped by costs.
>
> (Pool *et al.* 1984: 16)

Each of these points may usefully be amplified. As Figure 3.4 shows, it was
discovered that the volume of information flows in both Japan and the USA
was indeed such as to justify rhetoric about an information explosion. Supply
of information per capita in the United States was much higher than in Japan,
mainly as a result of differences in the stages of development of the mass media.
The number of words being *consumed* was also going up in both countries,

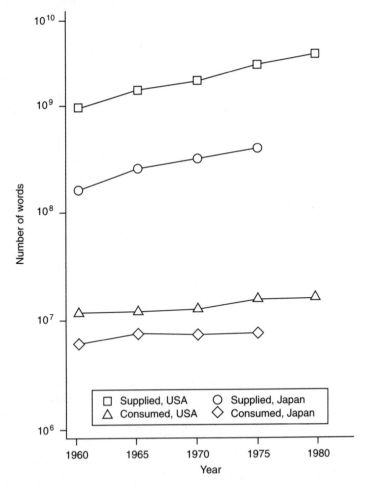

Figure 3.4 Supply and consumption per capita of all media. Source: Pool *et al.* 1984: 19

albeit at a much slower rate. Pool *et al.* (1984: 21) speculate that, since there must be absolute physiological limits on consumption, social trends such as the growth in leisure time over the time frame and people's tendency to indulge in two or more media simultaneously (e.g. television and telephone) could explain this phenomenon. However, the gulf between consumption and supply was vast and widening in both countries. Pool *et al.* helpfully brought their fabulous totals down to earth by working out that the number of words supplied in 1980 to the average American, by all media combined, was nearly eleven million per day; of these, only 48,000 were consumed. Thus, the scenario was one of huge 'information overload' – as the man on the Clapham omnibus had long suspected.

The comparative study also corroborated the MPT's finding that the fortunes of the individual media were a function of their costs. As can be seen from Table 3.4, there was a wide variation in the cost of transmitting 1,000 words in the USA over the period 1960–80. Cinema, school education, newspapers, magazines, and books became comparatively expensive vehicles of dissemination. On the other hand, telephone, television, facsimile, and data transmission became more cost-effective – the last of these dramatically so. As a general rule, the electronic media were triumphing over print media. Table 3.5 shows changes in their share of total information supply and consumption, for both the USA and Japan. In 1960, electronic media accounted for 92.2 per cent of information supplied in the USA; by 1980 they accounted for 97.6 per cent.

Table 3.4   US costs (in [1972] cents) of transmitting 1,000 words

	1960	*1980*
Radio	0.0005	0.0002
Television	0.005	0.002
Cable television	0.13	0.025
Records and tapes	n.a.	74.8
Cinema	0.48	0.57
Education	6.5	14.5
Newspapers	0.053	0.058
Magazines	0.16	0.18
Books	0.74	1.0
Direct mail	0.51	0.59
First class mail	19.0	24.6
Telephone	23.1	19.0
Telex	9,354	4,095
Telegrams	5,008	5,515
Mailgrams	[Did not exist]	1,033
Facsimile	1,914	221
Data	129	10

Source: Pool *et al.* 1984: 19

n.a., not available

Table 3.5   Change in balance of print and electronic media

Per cent of	USA Volume supplied 1960	1980	USA Volume consumed 1960	1980	Japan Volume supplied 1960	1975	Japan Volume consumed 1960	1975
Print media	7.6	2.3	31.4	17.0	14.1	7.8	28.9	24.6
Electronic media	92.2	97.6	58.3	76.2	84.6	91.9	57.4	68.4
Other media[a]	0.2	0.1	10.3	6.8	1.3	0.3	13.7	7.0

Source: Pool *et al.* 1984: 26

[a]Cinema and education were not classified as either print or electronic media

Table 3.6   Growth rates in 1970s compared with full period

		Mass media Words supplied (%)	Words consumed (%)	Point-to-point media
USA:	1960–80	8.4	3.2	5.8
	1970–75	8.2	3.8	5.3
	1975–80	5.9	2.6	6.9
Japan:	1960–75	9.5	3.2	9.5
	1970–75	10.5	4.2	11.5

Source: Pool *et al.* 1984: 52

That is to say, for every two or three printed words in the USA, there were, even as long ago as 1980, nearly 100 electronic words shooting across the info sphere; and Japan was not far behind. A process of 'electronic informationisation' was evidently well advanced in both countries.

As with the earlier MPT censuses, however, the American research team also registered a recent migration away from the electronic mass media. According to Table 3.6, the growth rate in the supply of mass media words in the USA decreased from 8.2 per cent in 1970–5 to 5.9 per cent in 1975–80. The consumption figures also fell, mainly as a result of a smaller proportion of radio and television being consumed. In short, the electronic mass media in America had reached the 'familiar saturation phase of an S-shaped growth curve' (Pool *et al.* 1984: 32). Figure 3.5 shows exactly how individual media have fared in the USA over a twenty-year period: the patterns – movies in trouble, telegraphy plummeting, cable TV and data communication prospering, and so on – have much in common with the situation in Japan.

The comparative study, like the MPT blueprint, singled out computer networking as an electronic point-to-point medium of great promise and significance. It will be recalled that, back in 1962, Machlup had spoken lyrically of the nascent 'electronic-computer industry' as a 'story that must not be missed'. Thirteen years later, Tomita (1975: 349) spoke of microelectronics 'ushering in

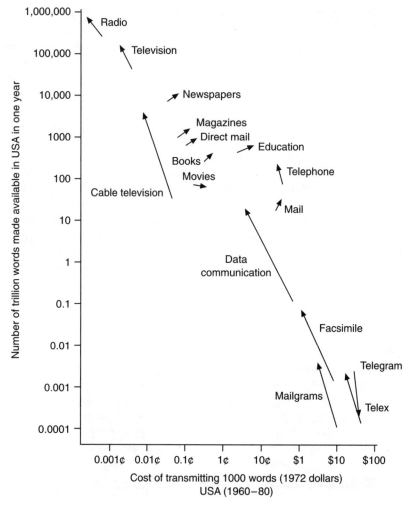

Figure 3.5 Volume and costs of communication by media. Source: Pool *et al.* 1984: 18

the present computer age'. Here we hear Pool and his collaborators reporting excitedly that, in the latter part of their time frame, 'computer communication began an explosive growth', of the order of 'about 28% per annum' (1984: 27). Indeed, they set computing alongside writing, printing, and telegraphy as one of the four great communications revolutions of history, and one which would be instrumental in 'raising the total volume of communication in society by orders of magnitude, as printing did at an earlier time and as radio and television did more recently' (Pool *et al.* 1984: 31). The vital truth about networked computing was that it was bringing the costs of point-to-point communication down to the level of the mass media. 'For the first time,' Pool *et al.* state (1984: 30), this new technology 'bridges the uses of mass media and point-to-point media, competing with both'. That is to say, the contributors to this unique piece of bilateral information census research believed in what is commonly known as the 'information revolution'. In the assigning of a starring role to the computer, the versions of the information society thesis examined so far speak with one voice.

Some recent MPT findings

Communications Flows was the first substantive Western involvement in information flows research: it was also the last (Dordick and Wang 1993: 51). The MPT Information Flow Census has, however, been faithfully maintained, with recent findings more or less corroborating the trends identified in the 1970s. The census methodology has diversified over the years, and now incorporates measures of international information traffic, as illustrated in Figure 3.6. The MPT has also begun measuring information stocks. How relevant these are to 'informationisation' is not yet entirely clear. Japanese authors have tended to confine their understanding of Johoka to increases in the amount and speed of information *flows* in society, but in one of his most influential

Figure 3.6 Volume of information sent between Japan and other countries. Source: Ministry of Posts and Telecommunications 1995

papers Ito defined Joho Shakai as 'a society characterized by abundant information in terms of *both stock and flow*' (1981: 672, my italic). Figure 3.7 shows the situation in 1993, with 'information stock' defined as information held for at least one year for reuse, and including books, library resources, and recordings of TV broadcasts. Japan's total stock was 1.51×10^{15}, of which books in homes accounted for a massive 73.6 per cent (MPT 1995: 15). It is interesting to speculate that if information stocks were themselves measured on an international scale Japan might fall steeply down the Johoka 'league table', behind not only the USA but also many venerable bibliophilic European countries like France and the UK. Perhaps this is why the White Papers do not include, and the MPT has no stated plans to include, comparative stock statistics.[4]

The latest figures for information flows, supplied in the 1998 *White Paper on Communications in Japan*, reveal that information continued to explode between 1986 and 1996:

> The results show that the amount of all types of information distributed rose significantly over the ten-year period, by an average of about 9%. This exceeded the 3.1% average growth rate of real GDP over the same period. The rise in information flow is attributable to the rapid increase in personal media using telecommunications, as well as growing use of the Internet and media with large data transmission capacity.
>
> (MPT 1998: 46)

In other words, Bunshu Shakai, the segmented information society, has now become a reality in Japan. Perhaps then this is the way that all information societies are destined to go?

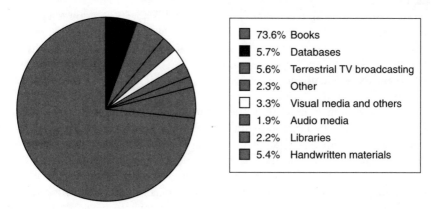

73.6% Books
5.7% Databases
5.6% Terrestrial TV broadcasting
2.3% Other
3.3% Visual media and others
1.9% Audio media
2.2% Libraries
5.4% Handwritten materials

Figure 3.7 Proportion of information stocks of various media. Source: Ministry of Posts and Telecommunications 1995

The Information Flow Census as a contribution to Information Society Studies

If the task of expounding Joho Shakai methodology was unencumbered by a large English-language secondary literature, this is true *a fortiori* of its evaluation. In spite of several decades of large-scale research, the Information Flow Census is apparently not considered in the West to be either a worthy subject for theoretical examination or a viable technique for practical information society research. With the exception of De Sola Pool's study, it has been ignored – eclipsed, no doubt, by the Machlupian methodology. John Bowes, at the close of a short 'critical perspective', had this to say:

> What is surprising, given the scope of their activity and the value inherent in their research perspectives, is the comparatively slight awareness of [Joho Shakai] information research among the North American communication research community.
>
> (Bowes 1981: 708)

Exactly the same charge can be laid at the doors of the English-speaking information science and sociology communities, although in both these cases 'comparatively slight' would be too generous.[5] The aim now is to begin to rectify this lamentable state of affairs, and to see whether a non-primitive information flows version might not be at least as feasible a methodology for Information Society Studies as the information sector version discussed in Chapter 2. It is conceded that what is offered below is based largely on readily available translations, and cannot therefore amount to anything more than a *preliminary* evaluation.

Perhaps I can start by proposing that the measurement of information flows on the 'macro' level is much more than a trivial exercise in informetrics. Notions of information explosion, information overload, info rich *versus* info poor, and the like are a non-negligible constituent of contemporary belief. Now are they veridical or chimerical, true or false? Answering this question requires a proper investigation – such as an Information Flow Census. As Ito points out, the census 'clarifies changes in our society that were previously thought of impressionistically or intuitively' (1981: 692). Perhaps this can be put aphoristically (while adapting, of course, Marx's last thesis on Feuerbach) as: *everyone talks about the information explosion, the point is to quantify it.*

The contention here is that the Information Flow Census has at last scientifically confirmed that individuals in modern societies are being subjected to an ever-increasing – with some media, exponentially increasing – volume of words and images. By focusing not on the nodes of the information society but on its channels – on what Pool and his colleagues referred to rather clumsily as 'communications flows' – the Joho Shakai methodology has supplied a completely new perspective on the phenomenon of informationisation. As Steinfield and Salvaggio's helpful if brief commentary concluded, 'the *Johoka shakai* research perspective encourages us to look beyond the occupational structure, and incorporate the communication and information behaviors of people into our definitions of information societies' (1989: 6). In so doing it has vouchsafed a *general* theory of the information explosion, one which makes as much sense to the man on the Clapham omnibus as to the scholarly researcher or the acquisitions librarian. The measurement of information flows in this comprehensive sense is a much more arduous task than re-interpreting the national income statistics, but the insights it has already yielded surely show that the effort has been worthwhile.

In addition, the Information Flow Census has provided the outlines of a theory of *phases* of informationisation. Unlike many Machlupians, who seem to think that information economies and societies appeared *ex nihilo* in the second half of the twentieth century, the Joho Shakai theorists have always been aware that 'any society is largely involved in information activities', and that, therefore, 'information societies have existed since man established the first community' (Tomita 1978: 19–20). Information Society Studies must now recognise that the agrarian societies of the past were genuine information societies, and that the industrial revolution, in turn, produced a new *type* of information society. Today, in the twenty-first century, another significant change in the pattern of information supply and consumption is taking place. Japan and the USA, and, by implication, a gathering host of other nations, have moved from being information societies driven by the electronic mass media to being information societies featuring electronic point-to-point communication and the pursuit of what Ito, in his theory of Bunshu Shakai, calls 'extracted information'. This is not to make the no doubt false claim that Joho Shakai researchers were the first to notice the trend towards customisation, but they do appear to have been the first to document it in a systematic manner – to delineate, in painstaking detail, the contours of an information-rich country. Henceforth, the information society thesis should be construed as a thesis not only about how information plays a larger and larger role in society, but also about changing *configurations* of information in the media landscape.[6]

All of this can justly be described as a major contribution to Information Society Studies. However, Joho Shakai has certain conceptual and methodological problems which still need to be addressed. It was argued in Chapter 2 that the information sector version does not work nearly as well as its army of subscribers would like to think, but is this information flows methodology above reproach? The Joho Shakai theorists themselves have never had any doubts. Back in 1975, Tomita had begun his benchmark paper by conceding that the Information Flow Census research was so difficult that 'of course, we do not think that we have succeeded in quantification'. However, he then immediately proceeded to exude the methodological optimism which seems to surround all versions of the information society thesis, even in their formative period:

We are confident that we derived much from the survey results … By continuing this kind of survey in a more precise manner in the future, we shall be able to obtain more accurate information on the functions of information in society.

(Tomita 1975: 345)

His own later writings, the official reports of the MPT, and most English-language materials referring to the censuses assume that any quantification problems have been solved. However, if this is the case, we are forced back to the question of why the methodology has not been taken seriously outside Japan.

It has been suggested that 'the complexity of this approach to measuring information has probably limited its application to other countries' (Dordick and Wang 1993: 52). The puzzle, however, is to ascertain wherein the alleged complexity resides. As we have seen, the census requires sums of breathtaking scale, but these are scarcely insurmountable obstacles for Western scholars. Unlike the information sector version, the Information Flow Census also demands some original experimental research; but, again, while this means extra resources of time and money, it can hardly be called excessively *complex*. The difficulty with the census really turns on one and only one aspect of the methodology, namely that of converting all media into a common unit. As Yasuto Yoshizoe writes, this is the 'crucial problem', for 'if these conversion ratios are not adequate, the significance of the Information Flow Census itself would become ambiguous' (1988: 54). But here again the difficulty should not be exaggerated. We noted that the Joho Shakai pioneers quickly exchanged binary digits for words as their information object. This did not ensure that technical and logistic challenges disappeared overnight, but it surely opened the way for a viable methodology. At any rate, the use of words as a single unit for the measurement of all information flows is no more far-fetched than the Machlupian technique of viewing all industries through a prism of knowledge intensivity.

Technicalities aside, however, the information flows version must address some axiological issues. By dealing exclusively with quantities, the Information Flow Census ignores the *value* or *quality* of information. Equating, for example, the informational content of a television 'soap' with that of a scientific treatise seems as absurd as Machlup's equation of a meeting of the Camp Fire Girls with a conference of university professors. Pressed face-to-face on the issue, Tomita had this to say:

My standpoint is neutral. We just measure volume of information. We don't measure information quality.

(Cited in Edelstein *et al.* 1978: 25)

Such disclaimers are not good enough. An axiologically reductionist doctrine of information is so violently counter-intuitive that it requires a proper defence. Pool *et al.* did point out that an index of information flows is no more than an instance of the 'classic problem of index number formation', i.e. the problem of treating heterogeneous objects as if they were homogeneous (1984: 2). They suggest that verbally equating background music with the Gospel of John is no worse than an index of unemployment counting a family head who has just lost his job alongside a high school student who has recently started applying. Again, this may be true, but one cannot help feeling that a more positive defence is required.

Moreover, in common with the information sector version, the Joho Shakai theorists seem to be smuggling undeclared value judgements into their position by locating the information society at the terminus of an historical trajectory. Agrarian society is supplanted by industrial society, which is in turn superseded by post-industrial information society. It seems to be assumed that the further along this trajectory a society moves, the more advanced, and therefore better, that society becomes. Tomita, for example, stated that 'in this "post-industrial" society the volume of information in circulation increases explosively, information processing is automated, and the value of information is said to be elevated when compared with material values' (1975: 339). Yoneji Masuda (1981) makes much of the alleged penchant for intellectual and spiritual values, giving it a distinctly utopian slant, while Yasusada Kitahara (1984) could even speak proudly of his nation as a 'very advanced information society'. However, there is no self-evident reason why more information is a superior state of affairs to less information, especially when the mass media are factored into the equation and scientific knowledge is not weighted. A society awash with 10^n words is not necessarily more advanced than a society with 10^{n-1} words. Indeed, many a left-wing moralist would be emphatically *against* Joho Shakai's preoccupation with the consumption of information, with the implicit disdain for physical labour. I am proposing, in short, that information flows theorists could be more careful with their insinuations about normative social progress.

There is another side to the axiological status of the information society. For most of the time, Joho Shakai theorists confine themselves to descriptive and empirical statements, but on some occasions they suddenly inject requirements of access or participation. This tension is apparent in Ito's work, for example. In one article (Ito 1994: 233), he states plainly that the concept of the information society is 'technical' rather than 'normative'. However, elsewhere he speaks of 'a society characterized by abundant information in terms of both stock and flow, quick and efficient distribution and transformation of information, *and easy and inexpensive access to information for all members of society*' (1981: 672, my italic). He seems there to be implicitly enlisting a particular (egalitarian) theory of social justice. Certainly, the third clause is of a quite different order from the first and second. Indeed, it could well be argued that many societies are information rich, in the sense of having a massive grand total of words, and at the same time distributively unjust: neither Japan nor the USA, the two countries for which we actually have figures for information flows, is regarded as seriously egalitarian in the distribution of money, power, information, or any other social resource. Thus, there are basically two routes for theory. One can restrict oneself to a purely technical definition, and then if one wishes to criticise a distribution of informational goods or services one has to speak of an *unjust* information society. Alternatively, one can build social justice into the definition and refuse to grant information society status to a society whose distributional setup violates the axiology. But one cannot have it both ways.

This brings us round to the delicate question of disciplinary orientation. I argued in Chapter 2, in the context of Machlup's treatment of communication media as a branch of knowledge production, that the mass media may pose problems for Information Society Studies. To recapitulate crudely, if there is in fact nothing about the behaviour of information in modern societies that communication people cannot deal with perfectly satisfactorily alongside their studies of television and radio (or whatever), then it would seem to follow that much information society theorising – i.e. theorising about a putative new social formation – is misconceived. Thankfully, some Joho Shakai theorists have grasped this point. Ito (1978: 254) notes that the difference between American communication research and Joho Shakai is that 'the former is more concerned with social effects of the *content* of mass communication, whereas the latter is more concerned with the social effects of the *amount* of information flow'. Similarly, the Japan Computer Usage Development Unit (JACUDI) has stipulated that 'the information society centring around computers is different from the society characterized by projected images that are passive, sentimental and sensible such as mainly represented by TV' (cited in Bowes 1981: 702). This is not to deny that there will be overlaps, nor that the information society thesis can gain from the insights of communication and media studies. If a pervasive and multifaceted process of 'informationisation' is indeed impinging on economically mature societies, then we must positively expect varying ways of studying the process to generate findings and conclusions which are at least mutually compatible. All I am suggesting here is that the information flows research tradition, in so far as it is an approach to what has come to be known as the 'information society thesis', needs to remain meticulously clear about the ways in which that thesis is distinct from theses of older vintage. This is not merely a matter of semantics or academic territorialism. It is to do with whether the whole idea of the information society is a genuine innovation or in essence little more than Marshall McLuhan's 'global village' revisited; it is about whether we are indeed witnessing a new social formation, or a variant of an older, much more familiar, social formation.

A different kind of problem for Joho Shakai theorists is that of determinism. In Chapter 2, it was noted that the information sector version must be economically deterministic in the sense that it predicates societies on the nature of their economies, and especially on the occupational patterns in their economies. The information flows version, on the other hand, seems to predicate societies on non-economic or at least non-occupational factors. Researchers working inside or around this tradition thus need to come forward with another version of determinism, an explanation of how propositions about an information society (or, as in Bunshu Shakai, a new species of information society) can be derived from propositions about increasing (or changing) information flows. We need to see evidence of the kind of argument deployed by Irving Horowitz in his classic essay on the significance of electronic publishing, where he wrote (1986: 55) of a 'shift [of] emphasis from the means of production as a critical variable in the social order to one based on means of communication'. There are a few scattered claims roughly to this end in the Joho Shakai literature. Ito affirms that 'human behavior is a function of information that each individual receives or acquires from his or her environment', and that 'the mode of communication technologies basically determines the nature of society' (1991a: 41–2); but he is not forthcoming with a justification of these potent premises. Indeed, later in the same paper he appears to revert to traditional economic determinism, opining that 'Marx was right when he said "Economy determines ideology" ' (1991a: 54). The *prima facie* contradiction is left unresolved. In other words, Joho Shakai, even in its most methodologically ambitious and advanced form, meets the *synecdoche problem*: it represents a whole, i.e. society, by only one of its parts, i.e. the 'info sphere' (see Harsel 1981: 713). This does not matter from a rhetorical point of view, any more than it matters that in ordinary speech we refer to the British government as 'Britain', but in strict logic it is worrying. The Information Flow Census reaches far beyond standard informetrics in the scope of its inquiry, but it has not yet mustered enough conceptual ammunition to deliver a robust information society thesis.

Before closing, it is necessary to comment briefly on the documentational pedigree of the information flows research. In his article on the origins of Joho Shakai in Japan (1991b: 6), Ito makes the revealing observation that 'subscribers to *Hoso Asahi* and *Chuo Kohron* [the periodicals which first discussed the information society] were mostly journalists, social critics and "journalistic scholars" ', and that 'these origins of the birth and early diffusion of the information society concept later caused resistance by "ivory tower scholars" '. Perhaps this distinction between 'journalistic' and 'ivory tower' scholars also needs to be respected a little more widely in Information Society Studies. 'Journalistic scholars' may not be an oxymoron, but those individuals for whom it is a suitable descriptor cannot invariably be classed as skilled thinkers. Leaving aside all of its facetious connotations, the point about an ivory tower is surely that it is an environment which is sufficiently neutral and leisured to allow deep thought. Thus, questions must indeed be posed as to the intellectual standing of a tradition which was not only *cradled* outside the tower, but also *developed* almost exclusively inside government offices and reported in official white papers. In Chapter 2, I suggested that the level of peer review to which Machlup's work was subjected was less than ideal. However, *The Production and Distribution of Knowledge in the United States* was at least published by a highly respected academic press and discussed in the review sections of reputable journals, and of course Porat's sequel originated as a doctorate. Compared with that, the information flows version is still in its infancy.

Notes

1 It was mentioned in Chapter 1 that Joho Shakai has also been translated as 'communicating society' (Wiio 1985). Other recent renditions include 'info-communications society' (MPT 1995) and 'intelligent society' (Dedijer 1996).

2 Two of Youichi Ito's articles (1981, 1991b) are the chief source of data in this section.

3 The proceedings of the conference were published as *Information Societies: Comparing the Japanese and American Experiences* (Edelstein *et al.* 1978), which is believed to have been the first English-language book to use the term 'information society' in its title.

4 I am very grateful to Sachio Fukuda, First Secretary, Posts and Telecommunications at the Japanese Embassy in London, for assisting me in the procurement of recent printed census material. The *White Papers on Communications* have now been put online at http://www.info2.mpt.go.jp/policyreports

5 A notable recent exception to this rule is sociologist Manuel Castells. In *The Rise of the Network Society* (1996) Castells cites some of the Joho Shakai research, and generally appears sympathetic to information flows approaches to measuring the 'information age'.

6 The subject of this investigation is methodological problems as distinct from social issues, but it may be worth noting that Joho Shakai has already provided a rich matrix for ethical and socio-philosophical reflection. Youichi Ito, its finest exponent, has explored the implications of the Information Flow Census for issues as diverse as modernisation, democracy, juvenile delinquency, racism, the comparative ethics of socialism and capitalism, and even European federalism (Ito 1991a, 1994).

4 The information technology version of the information society thesis

Introduction

In the present chapter, the inquiry is pursued further by treating a third methodology for understanding the alleged progress of informationisation, namely the information technology version of the information society thesis. This is, at first glance, the most straightforward approach to the information society, and, probably for that reason, it is also the most frequently encountered one. The information technology (IT) version contends that the information society is a society which has gone through a so-called 'information revolution' or 'information technology revolution'. In the mind of the man on the Clapham omnibus, there has never been any ambiguity: for him, 'information society' has always, and only, meant a computerised society. As we saw in Chapter 1, newspapers are full of items like 'Fibre optics play politics technology', 'Keeping up with today's technology', 'Visions of the cabled future', 'MI5 appeals for power to tap digital phones', 'Kiosk gives the jobless a link into cyberspace', and so on. Information society-related features and readers' letters focus not on 'knowledge production' nor on 'communications flows', but on *technology*, the tangible elements of informationisation.[1] 'The most common definition of the "information society" ', as Frank Webster recognises, 'lays emphasis upon spectacular technological innovation', its key idea being that 'breakthroughs in information processing, storage and transmission have led to the application of information technologies (IT) in virtually all corners of society' (Webster 1995: 7).

However, it is important to understand at the outset that despite its popularity, the IT version represents a significantly less cohesive research tradition than was the case with either the information sector version or the information flows version. *The Production and Distribution of Knowledge in the United States* was such an original text, and its author such a luminous academic figure, that it more or less inevitably generated a tradition of research which is still operating largely within the pioneer's own methodological parameters. The literature of the information flows version, scant though it may be, also adheres more or less faithfully to the blueprint laid down by the early Ministry of Posts and Telecommunications (MPT) reports. However, no similarly authoritative benchmark work and derivative literature exists for the IT version.

This is not to say that there is not an extensive library relating to the IT version. On the contrary, more has probably been written on the socio-economic impact of IT than on both Machlupism and Joho Shakai combined, but in the absence of a classic text around which to gather this literature lacks structure. It can best be divided into three types.

First, there are works nominally about the information society but in reality confined mainly to discussions of technological developments. A good example is Kenneth Laudon *et al.*'s *Information Technology and Society* (1994). Authored by computer scientists, most of this 600-page textbook is devoted to descriptions of the 'central processing unit', 'storage technologies', 'problem solving with programming', and the like, and only in the last of its fifteen chapters are the 'ethical and social issues in the information age' broached. Such works, while containing useful (albeit rapidly dating) information, cannot be regarded as contributions to Information Society Studies, at least in the sense I have been trying to promote. The same is true of the vast quantity of self-contained empirical studies of IT. Scattered across the literatures of a very wide range of fields, including information management, information science, management studies, and computer science, these 'impact studies' deal with observed effects of specific types of IT on particular organisations or industries. 'Optical disc technology in bank customer service units' by Caroline Savage (1994) and 'The dissemination of information by local authorities on the World Wide Web' by Harjinder Gill and Penelope Yates-Mercer (1998) are two random examples. Such papers are often peppered with allusions to 'information society' or a synonym, but no matter how methodologically sound they may be, they do not – cannot – operate at the level of generality required for the information society thesis. Even if all of this research were somehow collated it would not necessarily take us, conceptually, to the information society.

Second, there is what Youichi Ito would call journalistic scholarship, that is to say works on the 'information age' issuing from the pens of an assortment of media commentators and pundits. This genre, of which Alvin Toffler's *The Third Wave* (1980) is perhaps the most famous example, comprises heavily speculative works purporting to discern the shape of an emergent social formation. Unlike the impact studies mentioned above, such books do aspire to the macrolevel where the information society thesis belongs, but they do not achieve that objective. They certainly contain rich descriptions of new technological and social phenomena, but they lack the necessary level of methodological rigour. They neglect to establish their assumptions or to set clear-cut parameters, they fail to marshal quantitative data in a convincing manner, their erudition is often painfully limited (although this is not true of Toffler), and their conclusions are almost never entailed, in any strict logical sense, by their arguments. They also generally fall foul of the vital conceptual point that 'though the large-scale deployment of information technology and digital information may have major social consequences, this does not of itself create an information society' (Meadows 1996: 278). Such work may absorb the person on the Clapham omnibus or in the airport lounge, but it too has little to offer to the academic field of Information Society Studies.[2]

There is, however, a third species of literature which operates at the macrolevel with at least some degree of success. The most famous text in this category is probably *L'Informatisation de la Société* by Simon Nora and Alain Minc (1978), hailed as 'the first comprehensive work to recognize that information technology would profoundly affect society' (Dordick and Wang 1993: 13).[3] Despite its provenance in officialdom, the Nora and Minc report was widely discussed and became a fruitful source of new terms, notably that 'French barbarism' (Minc 1987: 134), 'la télématique' – in English, telematics. However, Britain too can boast an outstanding pioneering exponent of this kind of work. Ian Miles, formerly of Sussex University's Science Policy Research Unit, and now the director of PREST (Policy Research on Engineering, Science and Technology) at the University of Manchester, has produced, in many cases with the help of associates, an exceptionally robust information technology version of the information society thesis. In books such as *Home Informatics: Information Technology and the Transformation of Everyday Life* (1988a), as well as numerous journal articles and policy reports, Professor Miles has developed a position which is exceptional in both the depth of its conceptuality and the rigour of its methodology; a position which also, I will argue, incorporates enough hard data to refute allegations that the information technology version 'is not characterized by empirical research' (Chang 1995: 27). This *corpus* belies Miles's own self-effacing statement that 'Europeans' have provided 'few original contributions' to Information Society Studies (Miles and Robins 1992: 5). The present chapter evaluates what will be called, in long overdue recognition of its importance, *Milesianism* – the neologism, needless to say, has no connection with the Milesian school of Pre-Socratic philosophy.

Ian Miles as an information society theorist

It is advisable to begin by checking that Miles does actually see himself as an information society theorist. In 'The new post-industrial state' (1985), arguably his first important paper on this subject, he juxtaposed the term 'information society' with 'post-industrialism' as the 'high-technology interpretation of post-industrial society' (1985: 599). He also employed one of the verbal derivatives dear to Nora and Minc and many other information society insiders, namely 'informatization' – understood here in a conventional Machlupian sense as the growth of an information workforce: along with 'informalization' (the expansion of self-service and other types of informal work), informatization is portrayed in this article as one of the empirical trends which explain the socio-economic restructuring of the 1970s and 1980s.[4] However, Miles refrained from a wholehearted endorsement of the information society thesis, referring to the ideas of 'information society … theorists' (1985: 611) in an objective, almost remote, way which suggested that he did not wish to be numbered among them; and he also sometimes fenced the term 'information society' inside quotation marks. In short, his initial position seemed to be agnostic.

The next item, chronologically, and incidentally one of the most influential, was 'The social economics of information technology' (1987), written with

Jonathan Gershuny. In the opening pages of this paper, Miles's stance on the information society had become antagonistic. Under the somewhat sardonic heading 'Information society: a second coming of post-industrial society?', the first section dismisses the information society as a 'currently fashionable concept' whose exponents had foolishly adopted many of the exploded assumptions of post-industrialism. By the middle of the article, however, modern societies are said to be undergoing a 'transformation ... involv[ing] more than just technical change ... [to] a new socio-technical system' (1987: 216–17). Moreover, 'information society' appears in the titles of sections 3 and 4, as it had in section 1, but the inverted commas are now conspicuous by their absence, and the discussion has turned from debunking the information society thesis to posing the kinds of questions about social choice that are the stock-in-trade of the conscientious information society theorist. On the final page, we read that 'the reduction of major inequalities should be explicitly incorporated as a goal in the design of information society' (Miles and Gershuny 1987: 222). This statement is pregnant with meaning – indeed, it is arguably the most important single line ever written about the information society – but for our present purposes, which are interpretative rather than ethical, its significance lies simply in the fact that it implied that Miles was now a believer.

However, a year later, in another co-authored work entitled *Information Horizons* (Miles *et al.* 1988), the opening pages are again negative, featuring a sceptical attack on the 'prophets' and 'instant authorities' of the 'information revolution'. But then in a later section, quaintly entitled 'Planting our flag', Miles declares that he is in broad agreement with 'the idea that IT is a revolutionary technology' (Miles *et al.* 1988: 8). As regards 'information economy', a term which, as was noted in Chapter 2, often acts as a stepping-stone to, or even synonym for, 'information society', Miles claims that 'it makes little sense'; however, he is comfortable with 'information-based service sector' and 'information services sector' (1988: 100, 138, 139). 'Information society' itself is also treated ambivalently, sometimes hiding behind sneer quotes, at other times appearing without its quotation marks on but in contexts which suggest neutrality on Miles's part, and on yet further occasions being happily employed as though it were a regular societal descriptor. 'To talk of "the" information society,' Miles concludes, 'is misleading. There may be many information societies' (1988: 245). So now we have pluralism: it is only monism – the definite article – that is at fault.

Similar patterns of ambiguity infuse the whole of the Milesian *oeuvre*. It would be tedious to go through each item microscopically, but one point must be clarified. With co-authored works, it is obviously almost impossible to know who is really speaking. Most of the remaining textual evidence, however, suggests that Miles himself is more 'pro' than some of his associates. In *Mapping and Measuring the Information Economy* (1990), a report bearing no fewer than eight names on the title page, 'information society' is back behind sneer quotes, and even 'information economy', despite its titular enshrinement, bobs uncomfortably in and out of inverted commas. By contrast, Miles's monographic report, *Information Technology and Information Society: Options for the Future* (1988b), conveys the unmistakable impression of being the work of an engagé information society theorist, even to the extent of inventing the acronym 'IS'. Then in a more recent solo article, 'Measuring the future: statistics and the information age' (1991: 916), Miles coins the term 'InfAge' as shorthand for information age. There are few clearer signs of an author's attraction to a concept than his transmuting it into an acronym (or semi-acronym). Probably, therefore, we are entitled to conclude that, despite recurrent intellectual misgivings apparently resulting from a subtle form of peer pressure, Miles is a *soi-disant* information society theorist.[5] (In Chapter 5, I draw attention to a similar ambivalence concerning 'information society' in the writings of Daniel Bell.)

The rejection of Machlupism

Miles can be regarded as a subscriber to the *concept* of the information society; what needs to be established next is his *conception* of its nature – that is to say, his *version* of the information society thesis. He is astute enough to acknowledge that 'most discussion' of issues relating to the information society 'has been conducted within a tradition of counting up the "information workforce" ' (1991: 915). That is to say, he recognises that the Machlupian version represents the benchmark in Information Society Studies. Consequently, his own work needed to be 'guided by an analysis of what the term "information economy" means' (Miles et al. 1990: 3).[6] At the time of 'The new post-industrial state', Miles had apparently not yet learned to distinguish between the information sector and the information technology versions. Describing the way in which the information society thesis had superseded post-industrialism, he wrote:

> Now it is the 'information sector' whose growth is emphasized, rather than the tertiary sector; 'information workers' become the 'service class'; it is demand for IT-based products (information services of many sorts) rather than 'immaterial goods', broadly defined, that is seen as the key to economic growth.
>
> (Miles 1985: 591)

The problem here is that there is no necessary logical connection between information workers and information technology. As noted in Chapter 2, a large portion of Machlup's information sector was uninvolved with IT, and there is even an obvious *prima facie* tension between the growth of IT, which is presumably designed to be labour-saving, and the expansion of any kind of human work. Oddly enough, Miles recognised in this paper that 'IT places a question mark' (1985: 591) over the assumption that labour displaced from the manufacturing sector would be soaked up by the service sector, but he did not at this stage see that IT also impugns the information sector.

The conflation soon stopped, however, and from 'The social economics of information technology' (Miles and Gershuny 1987) onwards, Miles articulately opposed the Machlupian approach. His critique centred around the claim that the information sector version of the information society thesis had inherited many of the dubious dogmas of post-industrialism, particularly the idea that modern societies were witnessing a 'march through the sectors' from industry-based to services-based economies. Machlupians, according to Miles and Gershuny, had merely extended this idea by adding a quaternary information sector; but, like the post-industrialists, they provided little substantial analysis of the growth of what are in reality heterogeneous occupations. In a much-quoted judgement, they contended that 'lumping together a variety of "new" activities under a common heading is a gesture of recognition to the problem, not a step toward solving it' (1987: 213). Miles now appreciated that 'employment in many of the "information occupations" of the traditional services is likely to be reduced by the application of informatics' (1987: 218). In a later text, he also came to see that, since *practically all* jobs involve an element of information processing, 'the application of IT to industry (e.g. robots) can affect all classes of workers', rather than just the tertiary and quaternary sectors (Miles *et al.* 1990: 918). In his last major paper on the information society, while he was still observing the statutory genuflection to Machlup's 'pioneering study', Miles put forward the idea that 'the popularity of the [Machlup–]Porat approach reflects the appeal of being able to flourish a single estimate of the scale of the information sector, which can be relatively easily produced by reworking existing employment and/or national account statistics' (Miles 1991: 917–18). This explanation of the information sector version's ascendancy may seem uncharitable, but it is probably accurate, and it supports the claim made in Chapter 3 regarding the comparative unpopularity of Joho Shakai methodology in the West.

Having faulted the chief alternative, Miles argues for 'a different approach, focusing on the generation, diffusion, and application of new information technology (IT)' (1991: 915). On this view, informatisation, rather than being a function of a burgeoning information workforce, 'hinges upon the application of new IT' (Miles *et al.* 1990: 10). The information society then emerges as a genus whose species have in common an experience – although not necessarily an epoch-making one – of information revolution:

> Seeing IT as a revolutionary technology suggests a specific perception of information society. IS is seen as a complex of new and restructured social and economic practices (re)constituted around the potential of IT – not forgetting that these may take various forms and lead to quite distinct information societies.
>
> (Miles 1988b: 10)

Miles also suggests that it was the information revolution, rather than any widespread perception of the growth of an information economy, which explains the prevalence of the very concept of an information society. This is again highly plausible, since the information revolution is by all accounts a popular phenomenon, whereas Machlupian taxonomy is an esoteric, albeit multidisciplinary, affair.[7]

The *sui generis* conception of the information economy rising out of the Milesian rejection of Machlupism is lucidly summarised in *Mapping and Measuring the Information Economy*:

> It is our contention that the information economy is best conceptualised as involving a particular stage in the development of industrial society. 'Information economy' is a shorthand description for this complex of changes associated with – not caused by in a simple deterministic sense – IT and its diffusion through the formal economy and society at large. Mapping and measuring the information economy then becomes, in part, an empirical analysis that can help us to ascertain the features of this new 'sociotechnical system'.
>
> (Miles *et al.* 1990: 11)

In the sections below, the main features in this redoubtable intellectual manifesto will be examined, beginning with the definition of IT, and proceeding successively to the problem of technological determinism, the relation between IT and industrialism, and the proposal that the information society thesis should be construed as a thesis about a change of 'sociotechnical system'.

The definition of information technology

'Among information technologies,' writes Manuel Castells at the start of his magisterial treatise *The Information Age: Economy, Society and Culture*, 'I include, like everybody else, the converging set of technologies in microelectronics, computing (machines and software), telecommunications/broadcasting, and optoelectronics. In addition, unlike some analysts, I also include in the realm of information technologies genetic engineering...' (Castells 1996: 30). His inclusion of genetics is a startling reminder that the determination of the parameters of 'information technology' is far from being a straightforward matter; and even if genetics is left aside, it is not clear precisely which new or not-so-new technologies or media should count. 'IT' used to be confined to various manifestations of the computer, particularly the electronic computer, but many recent commentators (an exception is Garnham 1996) argue that computing technology cannot meaningfully be disentangled from developments in telecommunications, with the result that terms like 'wired nation' and 'telematic society' are routinely used as synonyms for 'computerised society'. Indeed, the statement that 'an efficient telecommunications network is the single most important element in a successful information society' (Moore 1997: 276) does not nowadays seem at all odd. Of course, the question then becomes: what is to count as telecommunications? Theorists such as Haywood (1995) include some or all of the older mass communications media. For others, however, television and the like are inadmissible, as in the JACUDI principle quoted towards the end of Chapter 3. There is, evidently, a range of mutually incompatible opinions regarding the definition of IT.

Now one of the ways in which Miles has distinguished himself from the majority of information society theorists is the extent to which he is prepared to grapple with semantics. 'Even defining new IT,' he asserts (1991: 919), 'is contentious'. This admission opens up the whole problem helpfully. Are we talking about IT as a new phenomenon or about new IT in the sense of new forms of an old phenomenon? Either way, we will have to allow for the awkward truism that ' "new" is not exactly a clear and sound empirical category, since the empirical basis on which it is founded changes constantly' (Burgelman 1994: 193–4). In *Information Technology and Information Society*, Miles refers to 'information-processing' as 'an integral feature of human activities', contrasting historic information-processing technologies, such as writing and the abacus, with 'new information technology (IT)' (1988b: 1). Then he lays out what he calls the 'specificities':

> New IT, often defined as the convergence of computing and telecommunication, is made possible by the increased power and reduced cost of information-processing via microelectronics. Modern computing and telecommunication – and many applications of these heartland technologies, such as the compact disc (CD) player or teletext systems – treat data in digital form. This facilitates the process of convergence, as the same data can be processed by many devices and media. Analysis of this potential is crucial to understanding IS.
>
> (Miles 1988b: 7)

Three conceptual points are important here. First, Miles endorses the definition of (new) IT in terms of a convergence of computing and telecommunications. Second, he relates the whole process to microelectronics and digitisation. Third, he draws a distinction between 'heartland technologies' and 'applications'. However, while this is a promising start, it soon becomes evident that Miles was not actually enjoying a state of clarification. In *Information Horizons*, published in the same year as *Information Technology and Information Society*, he declared that 'there are numerous dictionaries of IT with thousands of entries, which suggests our task [of definition] is enormous if not impossible' (Miles *et al.* 1988: 22): no 'specificities' are offered, and in the book's index, 'definition of' is conspicuous by its absence from the forty-eight subentries under 'information technology'.

Information Horizons further complicates matters by proposing a dubious additional distinction between 'core' and 'integrating' technologies, of which IT is here cast as a compound. Miles does not give definitions of these terms, only features and examples. Thus, core technologies are 'generally hidden from view' and perform the basic information-handling activities of data production, storage and retrieval, processing, transmission, and display; examples are silicon chips, optical fibres, and satellites. Integrating technologies, on the other hand, 'bind together several core technologies' and thereby enable them to be 'applied to a myriad of tasks', examples being computers and ISDN (Miles *et al*. 1988: 24, 40, 49). However, is it not slightly strange that computers, a 'heartland' technology in *Information Technology and Information Society*, are here an 'integrating' as opposed to 'core' technology, for what is the word 'heartland' if not a near-synonym for 'core'? In any case, the distinction falls apart upon close analysis. Silicon chips constitute a raw material and can hardly be lumped with finished manufacturing marvels like satellites. Indeed, surely a satellite is, if anything, an 'integrating' technology: computers do of course integrate many components, but satellites integrate vastly more. Furthermore, ISDN seems to sit most uneasily with computers in any core-integrating dichotomy. To make matters even worse, Miles briefly concedes that optronics is emerging as a rival to microelectronics, thus throwing into the air the whole understanding of (new) IT as a microelectronics-based phenomenon. This illustrates, of course, the ever-present danger of giving an example in *lieu* of a definition: if the example becomes obsolete the 'default' definition collapses. Then near the end of *Information Horizons*, without any explanation or justification, Miles suddenly starts referring not to 'IT' but to 'ITs' (e.g. Miles *et al*. 1988: 272). By failing to rationalise this huge terminological shift, he demonstrates that he is still in the dark semantically.

Confusion can be found in *Mapping and Measuring the Information Economy* too. Miles begins by aligning himself with smart epistemology, noting that the meaning of IT cannot be regarded as self-evident since 'what turns out to be self-evident for different readers may prove to be distinctly variable' (Miles *et al*. 1990: 12). He rejects the notion that IT is any technology which handles information: to incorporate paper stationery and the like is, he now argues, palpably inappropriate for a technological approach to the information society. On the other hand, he also rebuffs a very exclusive definition which stipulates that IT must involve machine-based 'active information-processing', as opposed to mere storage or transmission; this one certainly rules out pen and paper, but it also casts doubt on CD-ROM. Surprisingly, Miles proceeds to impugn definitions in terms of technological convergence, suggesting that they are impaled on the horns of the following dilemma: if convergence means only systems which combine computers and telecommunications, this would exclude standalone computers; but if convergence means either combined systems or standalone computers or telecommunications systems, then it would have to include older technologies like the abacus and smoke signals (1990: 14–15). Nevertheless, Miles contends that 'C & C' (computers and telecommunications) can help us to understand information technology aright, formulating his position in the following syllogism:

(a) Some process is leading to the convergence of computers and telecommunications, (b) this process is at the heart of new IT, and thus (c) to the extent that computers and telecommunications have been transformed by this process they are at the core of IT.

(Miles *et al*. 1990: 15)

Regrettably, the argument does not succeed. It confuses subject and predicate (is the process or the convergence the core of IT?); it equivocates in its use of the terms 'heart' and 'core'; and it illegitimately introduces the qualification new (in 'new IT') half-way through.

Moreover, when *Mapping and Measuring the Information Economy* goes on to name microelectronics as the underlying process, the issue of obsolescence must again rear its head. Identifying microelectronics as the process and the convergence of computers and telecommunications as the manifestation certainly has an impressive pedigree, but it puts out technological hostages to fortune – and with the rise of optronics, those hostages are duly being sacrificed. It is therefore not surprising that further cracks begin to appear in Miles's position, as when he confirms that 'the development of microelectronics ... is central to the information economy ... [and] at the core of the majority of IT developments' (Miles *et al.* 1990: 17). The word 'majority' gives the game away, for if microelectronics were really the core of IT it would necessarily follow that all, not merely most, IT developments are based on it. Miles admits that such 'would seem a logical demarcation criterion', but then suggests, evasively, that 'perhaps we do not need to draw such all-or-nothing boundaries'! After another page or two of strained reasoning, he finally confesses that 'this definition may not stand the test of time – what if we develop non-electronic optical chips? – but it represents a starting-point for analysis of the information economy' (1990: 21). However, he still maintains that his 'fuzzy' information technology approach 'should prove more fruitful than received studies of the "information sector" ' (1990: 25). That may well be true, but it is beside the point. The question is not whether a microelectronics-based definition of IT is better than the Machlupian version of the information society thesis, but whether a microelectronics-based definition of IT is better than any other definition of IT.

However, while information technology is certainly, in some senses, a 'moving target' (Miles 1991: 933), it should be possible to arrive at a more stable definitional position than anything on offer in the Milesian *corpus*. Come what may, computers will play a central role in the information technology version, but the moral seems to be that we should not try to tie them too closely to microelectronics or to any other specific technological base: we should acknowledge frankly that we have no idea what will drive future computational 'generations'. Nevertheless, a construal in terms of so-called 'convergence' does represent the best way forward for the time being, perhaps combined with an insistence that telecommunications networks should be brought into the semantic frame only in so far as they are serving computers. As a result, 'information society' becomes more or less synonymous with 'computerised society', and 'informatisation' is more or less reducible to computerisation. That, after all, is what the man on the Clapham omnibus currently thinks of when he hears such terminology. However, whatever definitional route is to be taken, Miles's valiant attempts to master the recalcitrant semantics of 'information technology', his willingness to *problematise* the whole issue, must be warmly welcomed. His ruminations reveal that he is at least beginning to negotiate the question of *essentialism* – of what constitutes the essence of the information society. In this respect, as in others to be examined below, he shows himself to be very much alive to methodological niceties normally glossed over in information society punditry.

Structuralism: a sophisticated articulation of information– society relations

A competent technological version of the information society thesis must also provide, in addition to a durable definition of information technology, an account of the relationship between IT and society. This is a much more complex task. The two other versions have already been criticised for leaving the link between information (sector, flows) and society at least partly unexplained, and the same challenge looms menacingly now. In whichever way IT is construed, no one is in any doubt that there is a great deal of it lying around. But why should it be thought to have engendered a new type of society? What is the nature of the *causality* between the new technology and the putative new society? In what economic or sociological sense of the word 'revolution' has there been an information revolution? Miles is well aware of the danger. He laments 'the relative paucity of analysis of the interrelations of social and technical innovation' in the information society literature (Miles and Gershuny 1987: 219), and instead of washing his hands of methodology and passing on to speculate about the social issues, he pauses to try to work out how those interrelations might be explained. The following analysis endeavours to show that, in spite of some costly and unnecessary mistakes, Miles has contributed much to the debate on the linkage between IT and society. It comprises further proof that he is in a different league from many of the semi-skilled journalistic scholars active in the information technology version.

Continuism, transformism, and structuralism

Milesianism is articulated in terms of the schema set out in Table 4.1. The 'depth dimension', Miles explains, underlies the discussion of the social implications of IT, reflecting 'the debates between those who see IS as something fundamentally new and IT as all-pervasive, and those who stress the limited extent of change and who may reject the term IS' (Miles 1988b: 1). Within the schema, there are three competing schools of thought. The first is continuism, which emphasises the overlaps between different phases of industrialisation – including the phase signified by terms like 'informatisation' and 'information society'. Continuists are evolutionists, believing that 'IT represents an(other) incremental step on a long path of technological evolution' (Miles *et al.* 1988: 232). They are also social determinists, maintaining that technology does not have any in-built propensities for the shaping of society, and certainly not for shaping it in a socially progressive fashion. At the opposite pole is transformism,

Table 4.1 Information technology and society: the 'depth dimension'

Continuism	Transformism	Structuralism
Main features of society likely to remain unchanged. IS is fashionable hyperbole. Social and political initiatives may lead to change, but fundamental power structures will persist. IT is merely current stage in long-term process of developing technological capacities. 'Revolutionary' claims overstated. Rate of diffusion of IT is and will be much slower than claimed by interested parties. Likely to be many mistakes, failures, and discouraging experiences.	Major shift in society anticipated, similar to that between agricultural and industrial societies. IS will be an historical stage of social development. Changed bases of political power and social classes. Growing role of information workers and knowledge class. IT is revolutionary technology based on synergistic and unprecedentedly rapid progress in computers and telecoms. Positive demonstration effects, and proven success of IT in meeting new social and economic needs, will promote rapid diffusion and organisational adaptation.	Social change like that experienced in earlier 'long waves'; likely to be new organisational structures, styles, and skills but still industrial society. New opportunities will be presented, issues are likely to change, leadership may stem from new sources. IT has substantial implications for economic structure and may be used to reshape many aspects of social life. Diffusion of IT will be uneven. Some countries and sectors will be more able to capitalise on its potential

Source: Miles 1988b: 2–3

according to which IT is radically changing the nature of society and its institutions: it is doing this with a high degree of inevitability, and is doing it largely in a way which satisfies many of the standard criteria for social progress. Transformism is couched in the language of revolution. Advanced nations are purportedly in the early stages of a technological revolution which is bringing about a social formation – even an epoch, a civilisation – as different from industrial forms of life as the latter differed from agrarianism. Transformism, as Miles puts it, 'anticipates (indeed claims to see) a revolution that will sweep away old structures and bring about an information society' (Miles *et al*. 1988: 93).

So far this adds little except systematisation to the standard axes guiding commentary on information technology and society (e.g. Burton 1992: 16–33). However, according to Miles, there is a third position which represents an attempt to break the mould of stereotypical dualistic thinking about the interrelations of IT and society. This *via media* is called structuralism. Without naming Miles, Jean-Claude Burgelman traces the provenance of structuralist thinking to a felt need for greater conceptual depth in Information Society Studies:

One must admit that the existing frameworks of analysis are, to a certain degree, not sophisticated enough ... Consequently, there might be a need, just as in the area of media policy ... for a new or more sophisticated theoretical framework, sometimes labelled as structuralist.

(Burgelman 1994: 192–3)

According to Miles, structuralism maintains, with transformism, that 'IT represents a revolutionary technology', and that talk of a new 'IT paradigm' is valid (Miles *et al.* 1988: 7, 247–8). It also agrees that society is going to be significantly changed by the information revolution, and that the term 'information society' will be an accurate descriptor for the resulting formation. It readily acknowledges that, on even the most conservative scenario, we face 'a vision of the future which implies immense social change'. However, structuralism *rejects* the view of the information society 'as being as distinct and epochal a formation in human history as agricultural and industrial civilisations are commonly viewed as having been' (Miles *et al.* 1990: 9–10). Instead of embracing transformist talk of a completely fresh social formation, structuralists argue that ' "information society" does represent a new organisation of *industrial* society' (Miles *et al.* 1988: 271, my italic). That is to say, the information revolution is conceptualised as taking place within the framework of the industrial revolution, as a kind of mini-revolution, and the information society as being a species or phase of advanced industrialism. In an important formulation in 'Measuring the future', Miles suggests that 'the InfAge may be a more industrialised society, a super-industrial or meta-industrial society, rather than a post-industrial one' (1991: 927). Structuralists, as Tom Forester sees it, 'steer a middle course, arguing that IT is a revolutionary technology, but it is one which can be accommodated within the existing structure of industrial society' (1989: 3).

This moderate position sets Miles apart from most partisans of the information technology version of the information society thesis, and is a substantive contribution to Information Society Studies. Too many theorists glibly assert that the information revolution enjoys parity of status with the industrial revolution, making the assumption that the information society thesis is predicated on changes whose scale and significance permit discourse about information society wholly to supplant discourse about industrial society. Indeed, there is a tradition of actively *modelling* the idea of informatisation on that of industrialisation, one which goes back at least as far as Yoneji Masuda's paper on 'The pattern model for industrial society' (1970). More recently, Castells has written in the same vein:

The prophetic hype and ideological manipulation characterizing most discourses on the information technology revolution should not mislead us into underestimating its truly fundamental significance. It is, as this book [*The Rise of the Network Society*] will try to show, at least as major a historical event as was the eighteenth-century Industrial Revolution, inducing a pattern of discontinuity in the material basis of economy, society, and culture.

(Castells 1996: 30)

By contrast, Miles's view is that the information revolution is essentially only a variation on the industrial theme. In short, and adapting the title of Masuda's *The Information Society as Post-Industrial Society* (1981), Milesian structuralism is about *the information society as hyper-industrial society*.

In terms of the standard technological–social determinism axis, too, structuralism steers a middle course, agreeing that informatisation is an inevitable and global trend, but failing to see any simple causal connection between IT and society. It is fully aware of the regular accusation that the IT version is, in Webster's words (1995: 10), 'unavoidably technologically determinist ... and as such an oversimplification of processes of change'. In all of his writings, Miles moves decisively to distance himself from technological determinism, as though it were some kind of intellectual temptation to be avoided. It is 'possible,' he informs us, 'to understand current developments without *falling into* a technological determinism' (Miles 1985: 608, my italic). He sternly repudiates what he calls 'crass technological determinism', fortified by the plausible dogma that 'new technology does not drop out of the sky', nor 'arrive ... like the fifth cavalry at the whim of a benevolent scriptwriter' (Miles *et al*. 1990: 11; Miles and Gershuny 1987: 218). At the same time, Milesian structuralism is not so socially determinist as completely to deny the causal efficacy of information technology. In the books on *Home Informatics* and *Information Horizons*, especially, IT is portrayed as playing a significant part in the changing of society. Indeed, at the end of the latter Miles admits that 'it may seem that we have veered towards technological determinism, and we cannot and would not wish to deny that technological development will continue to be a substantial factor in the making of the future'. However, he then adds the rider:

> Nevertheless we are not seeking to argue that technology is in itself the main force of change. Technology is a product of human action upon the world, and is inextricably part of the web of social interests within which we individual humans and the social groups we belong to are formed.
>
> (Miles *et al*. 1988: 224)

By thus dealing in nuance and caveat, as opposed to black-and-white rhetoric, Milesianism seeks to craft a defensible position.

As well as sharing continuism's hard-headed appreciation of the powerful interests that shape the social contexts in which technological innovations must strive for acceptance, structuralism manages to think pluralistically rather than monistically. Its 'horizon' certainly contains information societies, but these are viewed as being likely to vary very significantly in their fundamental nature. Instead of pontificating about 'the' information society, it maintains that 'there may be many information societies' (Miles *et al.* 1988: 245), or, in a formulation burdened by the recurrent quotation marks, 'many imaginable "information societies" ' (Miles *et al.* 1990: 241). In concrete terms, structuralists recognise that examples of informatised societies can be found in North America, Scandinavia, and other European states, whereas transformists have tended to focus on Japan as 'the most likely precursor of "information society" ' (Miles *et al.* 1988: 269). Pluralism perhaps follows logically from the structuralist position on determinism. If it is the case both that IT is a significant factor in social development and that this does not involve a simple unidirectional causality, it would seem to follow that more than one information society could come into being. In sum, Milesian structuralism adopts what David Lyon, a normally dependable commentator, calls 'an interactive model of the relations between technology and society' (1987: 468).

A tripartite typology undoubtedly represents an improvement upon 'either/ or' thinking, and is thus a step in the right direction for Information Society Studies, but it is in itself no more than an opening move. Immediately, structuralism faces the next question: how *exactly* does IT relate to the 'web of social interests'?, or, put another way, what is the ratio between social and technological factors in the shaping of societies? Miles explicitly denies that his *via media* is just 'averaged-out' continuism and transformism, or that it means that 'anything can happen' (Miles *et al.* 1988: 8; Miles and Gershuny 1987: 219), but at times his formulations do appear to lack precision. For example, positioning himself in the optimism–pessimism debate, he rightly criticises certain theorists on the grounds that 'all they can conclude is that the implications of IT could be *either* centralising *or* decentralising; *either* de-skilling *or* upgrading; *either* enhancing *or* threatening democracy, and so on'. But he goes on:

> Although we have favoured the structuralist viewpoint, we acknowledge that all three bodies of analysis have something to offer. (By the same token all three are open to criticism.) The world stubbornly refuses to sleep in the conceptual boxes we build for it.
>
> (Miles *et al.* 1988: 226)

This sounds weak, as though Miles is evading conceptual commitment and is incapable, after identifying all of the variables, of fusing them confidently into a proper synthesis. Similarly when he said in 'The new post-industrial state' that the terminology of 'social *implications* of IT' was acceptable, but the allegedly more deterministic language of 'social *impact* of IT' was unacceptable (Miles 1985: 592, 601, my italic), his distinction seemed fastidious, more academic than real. 'There is an obvious danger here,' in Robin Fincham's words, 'of simply falling back on relativism and a pluralist rationale in order to counter determinism' (1987: 465). Indeed, do we not sometimes feel prompted to ask in Popperian manner: if Milesianism is so judiciously open-ended, can it produce any *falsifiable* propositions about information societies? And if not, what use is it? Frankly, a good proportion of what has so far been encountered in Milesian structuralism could be explained as the intellectual's standard Pavlovian rebuttal of technological determinism combined with an eclectic appropriation of the most intuitively attractive elements of both continuism and transformism.

Mediating concepts

As Miles's writings are probed further, however, ideas and arguments are uncovered which manifest at least a serious attempt to explicate the fine detail of the linkage between IT and society. The attempt is not fully successful, but it certainly acquits Milesianism of any charge of 'averaged-out-ism'. It can be seen from Table 4.1 that Miles's account of structuralism makes an appeal to a theory of economic 'long waves'. This is nothing to do with Alvin Toffler's popular 'Third Wave' hypothesis, because, as has already been noted, Miles rejects the idea that contemporary upheavals are as acute as those which turned pre-agricultural societies into agricultural societies or agricultural societies into industrial societies. The reference is instead to a rather more esoteric wave theory first propagated in the 1920s by a Russian economist called Nikolai Kondratiev. Very little is said in Miles's papers and books about Kondratiev himself; indeed, if we were to judge solely by Miles's allusions, Kondratiev's thought can be summed up in the dubious generalisation that all economies are necessarily subject to periodic booms and depressions. Nevertheless, Miles strongly believes that an updated formulation of 'Kondratiev waves', one which blends the theory of long waves with Joseph Schumpeter's better-known theory of the role of major technological innovations, offers 'an alternative to both the incremental and the revolutionary views of socioeconomic and technological restructuring' (1985: 604).[8]

Now whatever is to be made of Miles's recourse to recherché Russians and their latter-day champions – and this is not the place for a general examination of 'neo-Schumpeterianism' – it should be recognised that certain concepts which Miles carries away from his engagement with long waves are extremely useful, if not indispensable, for a deepening understanding of the link between IT and society. It was mentioned above that structuralists endorse the transformists' claim that there is a new 'IT paradigm' (Miles *et al.* 1988: 247–8). This word 'paradigm' admits of a vast number of meanings, ranging from its basic dictionary sense of an 'example' to its Kuhnian sense of an all-encompassing 'world-view', and identifying exactly what Miles has in mind will take us to the heart of his position. It transpires that no fewer than three overlapping types of paradigm are incorporated into Milesian structuralism, namely 'technological paradigms', 'techno-economic paradigms', and 'socio-technical paradigms'. They are depicted, juxtaposed, in Figure 4.1. Of the three, the idea of a technological paradigm is the most elementary. It refers to 'a set of evolving practices and techniques' relating to a particular technology, and involves 'a reorganization of ways of doing things across many economic sectors, following on basic innovations which can substantially change the costs of key

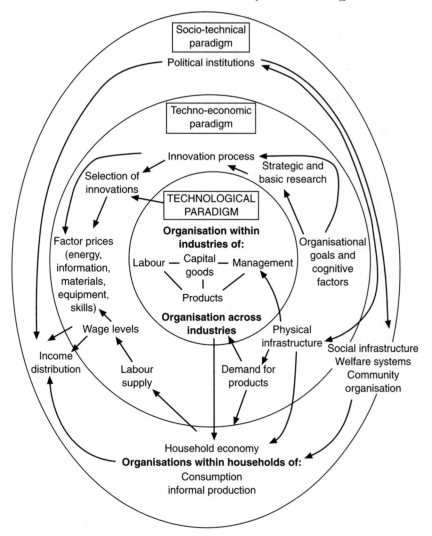

Figure 4.1 Three increasingly encompassing approaches to structural change. Source: Miles 1985: 607

activities, which can diffuse widely, which call for different patterns of skill and labour use, and the like' (Miles 1985: 604). In other words, in order to qualify as a technological paradigm, a new technology cannot be confined (as most in fact are) to one or two industries: it needs to be *pervasive*. Information technology, a versatile technology with an almost infinite number of economic applications, would obviously appear to meet this condition with little difficulty.

Milesian structuralism also posits a new 'techno-economic paradigm', a category which goes well beyond the realm of the merely technical or technological. A techno-economic paradigm is described as constituting 'more than just particular groups of technical innovation in production, rather as a complex of practices including typical products and processes, methods of management and organization' (Miles 1985: 605). *Information Horizons* lists approvingly Carlota Perez's specifications for the kind of technology responsible for paradigm shift, in this stronger sense of 'paradigm': a low and descending relative cost; no serious constraints on supply; the potential to be used across sectors in a wide range of applications; and the ability to lower the costs of capital, labour, and products as well as to change them qualitatively. Taken together, these conditions amount to a 'shift in what is perceived to be the expected structure of costs, and the "commonsense" way of organising production' (Miles *et al.* 1988: 8–9). They are such as to allow a fairly wide range of inventions, including steam engines, low-cost steel, and oil, to qualify as revolutionary technologies, implying that changes of techno-economic paradigm typically occur as frequently as once or twice per century. Miles very plausibly argues that information technology also meets these conditions, affirming that 'IT is at the heart of a technological revolution' which has redrafted the 'calculus of economic decision-making' (Miles *et al.* 1990: 10).

The outcome of construing information technology as a new techno-economic paradigm is a *sui generis* conception of the 'information economy'. Despite its misuse at the hands of the Machlupians, Miles retains this term on the reasonable grounds that it is 'a useful one for indicating the distinctions between economic affairs before and after the development and diffusion of new IT' (Miles *et al.* 1990: 10). In the present context, the information economy is not restricted to certain sectors within the economy, certainly not to a standalone quaternary sector, but denotes the economy as a whole. As Miles puts it, 'all sectors are potentially IT-using sectors – and in advanced industrial societies devices such as personal computers have already been used to effect in every branch of extractive, construction, manufacturing and service industries'. Figure 4.2 pictures the information economy according to the information technology version, identifying the multiple sectoral situses for IT and its applications. All six sectors, from the extractive sectors and capital goods sectors to the consumer services and household sectors, are involved with information technology in one way or another. Table 4.2 then gives a complementary perspective which relates IT to the information economy in a more direct and detailed manner. As the key explains, the plus symbols indicate the anticipated extent of use of a range of types of information technology in each of seven sectors, over the period 1985–2010. 'We would argue,' Miles writes, 'that there are important information activities in *all* spheres of the formal economy, and that it makes little sense to classify many diverse activities as constituting an "information economy" distinct from the rest of economic life' (Miles *et al.* 1988: 100, my italic). Models such as these may not account for the totality of economic activity – money flows, for example, are left out – but they are nevertheless a valuable framework for developing an understanding of IT as a new 'techno-economic paradigm'. In particular, they are useful in showing the pervasiveness – what might even be called, invoking theological language, the 'immanence' – of information across the whole economy.

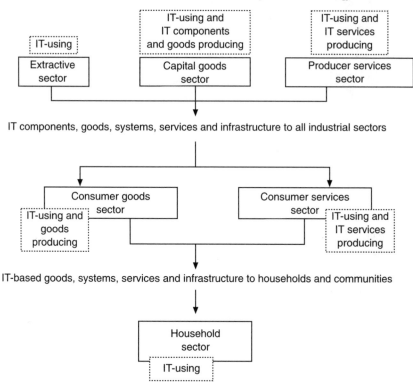

Figure 4.2 The information economy. Source: Miles *et al.* 1988: 19

The new socio-technical system

However, while the foregoing exposition yields a clearer idea of the information *economy*, we are still a long way from the information *society*. Miles says that the difference between a technological paradigm and a techno-economic paradigm is that the latter 'is social as well as technological in nature' (Miles 1985: 605), but nothing has hitherto been seen which could be identified as 'social' except managerial and organisational practices within the economy. If it is truly the case that 'the "information economy" is a shorthand description for this complex of changes associated with – not caused by in a simple deterministic sense – IT and its diffusion through the formal economy *and society at large*' (Miles *et al.* 1990: 11, my italic), then we must press hard for an account of how 'society at large' may have been affected. It has been insisted all along that information society theorists must not be allowed to slide with impunity from the economic to the social realm; if, like Machlup, they produce only an information economy thesis this should be clearly understood and they should not be credited with anything more extensive. The claim that IT is a new techno-economic paradigm is, I am suggesting, plausible, but if this amounts to little more than a claim

Table 4.2 The information economy in more detail

System type	Sector						
	1	*2*	*3*	*4*	*5*	*6*	*7*
Integrated text and data processing	+[a]	+	+	++	++	+++	+++
Transaction clearing	+	+	+	+	+++	+++	+
Online inquiry systems	+	+	+	++	+++	++	+++
Management information systems	+	+++	++	+++	+++	++	++
Professional problem-solving	++	+++	++	++	+	++	+
Professional databases	+	++	++	++	+	+	++
Electronic mail and teleconferencing	+	++	+	++	++	++	++
Material planning, stock control, scheduling systems	++	++	++	+++	+++	+	+
CAD and draughting	+	++	+++	+++	+	+	+
Computer-aided manufacturing	—	+	++	+++	—	—	—
Computer-aided fault diagnostic systems	++	+++	+++	+++	++	+	—
Remote sensing devices	++	+++	+++	+	++	+	—

[a]Plus symbols indicate level of application of IT anticipated in specific sectors over the period to 2010: 1, agriculture; 2, extractive; 3, construction and utilities; 4, manufacturing; 5, goods services; 6, information services; 7, people services

Source: Miles *et al.* 1988: 64–5

about ways of structuring costs and practising management, albeit across the economy as a whole, then a change of techno-economic paradigm must come short of the conceptual threshold for a theory of societal change. In short, does Milesian structuralism, or does it not, go the additional conceptual distance required for a proper information society thesis?

In various parts in his *oeuvre*, Miles does indeed speak of IT's effects in a more rounded way, demonstrating an appreciation of its broader social context and pointing to a more red-blooded conception of paradigm shift. 'A better understanding of information-related activities,' he averred in an important statement, 'and the potential transformations that may be associated with the introduction of informatics, really requires an analysis of large-scale processes of social change' (Miles and Gershuny 1987: 213–14). In *Information Horizons*, Miles argues that 'these technological revolutions since the Industrial Revolution [have been] associated with major social change, shifts in the balance of power between nations, new ways of life, and so on' (Miles *et al.* 1988: 9). That is to say, despite the fact that he has already put the information revolution in much-needed perspective by stripping it of any epoch-making significance, and has thus, as it were, 'downsized' the information society thesis, Miles is still wedded to a substantial-sounding *social* thesis. He tries to get from point A, the new technological or techno-economic system or paradigm, to point B, broader socio-cultural matters like 'new ways of life', by enlisting a third key mediating construct called the 'socio-technical paradigm' or 'socio-technical system'. 'Modern societies,' he writes, 'are undergoing a 'transformation ... involv[ing] more than just technical change ... [to] a new socio-technical system' (Miles and Gershuny 1987: 216–17). The idea of long waves is then re-interpreted in this context, 'in terms of the growth, maturity and stagnation of socio-technical systems, of which technical paradigms form just one, albeit important, part' (1987: 214). Notwithstanding, therefore, its official repudiation of technological determinism and of transformism, we find at the heart of Milesian structuralism a scenario of seismic socio-economic change resulting from technological innovation.

Formally, the concept of a socio-technical paradigm or system is invaluable for clarification-seeking about the information society thesis. It provides a way of answering Webster's charge that the information technology version, being 'unavoidably technologically determinist', fails to see the obvious truth that technology is 'an integral – indeed constitutive – part of the social' (1995: 10). But it does more than that. One may suppose that, if it were defined appropriately, the 'socio-technical system' – I suggest the word 'system' is preferable to 'paradigm' – could be said to be crucial to the makeup of any society (or at least any modern society), and hence that the essence of the information technology version of the information society thesis is that IT has played a significant part in the creation of a new socio-technical system. A general definition of socio-technical system might thus be: *The set of relations (which need not be unidirectional or causal) in any given society between its axial socio-economic structures (economic system, stratification system, etc.) and its level and modalities of technological development*. The perennial problem for the information society theorists in their articulation of the social role of information – that of turning an apparent elision into a tolerably intuitive step – would appear to have found at least a partial solution in the structuralist concept of the socio-technical system. However, this does not, of course, necessarily mean that Miles himself succeeds in presenting the best possible account of an IT-mediated socio-technical system, and, in fact, when he tries to spell out the kinds of changes he envisages in 'society at large', he is less than convincing – or so it will now be argued.

The social content of the new socio-technical system must, as has already been said, go well beyond management practices and any other social changes already accounted for by the techno-economic paradigm. We cannot expect changes in ways of life on the scale associated with those of the industrial revolution, since the structuralist view is that informatisation occurs within the framework of the industrial revolution; but there ought to be identifiable and non-negligible axiological and behavioural changes. Miles seems to recognise this when he writes that 'the design of products and infrastructures has considerable relevance to the ways of life that may evolve, *the values and practices that are integral to a new sociotechnical system*' (Miles and Gershuny 1987: 215–16, my italic). Figure 4.1 showed that the socio-technical system subsumes such major societal arrangements as the political setup, the distribution of income, the welfare state, and the household economy. However, in the text of the article from which that diagram is taken, Miles amplifies the implications of IT only for the last – and sociologically least important – of these. Thus he points out that the reach of the concept of a socio-technical system must extend beyond the production realm to the consumption realm, that, as he puts it, 'the "commonsense" of production has to relate to consumption' (1985: 606). In *Information Horizons*, he painstakingly catalogues a remarkable range of actual and potential domestic applications of IT, talking of such wonders as baby alarms, automated ovens, self-diagnostic systems for fridges, and homework aids on viewdata, and enthuses that 'there is hardly a household task to which microelectronics could not conceivably be applied' (Miles *et al*. 1988: 167). Indeed, 'home informatics' ended up as the title of one of his most influential books (Miles 1988a). More significantly, it embraces an area of the social world where Miles, apparently forgetting that he has officially distanced himself from the sensational scenario-making associated with transformism, cheerfully admits that 'our structuralist perspective leans mostly towards the transformist view' (Miles *et al*. 1988: 171).

Unfortunately, even if this enthusiasm is consistent with other aspects of Miles's position, which is doubtful, home informatics is far from being enough to carry his main thesis. If a change of socio-technical system is truly significant, we need to know more – we need, so to speak, not merely home informatics but also *homo informaticus*. While it is understandable that Miles may want to play Karl Marx to the transformists' utopianism, and refuse to give out too many precise 'recipes' for the 'cook shops of the future' (Marx cited in Sowell 1986: 158), more details would have to be forthcoming before we could even begin to agree that a change in socio-technical system is in the offing. But instead of doing this, Miles shies away from the issues, taking refuge in complexity and what Fincham would classify as 'pluralist rationales'. He confesses that the implications of his home informatics for such substantive sociological matters as social isolation, the sexual division of labour, and the generation gap are 'uncertain' (Miles *et al*. 1988: 173). Admittedly, his writings are sprinkled with insinuations that other major 'way of life' changes could occur, including a reduction in lifetime working hours, the decentralisation of organisations, a blurring of the line between private and public activities, and certain changes in social attitudes (e.g. Miles 1988a: 134–5), but they are made without systematic evidence or argumentation, and lack conviction. Even in Miles's most succinct and overtly pro-information society monograph, *Information Technology and Information Society*, uncertainty seems to reign, as when he says:

> Changes in ways of life defy easy summary. Simplistic assertions about growing isolation versus renewal of community do not capture the complexity and active nature of social change.
>
> (Miles 1988b: 17)

The upshot of such prevarications is that, despite the promises (or at any rate the insinuations), we are left with little that is clearly evidential – much less, probative – of any wide-ranging thesis concerning the 'process of structural change' (Miles 1985: 606).

Finally, and, it is suggested, decisively, Miles fails to provide any account of how IT is affecting the 'political institutions' and 'income distribution' systems mentioned in Figure 4.1. It would seem that for Milesian structuralism a change of socio-technical system can occur without any upheaval in, or even significant development of, the class system and the way social resources are shared. Indeed, at one point Miles states unambiguously that 'to be sure, the basic social relations of industrial capitalism persist' (Miles 1985: 605). But this surely gives the game away. If it is the case that the core aspects of a socio-economic structure can survive changes of socio-technical systems in general and the arrival of the 'IT paradigm' in particular, then the concept of a socio-technical system loses much of its force. Bluntly, it entails that 'IT' is not really very socially innovative after all, and leaves us, in all of the most important respects, in a continuist position. I am not seeking to deny that the study of the information society is a 'study of continuity and change' (Feather 1998). On the contrary, that is precisely what Information Society Studies ought to involve. However, certain methodological and epistemological parameters need to be observed, and surely one cannot meaningfully speak of a change of socio-technical system without incorporating judgements on these major systemic issues? Thus, the information society thesis still awaits complete vindication.

Informatisation: the informetric challenge

The outcome so far is a conception of the information society as a society in which IT is pervasive, in the sense of having allegedly created a new socio-technical system. The final task, which takes us down from high theory to informetrics, is, of course, that of measurement. The received wisdom holds that the information technology version 'does not support its analysis with accurate empirical data' (Burgelman 1994: 188). Webster adds his voice to the chorus of criticism of what he calls the 'technological definition' of the information society:

> We ask for an empirical measure – in this society now, how much IT is
> there and how far does this take us toward qualifying for information society
> status? ... [But] one quickly becomes aware that a good many of those
> who emphasize technology are not able to provide us with anything so
> mundanely real worldly or testable.
>
> (Webster 1994: 4)

Elsewhere, Webster (1995: 9) specifically cites Miles's work, contending that
'in Britain over a decade of social science research by PICT (Programme on
Information and Communication Technologies), which was charged with
mapping and measuring the "information society" [*sic*], has not as yet produced
any definitive ways of meeting its objectives'.[9] I will vigorously dispute this
view, and argue to the contrary that Miles's sophisticated formulation of the IT
version of the information society thesis is based on at least as much sound
empiricism as the dominant Machlupian version. Miles, in fact, goes out of his
way to stress that his project of 'mapping and measuring the information
economy involves an empirical analysis that can help us to ascertain the features
of this new "sociotechnical system" ' (Miles *et al.* 1990: 11).

A theory of statistical data

The informetric project has three requirements, two of which Milesianism more
or less successfully addresses. First, it should be grounded, at least schematically,
in a general doctrine of empiricism, and particularly a statement on what it is
going to understand by, and how it might verify, 'statistical data'. Second, it
must provide a practicable metric, one which enables measurements of the
diffusion of information technology, including, where relevant, extensive
diachronic and international comparisons. Third, Miles, and all theorists who
aspire to propagate the information technology version, should be expected to
venture a pronouncement on the precise point at which a degree of diffusion of
IT can be said to confer information society status – otherwise we are left
unsure as to whether society x or society y has 'qualified'. This third condition
may be stronger than is normally expected of analyses of socio-technical change
– theorists of industrialisation, for example, were rarely pressed for watertight
definitions – but that is surely no reason for not striving *now* for the highest
possible level of methodological rigour.

A virtue of Milesianism is its antipathy to the *a priori* approach manifest in
the average piece of discourse on the information revolution and the information
society. Miles calls such writing 'visionary':

> Despite the vast volumes of paper that have been devoted to celebrating
> or (less often) cautioning about this emergent socioeconomic structure,
> there is something of a dearth of statistical analysis of the issues raised ...
> There seems to be more interest in visionary exhortations about the InfAge
> than in close inspection of what trends and potentials are revealed by
> available data.
>
> (Miles 1991: 916)

Speaking forthrightly, the shape of the information society cannot be 'divined from chiliastic assumptions' (1985: 605). But neither, Miles also sees, can it be deduced from the hordes of empirical case studies, examples of which were cited in the introduction to this chapter. Miles does not need to be told that there is 'a deluge of detailed (but generally localized) case studies of technological and organizational change' (1991: 921–2), because he realises that these are not pitched at the holistic, macroscopic, society-wide level required for a cogent information society thesis. *Mapping and Measuring the Information Economy*, produced by a multidisciplinary team under Miles's leadership, was precisely a path-breaking effort to fill this gaping hole in the knowledge base. It was, as it claimed to be, 'the first attempt to provide an overview and route-map to the empirical material on this broad set of topics, and it provides a marked contrast to the provocative but speculative visions, and rich but restricted case studies, which constitute so much of the literature on the "information economy"' (Miles *et al*. 1990: iv).

Miles appreciates that in the end the problem of the existence of the information society must involve empiricism, in the form of an appeal to one or other species of statistical data. He knows that if 'production, diffusion and application of IT itself are the key to the information society', then it follows that the 'production, diffusion and, of course, the application of statistics on these activities are the key to understanding it' (Miles *et al*. 1990: 241). Moreover, he goes beyond the Machlup-style issuing of self-defensive caveats about 'the available data' by formally *problematising* the issues, and especially the issue of the relation between data and theory. Indeed, *Mapping and Measuring the Information Economy* is unique among the major original sources of the information society thesis in that it contains what might be called a theory of statistics. Data are defined as 'social products' which have been 'constructed' by 'social actors', with certain 'purposes' in mind, and using 'financial and intellectual resources' (Miles *et al*. 1990: 26). Miles notes that in the eyes of certain social scientists, such as those adhering to phenomenological, ethnomethodological, or deconstructionist schools, these social constructs can never be trusted. 'To such commentators,' he writes, 'data on the "information economy" tell us much more about how ideas about the latter are changing than about the latter itself – if indeed they accept that there is any social reality outside of concepts!'. As with his structuralist *via media*, Miles himself eventually comes down in favour of a moderate position which avoids both the Charybdis of radical scepticism and the Scylla of naive realism. Milesianism is able to accept that statistical data can in principle be veridical, but also requires that they be calibrated according to criteria such as: the degree of conceptual adequacy they evince; the appropriateness of instruments employed; technical rigour; and suitability of presentation. The result of these conditions is that facts may be construed as partly a true representation of reality and partly a function of the conceptual prisms through which we perceive them, with the corollary that the research process should acknowledge a 'dialectical relationship' between conceptual categories and appropriate indicators (Miles *et al*. 1990: 64).

As was noted in Chapter 3, a useful concept for measurement purposes is that of informationisation or informatisation. This 'ugly but apt neologism' (Miles 1988b: 9) allows for phases or degrees of development, instead of casting societies as either information societies or not information societies; it thus facilitates comparative analyses. However, in the information technology version informatisation refers not to the expansion in the volume of, nor changes in the patterns of, information flowing across society's media, but to the degree to which a society has been pervaded by IT. Miles, ever the proficient social scientist, recasts informatisation as a species of the familiar sociological notion of technological 'diffusion', explaining, plausibly, that 'the information economy develops by a process of diffusion of new technologies and associated practices', and that 'it makes sense to think of degrees of informatisation of different sectors or national economies' (Miles *et al.* 1990: 18).

Informatisation in the Milesian sense could harbour a wide range of indicators. It could refer to businesses utilising IT (the production sphere) or to individuals or households possessing IT (the consumption sphere); to expenditure per head or per institution; to takeup per head or per institution; and so on. Webster argues that this flexibility presents a 'formidable' problem, indeed a problem which calls into question the whole information technology version (1995: 9), but that is much too hard a line. Measuring diffusion is a routine practice in established social sciences and the burden of its philosophical justification cannot be visited upon a new specialism like Information Society Studies. Moreover, while Webster is correct that Miles's work does not supply a stipulation of the point on the 'graph' of IT diffusion at which an information society comes into being, his suggestion that this issue cannot be answered satisfactorily is again unfair (Webster 1995: 10). Critics of the information society thesis should realise that no amount of measurement of IT diffusion (or of Johoka), nor any level of sophistication in measuring methods, can possibly supply an answer as to the point at which information societies come into being, because that is a matter not for *discovery* but for *decision*. One must look at all the available data – in this case, various metrics for rates of diffusion – and then decide whether or not they are probative of, or perhaps just suggestive of, a new social formation. Where the line between industrial society and information society – or, in Milesian terms, between industrial and hyphenated-industrial society – should be drawn is indeed a key methodological issue; but it is not in the final analysis a problem for empiricism, nor one which can reasonably be regarded as overwhelming.

Informatisation in the United Kingdom

Milesianism, it must be stressed, is an authentic British product, so we must finish by examining how it has set about measuring informatisation in the United Kingdom. We saw in Chapter 2 that Machlup's use of official US statistical series was hampered by the fact that these were often not specific enough for dogmatic judgements about who is and who is not an information worker. Similarly, when Miles and his colleagues tried to execute their task of 'mapping and measuring' the UK information economy, they encountered a distinct shortage of appropriate, disaggregated data. While they found some relevant categories in official statistical series such as *Business Monitors* and the *Census of Production*, these did not give anything like a full picture of IT diffusion. Specific problems included the fixation of such series with hardware rather than software, with standalone systems as opposed to networks – it may be many years before the nature of technological convergence has been properly grasped by statisticians – and with levels of expenditure on equipment as distinct from assessments of technological capabilities (Miles *et al*. 1990: 118). Moreover, *Business Monitors* compounds industries producing integrated circuits with, *inter alia*, the electronic consumer goods and record industries, neither of which is entirely relevant to informatisation (Miles *et al*. 1990: 74; cf. Freeman and Soete 1990: 284–5). Another problem was that much more statistical work had been done in the UK on IT in the manufacturing sector than on IT in the services sector. This is particularly regrettable, given that contemporary lore about the information revolution attaches greater significance to services than to manufacturing, tending to highlight, for example, telebanking or telemedicine rather than factory automation. The patchiness of the official statistics, Miles noted, forced researchers to turn much of the time to unofficial sources, and these can, of course, lack the stability, objectivity, and professionalism associated with official publications.[10] A final age-old problem is commercial secrecy, with the reporting of 'leading-edge' technologies particularly prone to dissimulation (Miles *et al*. 1990: 130).

However, in spite of these informetric hurdles, Miles and his colleagues were able to supply a rough-and-ready snapshot of UK informatisation. It was a mixed picture. There was certainly ample evidence that a majority of UK businesses, or at least of medium-sized and large businesses, utilised IT at some stage in their value chains. As regards the consumption sphere, however, diffusion was markedly less impressive. At the time of *Mapping and Measuring the Information Economy*, household ownership of computers was approximately 15 per cent. Miles suggested that this figure 'makes the UK one of the most, if not the most, computer-intensive countries in the world' (Miles *et al*. 1990: 201), but even if this were true, it falls acutely short of a numerical majority – the likely cut-off point on most accounts of informatisation. When compared with figures for other consumer durables such as cars, washing machines, and televisions, microcomputer ownership looked even less impressive: even video recorders, at 36 per cent of households in 1990, were more widely diffused. The situation has changed since then, of course, but ten years later the most generous estimates for household PC ownership in Britain do not venture much beyond the 27 per cent mark. Thus, while the UK is no doubt slowly being informatised, it seems to be still a long way from any graduation ceremony for full information society status, understood in the present information technology sense.

Conclusion: benefits of Milesianism

In his paper 'How genre conventions shape nonfiction social analysis' (1994), Rob Kling argued that writing on the social impact of information technology is primarily the subject of popular and professional literatures that are heavily weighted toward the genres whose knowledge claims are least reliable. In this chapter I have expounded and analysed a sophisticated body of thought which may justly be regarded as an exception to Kling's generalisation. The rubric *Milesianism* is proposed for this eminent indigenous formulation of the information technology version of the information society thesis. In the concluding section, I wish to recapitulate some of the principal ways in which Milesianism can be said to have contributed to Information Society Studies.

Unlike amateur information society theorists, Miles understands that the matter of defining information technology cannot be quickly passed over, that it needs instead to be *problematised*. The hyperbole, mutual self-contradictions, and general false consciousness which have surrounded the launches of a succession of technologies, including teletext, online, CD-ROM, and, much earlier, microfiche, powerfully illustrate the presence of a definitional problem. The greatest temptation of the information society thesis in all its versions is to fall prey to a failure of *perspective*, and nowhere is this more evident than in the unbalanced iconising of what is seen in hindsight to have been merely an ephemeral manifestation of IT. The logical solution, it would seem, is to try to find the underlying nature – the essence – but this too, as Miles came to appreciate, proves extremely taxing. The Milesian rendition of IT in terms of microelectronics is simultaneously too broad and too narrow: too broad because the relevance of some applications of microelectronics to Information Society Studies is unclear, and too narrow because some *prima facie* relevant applications are not microelectronics-based. Perhaps the important lesson to be learned is that it is wise to refrain from fixing the definition of IT on to any single 'core' technology. Still, we need a working definition or we could not proceed at all, and Miles is probably therefore justified in concluding that the most viable approach at present is one which emphasises the *convergence* of computers and telecommunications networks. Certainly, 'C & C' is a technological development which is arousing the interest (and sometimes the concern) of *The Times* and *Sunday Times* – newspapers which can be seen as vehicles for the opinion of the man on the Clapham omnibus. It is the unprecedented *fusion* of node (computer workstations and terminals) and channel (the networks carrying information flows) which makes the information revolution the stuff of headlines.

Another of the formal requirements for a competent information technology version of the information society thesis is a credible account of the relations between IT and society. Milesianism provides some promising markers for the way forward in this regard, in particular through its invocation and partially successful articulation of various mediating concepts. Three types of paradigm or system are advanced, namely technological systems, techno-economic systems, and socio-technical systems. All of these are useful to Information

Society Studies, but the last is of great importance. Milesianism is best seen as a serious negotiation with the proposition that *a new socio-technical system has resulted from a set of social, economic and technological factors, including, centrally, the growth of informatics*. The Milesian conception of socio-technical system is too minimalist, but the general idea of a new socio-technical system has the potential to redeem the conceptuality of the information society thesis. That is to say, Miles has helped to focus the information society debate by showing that what we are looking for when we try to verify the information technology version of the information society thesis is evidence, not of a 'new society' – a term which is impossibly vague – but of a new socio-technical system.

The Milesian articulation of IT–society relations incorporates a doctrine called structuralism. This is formulated in such a highly nuanced way that while it cleverly circumvents the standard charge of technological determinism, it comes across as slightly evasive, as a compromise between technological and social determinism. A more glaring weakness of Milesian structuralism is that it is associated with an obscure theory of economic cycles called 'Kondratiev waves'. Miles does not demonstrate in anything remotely approximating sufficient detail the manner in which his information society thesis coheres with such ideas; but what is valuable in his position is not dependent on notions of waves, long or otherwise. Milesianism emerges from this intellectual dalliance with a truly sagacious perspective on the information revolution. The received wisdom about that revolution is that it enjoys epoch-making parity with the industrial revolution, but by taking the long view Miles is able to recast it as one occurring *inside* the industrial era: the information society is thereby reduced to a phase of industrialisation – to 'meta-industrial' or 'super-industrial' society. This allows the dismissal of hyperbole, and an endorsement of Herbert Simon's wry Clausewitzian conclusion that the information revolution is 'a continuation of the Industrial Revolution by other means' (1987: 117). The engagement with long waves can also be seen as evidence that Miles does at least recognise the need for 'theory', and a fully fledged information society thesis probably would need to delve into economics proper as well as epistemology, econometrics, and sociology.

Finally, its amenability to empiricism, its emphasis on sheer technology, is another of Milesianism's strengths. While it is unfair to allege that an information technology version necessarily involves anything so metaphysically melodramatic as a 'hypostatisation of technology' (Webster 1995: 10), the material orientation does make a frequently abstract and hence unverifiable thesis much more *concrete*. The result is that the IT version is basically a more reliable way of grounding the information society thesis than the dominant Machlupian tradition. It has a brighter future, that is to say, than virtually theological argumentation to the effect that everyone is now an information worker, because such argumentation will always remain not just intuitively unprepossessing but inherently unprovable. Moreover, in addition to meeting, or at least trying hard to meet, many of the formal conditions inherent in a cogent methodology of the information society thesis, Milesianism also points the way forward in very practical terms. *Mapping and Measuring the Information Economy* marshals a more or less comprehensive bibliography of statistics germane to the study of informatisation in the UK, while *Information Horizons* and *Home Informatics* furnish detailed descriptions of the effects of IT on the main sectors of our society. Milesianism provides, in sum, a promising cartography for an emergent information society.

The preceding pages have emphasised the rich content of Miles's work, and have not examined the media in which it was published; but since the other versions were thus interrogated, something should be said by way of end-piece about the bibliometric dimension of Milesianism. A strong case can be made to the effect that, like Machlupism and Joho Shakai, most of Miles's writings are beneficiaries of comparatively unrigorous outlets. *Information Horizons* was published by the minor, non-academic house Edward Elgar. *Information Technology and Information Society* is a report in pamphlet form. *Mapping and Measuring the Information Economy* is one of those workaday British Library-sponsored projects. 'Measuring the future: statistics and the information age' appeared in a journal of the arguably obscure specialism known as 'futurology' – as, in fact, does Miles's latest paper (1997).[11] And so on. Where, in all this, is the kind of peer review and quality assurance to which we might expect a senior British researcher to submit himself? Why did Miles not publish his information society work in refereed sociology or economics journals? Without intending suddenly to cast doubt on Milesianism as an intellectual force, I would simply suggest, in closing, that it is unfortunate that it too has been largely propagated in 'soft' media. Thus, the overall conclusion must be that what has been supplied is a brilliant case of '*Towards* an information technology version of the information society thesis'.

Notes

1 'Praise the Net and Pass the Modem', the title chosen by Trevor Haywood for the First Ameritech Information Society Lecture (1997), epitomised splendidly this popular preoccupation of the 1990s.

2 Of course, it may well be the case that some of the authors of books in this genre have also produced less well-known works of a higher academic calibre: I am judging here only the popular offerings.

3 The English-language edition was published in 1980 under the title *The Computerization of Society: A Report to the President of France*.

4 Dordick and Wang assert (1993: 13) that Nora and Minc invented the term 'informatisation'. In fact, as Ito points out (1994: 251), Nora and Minc published their report after visiting Japan and prosecuting some studies of the Japanese information society literature: their French word 'informatisation' was a direct translation of 'Johoka' (i.e. informationisation). Miles uses the term 'informatisation' rather than 'informationisation', sometimes spelling it informatization: he has been transcribed faithfully here.

5 It seems that Miles's interest in the information society has subsided somewhat, especially since his move to PREST. In 'Cyberspace as product space' (1997), for example, the focus is on interactive media and their markets: the societal dimension has been totally eclipsed.

6 Miles has some awareness of the information flows approach. He briefly cites Pool *et al.*'s study, describing it as unique, and speaking approvingly of its 'technometric' methodology (Miles *et al.* 1990: 24, 238–9).

7 Miles has his own account of the 'information sector', which is confined to personnel working as IT professionals; he estimated the 1989 UK IT workforce at only 293,000 (Miles *et al.* 1990: 171–5).

8 It should be pointed out that Miles was by no means alone in this enthusiasm. Sussex University's Science Policy Research Unit, with which he was closely associated as he developed his information society thesis, studied Kondratiev waves intensively in the 1980s, giving rise to many influential publications (especially Freeman *et al.* 1982). Webster has referred recently to its work as comprising 'a much respected school of thought' (1995: 8), but others scholars (e.g. van den Besselaar 1997: 379) are now sceptical. Certainly, this particular research front is less active today than it used to be.

9 The reference is to *Mapping and Measuring the Information Economy*. As Webster indicates, this report was commissioned by the Economic and Social Research Council's Programme on Information and Communication Technologies.

10 Miles makes an interesting case to the effect that official publications have been harmed by the politically motivated substitution of private sector alternatives for formerly publicly run statistical operations. For example, he provides evidence that in the area of telecommunications the quantity and quality of statistical data have deteriorated since the privatisation of British Telecom in 1984 (Miles *et al.* 1990: 92–3). It is somewhat ironic that at the critical stage of the information revolution in Britain and the USA, a revolution which was trumpeted loudly by the neo-conservative governments which were fortunate enough to preside over it, long-standing and respected statistical sources of direct relevance to that revolution may have been compromised.

11 I am very grateful to Professor Miles for drawing my attention to some of his more recent publications, including a contribution on 'Information Revolution' for the *Microsoft Encarta* CD-ROM Encyclopedia (1999). It was not possible to address this new work in the present study.

5 Synthetic methodology of the information society thesis

Introduction

It should now be very clear that there is a plurality of distinct research traditions sharing the term 'information society' and cognates. I have suggested that both Joho Shakai and the information technology version, and specifically the sophisticated variant of the latter expounded by Ian Miles and his associates, utilise more credible methodologies for grounding information society thinking and discourse than does the dominant information sector version. Now while it has never been implied that these various approaches are incompatible, commonalities have not so far been emphasised. So, it is time now to consider whether a combination is really feasible, whether there exists a multifaceted version which successfully incorporates some or all of the insights offered by the schools of thought examined in the foregoing pages. In this chapter, therefore, the theme will be synthetic methodology of the information society thesis.

As with the other versions, it is necessary to select the author who has produced the most intellectually cogent account, and in this case there can be no hesitation in choosing Daniel Bell as our new subject.[1] Bell, who was professor of social sciences at Harvard University and is currently a scholar-in-residence at the American Academy of Arts and Sciences, is without doubt the most academically illustrious person to have been associated with the information society thesis. A study of 1970 which used a 'reputational methodology' located his name in the top ten of the 'American intellectual elite', next to public figures such as Noam Chomsky, John Kenneth Galbraith, and Norman Mailer; alphabetical order actually ensured that Bell's name came first (Kadushin 1974: 30–1). In our own day, *The Times Literary Supplement*, one of the chief vehicles of the British intelligentsia, has listed two of Bell's writings, *The End of Ideology* (1960) and *The Cultural Contradictions of Capitalism* (1976), among '[t]he hundred most influential books since the war' (*Times Literary Supplement* 1995); they are juxtaposed with such seminal texts as George Orwell's *1984* and John Rawls's *A Theory of Justice*. Fellow sociologist Malcolm Waters writes in a monograph devoted to Bell (Waters 1996: preface) that his work is 'a central element in the sociological canon', one which 'infuses the discipline, often guiding the direction of sociological thought'; upon careful consideration, he ranks him as the third greatest sociologist of the second half of the twentieth century, after Talcott Parsons and Jurgen Habermas – a judgement endorsed by Dennis Wrong (1996: 8). A rigorous bibliometric study by Blaise Cronin and colleagues (1997) does not actually quite bear out such a high ranking, finding Bell's 'citation count' to be lower than that of several other post-war sociologists including Peter Berger, Anthony Giddens, and R.K. Merton, but this may be a function more of its time frame (1985–93) than of anything else. In any case, by all accounts Bell is a very considerable twentieth-century thinker.

Bell's contribution specifically to Information Society Studies has been immense. Even his sharpest critics acknowledge (e.g. Webster and Robins 1986: 32) that Bell's *magnum opus*, *The Coming of Post-Industrial Society* (1974), is a definitive work in this field. Few would dispute the claim of Jorge Schement and Terry Curtis that 'his original interpretation remains the dominant context for thinking about information and society' (1995: 25). Indeed, Bell's contribution is more influential even than Machlup's, despite Machlup being – as was argued in Chapter 2 – the chronological pioneer. A recent investigation, for example, found that journal articles on the information society cited *The Coming of Post-Industrial Society* four times more frequently than Machlup's *The Production and Distribution of Knowledge in the United States*, over the period 1972–93 (Tsay 1995). This was dealing with the literature of information science in particular, but there is no reason to think that its findings were atypical.[2] Webster, who is surely one of the most well-versed commentators in Information Society Studies, writes simply that Bell's 'is the most influential theory of the "information society" ' (1995: 14).

The *nature* of Bell's position as an information society theorist is, however, widely misunderstood. Leaving aside the ever-expanding literature which cites Bell, or Bell *inter alia*, merely as an act of literary genuflection, the scholarly commentary is largely of one mind: it represents Bell as the arch-exponent of post-industrialism whose work fits smoothly and sequentially into the information sector tradition. For example, Liam Bannon's recent paper on 'Conceptualising "the information society" ' explicitly links Bell with Machlup and Porat in the 'information economy' framework (1997: 302). This reading guides Webster too (1995: 14), and also Harris and Hannah (1993), Stehr (1994: 14), Martin (1995), and van den Besselaar (1997), to mention only some other fairly recent studies. The aim in this chapter is to go beyond such stereotyping, and instead systematically to expound and evaluate the nuances of Bell's methodological position on the information society. It will be argued, specifically, that his theory of the information society is *synthetic*, a compound which in particular ways incorporates the various versions of the information society thesis identified in preceding chapters.[3] Certainly, a doctrine of the post-industrial workforce is forthcoming in the Bellian *oeuvre*, but it can be shown to be interwoven with two other important strands: one concerning information flows and an information explosion, and the other involving computers and an information revolution. These three strands are interrelated, but as we have seen each has its own disciplinary provenance and approach to methodology, and makes a unique set of claims about informationisation and the information society.

Bell's work will also be treated here chronologically, rather than, as is usually the case, monolithically or proleptically. That is to say, his work will be shown to accommodate *evolving* views on the information economy, information flows, and information technology. Naturally, the investigation will focus on *The Coming of Post-Industrial Society: A Venture in Social Forecasting* (1973; the Heinemann edition of 1974 will be cited), but other key works will also be examined in detail. In particular, it will be demonstrated that Bell's article 'The social framework of the information society' (1980c), is critical for an understanding of his place in Information Society Studies. Many other writings, especially a little-known later article on 'The third technological revolution and its possible socioeconomic consequences' (1989) and some private correspondence (1996a, 1996b, 1996c), will also feature in what follows.[4]

Daniel Bell as a *soi-disant* information society theorist

As in the previous chapters, the first task is to establish whether or not Daniel Bell is a *soi-disant* information society theorist. Most commentators do not trouble themselves over such subtleties, instead making the assumption that because Bell is known as an apostle of the information society he must therefore think of himself as one. Exegesis, however, gives a rather more complicated picture, revealing that, rather like Miles, Bell actually adopts a range of attitudes at different stages in the development of his thought. In his early thinking, in papers such as 'Notes on the post-industrial society' (1967) and 'Technocracy and politics' (1971), the term 'information society' does not make an appearance, although there are tantalising allusions – to a 'class of knowledge workers', for example (1971: 4) – which suggest the seeds growing in Bell's mind. Two years later, *The Coming of Post-Industrial Society* was published, but while, as already noted, this is often considered a definitive source of the information society thesis, a close textual reading does not in fact disclose any clear-cut appropriation of the term itself.

> The question has been asked why I have called this speculative concept the 'post-industrial' society, rather than the knowledge society, or the information society, or the professional society, all of which are somewhat apt in describing salient aspects of what is emerging ... The sense was present – and still is – that in Western society we are in the midst of a vast historical change ... The use of the hyphenated prefix *post-* indicates, thus, that sense of living in interstitial time.
>
> (Bell 1974: 37)

These musings occur near the beginning. Later on, Bell moves closer to employing the term, writing that 'the post-industrial society, it is clear, is a knowledge society' (1974: 212). However, since, as will be seen, Bell himself draws a distinction between knowledge and information, this cannot be taken as watertight proof of a conversion to information society nomenclature. Towards the end of his long book, he edges even closer, but again without quite going the whole way. 'The post-industrial society,' he states, 'is an information society, as industrial society is a goods-producing society' (1974: 467). This must be read as a statement of *predication* rather than *essence*: Bell was saying that 'being an information society' or 'being informational' is an attribute, *inter alia*, of the post-industrial society, rather than that a modern society is essentially an information society. Nowhere, in fact, in *The Coming of Post-Industrial Society* can we find the unequivocal avowal with which Bell is commonly credited.

By the time of 'Teletext and technology: new networks of knowledge and information in postindustrial society' (1977, reprinted in 1980b), however, Bell was on the brink of embracing the term. The article's title puts 'information' and 'society' almost together, and the text employs a great number of the buzz words which have in various ways come to be associated with the information society thesis, including 'computers', 'information users', 'electronic library', 'paperless office', 'information industries', 'information explosion', and 'information retrieval'. Nevertheless, there is no actual mention in either title or text of the 'information society' itself. That was to happen, at last, in an article which appeared two years later, entitled 'The social framework of the information society' (1979, reprinted as 1980c). The title must of course be taken as it stands. However, even here there may be a latent ambiguity, for while the text makes liberal use of such cognates as 'economics of information', 'information economy', and 'information sector', references to the 'information society' itself are very rare – hardly confirming that Bell was thinking of himself as a committed, confessing information society theorist. Curiously, an acknowledgement in his collected papers, *The Winding Passage: Essays and Sociological Journeys 1960–1980*, reveals that 'Teletext and technology' was 'drawn from a larger manuscript on "The social framework of an [*sic*] information society", prepared for the Laboratory of Computer Science at MIT in 1975'. This is obviously more or less the same manuscript that was eventually published in 1979 under the slightly different title of 'The social framework of the information society'. It would appear, therefore, that by 1975 Bell had *privately* decided in favour of using the descriptor 'information society', but also that he was not prepared to champion it in the public domain until 1979 – and even then only sparingly.

Moreover, it transpires that Bell, having crossed the Rubicon and aligned himself with information society terminology, then hesitates – as did Miles. In 'The world in 2013', there is no mention of any 'information society', although there is a reference, safely fenced inside quotation marks, to the 'wired nation' (1987: 34). Similarly, 'The third technological revolution and its possible socioeconomic consequences' manages to avoid the critical phrase and all synonyms: indeed, Bell states there that 'on the axis of technology, both the United States and the Soviet Union are *industrial* societies' (1989: 176, my italic), seeming to imply (although this is misleading) that he had by the late

1980s lost sight not only of the information society but also of its post-industrialist matrix. If we move into the 1990s there is even less of a positive nature to report. One searches in vain Bell's major sociological paper, 'Social science: an imperfect art' (1995a), for a mention of the information society. A brief journalistic piece published in the same year does allude to 'the requirements of an information-based society' (1995b: 7), but the context is a philippic against Newt Gingrich and the 'star-trek sociology' undergirding populist republicanism in the United States: it can hardly be read as an endorsement of a strong information society platform. Then in his most recent publication, a preface to a reprint of a futurological report entitled *Toward the Year 2000: Work in Progress*, Bell reverts to an almost *verbatim* reiteration of the passage from *The Coming of Post-Industrial Society* quoted above: 'Why "post-industrial", rather than, say, "information society", the term that is now loosely used to characterize our "new" world?...' (Bell and Graubard 1997: xv).

Bell was approached privately for illumination on the matter. 'No term is wholly satisfactory,' he wrote initially (1996a), 'and I do not like the term "information society" to the extent that it assumes to be a term that "swallows up" all other dimensions'. This seemed at first simultaneously to confirm his disenchantment with 'information society', and to imply that he sees the label as a partially accurate societal descriptor; that is, as misleading rather than positively mistaken. However, pressed for further clarification, he referred in his second letter to 'what seemed to you [the author] a shilly-shallying in the use of the term "information society" ', and he ended with the emphatic and unambiguous denial: 'I don't think of myself as an "information society theorist" ' (1996b).

Thus, the question 'Does Daniel Bell see himself as an information society theorist?' can be answered more or less straightforwardly in the affirmative only for one brief period in the development of his thought. For the rest of the time, he either ignores the term, or eschews it, or cages it or its synonyms inside inverted commas. William Martin is therefore correct in his suggestion that Bell is 'apparently uncomfortable with the term information society' (1995: 2), but why should this be the case? Why does Bell prevaricate? Martin does not offer any enlightenment. A very likely explanation, however, is that Bell became *embarrassed* to be associated with the ardent utopians who have largely taken over the information society camp: the Alvin Tofflers, Tom Stoniers, and Yoneji Masudas, to name a few. Frankly, he despises anything that looks to him like 'star-trek sociology', anything that purports to tell us about a new society without having gone through the rigours of proper sociological analysis. Nevertheless, whatever the reason for his discomfort, the fact remains that Bell was and is widely regarded as a camp-leader. It may be worth recalling Karl Marx's ironic protest, 'je ne suis pas un Marxiste'. Clearly, no one could have been more of a Marxist than Marx himself; similarly, while Bell may now want to resist the label 'information society theorist', it remains the case that, objectively speaking, this is what, among other things, he is. However, it is time now to proceed to examine the ways in which information enters into the *substance* of the Bellian version of the information society thesis, beginning with that famous legacy of Fritz Machlup: the information economy.

The information sector element

'We are now, one might say,' Bell had intimated in 1967 (1967: 27), 'in the first stages of a post-industrial society' – a big, seminal thought which found classic expression a few years later in *The Coming of Post-Industrial Society*. Partisans of the information sector version of the information society thesis always cite this book as a cast-iron source of their position. Strangely, however, the text itself does not actually yield any doctrine of the information sector or economy. What it does do, though, is promulgate two interrelated claims which can be interpreted as being *conducive* to the concept of an information economy: first, a claim concerning a change in the US economy from a goods-producing to a service economy; and second, a claim concerning the pre-eminence of the professional and technical class in the US occupational distribution. In what follows, Bell's handling of these propositions is scrutinised with a view to ascertaining whether or not they are well founded, and whether, if they are well founded, they are indeed correctly understood as being supportive of information sector thinking.

From goods to services

The main source for Bell's theory of post-industrialism is a short chapter of *The Coming of Post-Industrial Society* entitled 'From goods to services: the changing shape of the economy. 'What is clear,' Bell declares, 'is that if an industrial society is defined as a goods-producing society – if manufacture is central in shaping the character of its labor force – then the United States is no longer an industrial society' (1974: 133). His evidence for this strong verdict takes the prosaic form of standard US Bureau of Labor statistics showing a growth of the services sector and a more or less simultaneous decline of the manufacturing sector. It can be seen from Tables 5.1 and 5.2 that whereas employment in the 'goods-producing' sector increased from 10.63 million in 1870 to 25.6 million in 1940, and was projected to reach 31.6 million in 1980, services employment in the USA went up much more rapidly over the same period, from 2.99 million in 1870 to 24.25 million in 1940 and 67.98 million (projected) in 1980. Bell also provides percentage figures – although, irritatingly, only for part of the time frame – and these indicate that the goods-producing proportion of the US workforce went from 51 per cent in 1947 to 31.7 per cent in 1980, while the services sector went from 49 per cent to 68.4 per cent (Table 5.3). As the tables make apparent, the services sector is a mixed-bag category which includes not only professional and technical workers but also transport workers and tradesmen, among others. However, Bell plausibly argues (1974: 133) that 'blue-collar' workers in the services sector are more than offset by 'white-collar' workers within the manufacturing sector, and cites a *Bureau of Labor Bulletin* to

Table 5.1   Sector distribution of employment by goods and services, 1870–1940 (in thousands) (from Bell 1974: 130)

	1870	1900	1920	1940
Total	12,900	29,000	41,600	49,860
Goods-producing total	10,630	19,620	23,600	25,600
Agriculture, forestry, and fishing	7,450	10,900	11,400	9,100
Manufacturing	2,250	6,300	10,800	11,900
Mining	180	760	1,230	1,100
Construction	750	1,660	2,170	3,510
Service-producing total	2,990	9,020	15,490	24,250
Trade, finance, and real estate	830	2,760	4,800	8,700
Transportation and utilities	640	2,100	4,190	4,150
Professional service	230	1,150	2,250	4,000
Domestic and personal service	1,190	2,710	3,330	5,710
Government (not elsewhere classified)	100	300	920	1,690

Note
Totals do not always add up because of small numbers not allocated, and rounding of figures

Source: *Historical Statistics of the United States (1820–1940)*

Table 5.2   Sector distribution of employment by goods and services, 1947–80 (in thousands) (from Bell 1974: 131)

	1947	1968	1980 (proj.)
Total	51,770	80,780	99,600
Goods-producing total	26,370	28,975	31,600
Agriculture, forestry, and fishing	7,890	4,150	3,180
Mining	955	640	590
Construction	1,980	4,050	5,480
Manufacturing	15,540	20,125	22,358
Service-producing total	25,400	51,800	67,980
Transportation and utilities	4,160	4,500	5,000
Trade (wholesale and retail)	8,950	16,600	20,500
Finance, insurance, and real estate	1,750	3,725	4,640
Services (personal, professional, business)	5,050	15,000	21,000
Government	5,470	11,850	16,800

Source: *The US Economy in 1980, Bureau of Labor Statistics Bulletin* 1970

Table 5.3 Sector distribution of employment by goods and services, 1947–80 (in per cent) (from Bell 1974: 132)

	1947	1968	1980 (proj.)
Goods-producing total	51.0	35.9	31.7
Agriculture, forestry, and fishing	15.0	5.1	3.2
Mining	2.1	0.8	0.6
Construction	3.9	5.0	5.5
Manufacturing	30.0	24.9	22.4
[Durable	16.0	14.7	13.3]
[Non-durable	14.0	10.2	9.1]
Service-producing total	49.0	64.1	68.4
Transportation and utilities	8.0	5.5	5.0
Trade (wholesale and retail)	17.0	20.5	20.6
Finance, insurance, and real estate	3.0	4.6	4.7
Services (personal, professional, business)	10.0	18.6	21.2
Government	11.0	14.6	16.9
[Federal	3.5	3.3	3.0]
[State and local	7.5	11.2	13.9]

Source: *The US Economy in 1980, Bureau of Labor Statistics Bulletin* 1970

the effect that the latter would reach 34.5 per cent (of manufacturing employment) by 1975. He concludes, although without giving his sums, that by 1980 the total manufacturing labour force would be only 22 per cent of the labour force, and that technological developments such as automation were bound to ensure that this figure would continue to decrease: *ergo* 'post-industrialism'.

Before going any further, it is important to register that while Bell is not quite guilty, as Mark Poster alleges, of 'transforming by the magic of rhetoric an assumption into a finding' (Poster 1990: 25), it *is* the case that this stunning revelation is arrived at after only two or three borrowed tables and a mere five pages of text, and that, instead of researching new empirical data, Bell just presents a rather tendentious new gloss on routine statistical sources. Of course, this is in a way perfectly legitimate. Bell is a social theorist in the grand sense of 'macrosociologist' or 'social philosopher', and, as such, he is not obliged to go out and gather his own facts and figures. However, where he can be faulted is in his *sense of proportion*. He takes these simple and one-dimensional tables at face value, and without in any way questioning their validity ventures to place an enormous weight of interpretation on them. It is *possible* that they can bear this weight, that is to say the weight of a theory telling us that industrial societies are no more, but Bell neglects to *establish* the point. This methodological problem has huge ramifications, for it was not as if Bell was an obscure scholar experimenting with *avant-garde* ideas. On the contrary, he was by the time of *The Coming of Post-Industrial Society* a major figure in social thought, and it was inevitable that his views on post-industrialism would be imbibed by disciples. That is exactly what happened, and the disciples include a great many avid information society theorists. For most of the latter, the adoption of Bellian post-industrialism has been totally uncritical, the result being that a palpably slender pillar of evidence – a few aggregated statistics – is supporting an inordinately heavy superstructure of opinion. This worrying state of affairs should be kept in mind as Bell's contribution to information sector thinking is probed further.

Bell proceeds – as had Machlup, all too briefly, with his penultimate chapter on the 'occupations approach' – to reinforce his post-industrialism by reformulating it in terms of what he calls the 'pattern of occupations':

> The changeover to a post-industrial society is signified not only by the change in sector distribution – the places *where* people work – but in the pattern of occupations, the *kind* of work they do. And here the story is a familiar one. The United States has become a white-collar society.
>
> (Bell 1974: 134)

The evidence for this putatively 'familiar' story again takes the form of standard serial statistics, such as those in Table 5.4 showing an expansion of white-collar workers from 17.6 per cent of the workforce in 1900 to just over 50 per cent (projected) in 1980. 'The central occupational category in the society today,' Bell states emphatically, 'is the professional and technical', made up of groups such as teachers, health professionals, scientists and engineers, and qualified technicians (1974: 136). Again, however, he does not convincingly demonstrate his point. Except for the material in Table 5.4, no further documentation is produced. Instead, Bell hurries on to speculate about the *implications* of these supposed 'historic shifts' for such social groups as the trade union movement, coloured people (referred to rather summarily as 'the blacks'), women, voluntary organisations, and – the apple of the 1970s sociological eye – the 'working class' (1974: 137f.). Moreover, all of the other chapters of *The Coming of Post-Industrial Society*, with one exception, are in various ways deductions or ruminations which assume rather than augment this empirical base, as their titles will attest: 'From industrial to post-industrial society: theories of social development' (chapter 1); 'The subordination of the corporation: the tension between the economizing and sociologizing modes' (chapter 4); 'Social choice and social planning: the adequacy of our concepts and tools' (chapter 5); ' "Who will rule?": politicians and technocrats in the post-industrial society' (chapter 6); 'Coda: an agenda for the future'. The exception is chapter 3, 'The dimensions of knowledge and technology'. However, while this one does marshal statistical material, it relates solely to the information explosion and information technology elements in the Bellian synthesis (discussed in their own right below), and in no way strengthens the case for a post-industrial workforce.

Again, as with the goods to services claim, my concern here is to draw attention to the fact that Bell was happily – and perhaps complacently – relying

Table 5.4 Percentage distribution by major occupation group, 1900–80 (from Bell 1974: 134–5)

Major occupation group	1900	1910	1920	1930	1940	1950	1960	1970 (proj.)	1980 (proj.)
White-collar workers	17.6	21.3	24.9	29.4	31.1	36.6	42.0	46.7	50.8
Professional and technical	4.3	4.7	5.4	6.8	7.5	8.6	10.8	13.6	16.3
Managers, officials, and proprietors	5.8	6.6	6.6	7.4	7.3	8.7	10.2	10.0	10.0
Clerical and kindred	3.0	5.3	8.0	8.9	9.6	12.3	14.5	16.9	18.2
Sales workers	4.5	4.7	4.9	6.3	6.7	7.0	6.5	6.0	6.0
Manual workers	35.8	38.2	40.2	39.6	39.8	41.1	37.5	36.3	32.7
Craftsmen and foremen	10.5	11.6	13.0	12.8	12.0	14.1	12.9	13.1	12.8
Operatives	12.8	14.6	15.6	15.8	18.4	20.4	18.6	18.4	16.2
Labourers, except farm and mine	12.5	12.0	11.6	11.0	9.4	6.6	6.0	4.7	3.7
Service workers	9.0	9.6	7.8	9.8	11.7	10.5	12.6	12.4	13.8
Private household workers	5.4	5.0	3.3	4.1	4.7	2.6	3.3	—	—
Service, except private household	3.6	4.6	4.5	5.7	7.1	7.9	9.3	—	—
Farm workers	37.5	30.9	27.0	21.2	17.4	11.8	7.9	4.6	2.7
Farmers and farm managers	19.9	16.5	15.3	12.4	10.4	7.4	4.0	—	—
Farm labourers and foremen	17.7	14.4	11.7	8.8	7.0	4.4	3.9	—	—

Source: *Historical Statistics of the United States (1900–1960)* and *US Department of Labor Bulletin 1970*

on someone else's 'story'. He was accepting as beyond question that a major change had recently occurred in the kind of work in which Americans engage, and was prepared to base a 500-page book on this assumption. This is surely an upsetting finding for Information Society Studies, for one would have thought that the *magnum opus* of the father of post-industrialism should contain a much greater proportion of empirical material. No doubt, Information Society Studies is not a purely empirical enterprise: no doubt, it must make room for normative dimensions that have more to do with ethics and social philosophy than with descriptive sociology or informetrics. But there is still surely a proportionality problem here. The analysis of a putatively emergent social formation really does require a significantly higher ratio of empirical to normative argument than that afforded it in *The Coming of Post-Industrial Society*. This basic exercise in textual analysis, in short, does nothing to dent the sceptical position that evolved in Chapter 2 of the present study with regard to the information sector version. It is hard indeed not to agree with Victor Ferkiss's mordant conclusion that 'the most charitable verdict that can be passed on the claim that services, and therefore skill and knowledge, are becoming more important is the Scottish "Not proven" ' (1979: 79; cf. Rose 1991: 32).

From services to information

The claims advanced in Bell's chapter on 'the changing shape of the economy' are only half of the story of informationisation, the other half being, as Ferkiss suggests, an account of how the (allegedly) expanding services sector relates to *information*. Thus, the question to be faced now is where in *The Coming of Post-Industrial Society*, if anywhere, does information sector thinking take over from the service sector thesis? Some elementary investigation is again extraordinarily revealing. 'Information economy' does not appear in the book's index; neither does 'knowledge economy', nor 'information worker', nor 'knowledge worker'. Marc Porat's name is absent of course, because *The Coming of Post-Industrial Society* preceded the publication of Porat's research. Fritz Machlup is cited, but, crucially, his claims concerning the production and distribution of knowledge in the United States are *not* endorsed by Bell. That is to say, *The Coming of Post-Industrial Society* more or less *rejects* Machlupism – as will now be demonstrated.

At the start of a key section on 'The structure of the knowledge society', Bell claims that the post-industrial society is a knowledge society in two senses: first, that theoretical knowledge is pre-eminent; second, that, as he puts it, 'the weight of the society – measured by a larger proportion of Gross National Product and a larger share of employment – is increasingly in the knowledge field' (Bell 1974: 212). Playing, as usual, the gentleman-scholar – Bell's old-world courtesy could actually be seen as a judgement on the blustering information-age modernism his writing promotes – he begins by paying respect to Machlup's 'heroic effort to compute the proportion of GNP devoted to the production and distribution of knowledge'. However, it soon becomes obvious that he regards the heroics as problematic, as laudable in intention but impossibly acrobatic in practice. Machlup's categories of knowledge are, he says, 'broad indeed', and this is obviously a euphemistic way of saying that they are far too broad. Bell expresses surprise that Machlup's 'education' category included education in the home, the church, and the workplace, that 'communication media' subsumed stationery, that 'information machines' included musical instruments and typewriters, and that 'information services' contained such familiar industrial classes as brokers and estate agents. 'Any meaningful figure about the "knowledge society" ', Bell counters, 'would be much smaller'; he goes on to suggest that it should be restricted to research (but not development), higher education, and the production of intellectual property and copyright materials (1974: 212).

Now these are precisely the kinds of parameters which were defended above (Chapter 2) on the grounds of their intuitive acceptability: the items on Bell's list, as opposed to much of Machlup's epistemologically overpopulated catalogue, are surely what common sense understands by the word 'knowledge'. This would not entail that Bell cannot be a believer in the knowledge economy or the knowledge society. He readily acknowledges the 'singular' fact, to which Machlup had first drawn attention, that the proportion of US GNP devoted to higher education had increased dramatically, moving from 3.1 per cent in 1929 to 7.5 per cent in 1969 (Bell 1974: 213). Using further data on university enrolment and the like, he assiduously charts the continuing growth of higher education, and arrives at the conclusion that 'by the year 2000, the United States will have become, in gross terms, a mass knowledge society' (Bell 1974: 242). But higher education was, as we saw, only a very small part of Machlup's education category, so what Bell means here by a mass knowledge society is a society with a 'mass higher education system' rather than a society with the lion's share of GNP devoted to knowledge work – two quite different ideas. Moreover, it transpires that it is only a fraction of this knowledge-producing sector that is axial to Bell's conception of the 'knowledge society'. 'The most crucial group in the knowledge society, of course,' he says, 'is scientists, and here the growth rate has been the most marked of all the professional groups' (Bell 1974: 216). He supplies impressive figures, such as those in Table 5.5, which indicate that the 'scientific population' had increased from 2.7 per cent of the workforce in 1963 to 4 per cent in 1970s, but professional scientists – 'scientists in the strict sense' – still constituted only 0.74 per cent of the workforce in 1970 – i.e. '300,000 persons' (Bell 1974: 229). Such an argument could scarcely be further removed from Machlup's thesis that approximately one-third of the US workforce were knowledge workers!

However, at the same time as he drastically reins in Machlup's parameters, Bell entertains a broader conception of the knowledge society. His 'knowledge class', in this sense, includes not only the creators of research and intellectual property but also many personnel outside science and higher education, such as the entire 'professional and technical persons' category reproduced in Table 5.6. Teachers are the numerically largest group, comprising a quarter of professional and technical workers, and of course primary and secondary teachers

Table 5.5 Forecast of skilled population and scientific personnel (from Bell 1974: 217)

	1963	1970	1975 (proj.)
Population of the United States (in millions)	190	209	227
Workforce (millions)	76	86	—
Civil employment (millions)	70.3	—	88.7
White-collar workers	31.12	—	42.8
(as percentage of civil employment)	(44.2%)	—	(48.0%)
Professional and technical	8.5	—	13.2
(as percentage of civil employment)	(12.2%)	—	(14.9%)
Scientific population (millions)	2.7	4	—
(as percentage of active population)	(3.6%)	(4.7%)	—
Scientists in the strict sense	0.5	0.74	—
Engineers	0.93	1.4	—
Technicians	1.0	1.6	—
Science teachers in secondary schools	0.25	0.3	—
Doctorate degrees (in thousands)	106	170	—
In science	96	153	—
In engineering	10	17	—

Source: Organization for Economic Cooperation and Development, *Reviews of National Science Policy: United States* 1968

far outnumber lecturers and other higher education personnel. So we have already moved towards a knowledge sector of more Machlupian proportions. The second largest group is engineers, but at this point the link with the knowledge sector (in any sense) is unclear, for not even unreconstructed Machlupians count *all* engineers as knowledge workers. Moreover, Machlup specifically ruled out dentists, also present on Bell's list. Similarly, Bell is including all nurses, something not even Porat had done. Thus we are confronted with conceptual disarray. On the one hand, Bell has rejected Machlup's 'broad indeed' parameters, with all their definitional absurdities – while simultaneously endorsing a 'knowledge class' which is in some ways even more inclusive than Machlup's. On the other hand, he promotes a knowledge class so diminutive that it numbers only a few hundred thousand talented persons. Sense 1, the knowledge society as a society with great swathes of the economy given over to knowledge work, is in tension with sense 2, the knowledge society as a society in which theoretical knowledge is predominant. Frankly, we are forced to the unhappy conclusion that Bell is inconsistent in his theory of the knowledge society, in so far as this is construed as a function of a knowledge sector. The case for an information society, in short, is not well made – despite the near-universal reliance on *The Coming of Post-Industrial Society* as an authoritative source of that case.

Table 5.6 The makeup of professional and technical occupations, 1960 and 1975 (in thousands) (from Bell 1974: 19)

	1970	*1975 (proj.)*
Total labour force	66,680	88,660
Total professional and technical	7,475	12,925
Scientific and engineering	1,092	1,994
Engineers	810	1,450
Natural scientists	236	465
Chemists	91	175
Agricultural scientists	30	53
Geologists and geophysicists	18	29
Mathematicians	21	51
Physicists	24	58
Others	22	35
Social scientists	46	79
Economists	17	31
Statisticians and actuaries	23	36
Others	6	12
Technicians (except medical and dental)	730	1,418
Medical and health	1,321	2,240
Physicians and surgeons	221	374
Nurses, professional	496	860
Dentists	87	125
Pharmacists	114	126
Psychologists	17	40
Technicians (medical and dental)	141	393
Others	245	322
Teachers	1,945	3,063
Elementary	978	1,233
Secondary	603	1,160
College	200	465
Others	158	275
General	2,386	4,210
Accountants	429	660
Clergymen	200	240
Editors and reporters	100	128
Lawyers and judges	225	320
Arts and entertainment	470	774
Architects	30	45
Librarians	80	130
Social workers	105	218
Others (airline pilots, photographers, personnel relations, etc.)	747	1,695

Source: *Bureau of Labor Bulletin* 1969

Social framework of the information society

As mentioned above, the high-water mark for Bell as an information society theorist was 'The social framework of the information society' (1980c). Not only is this the sole work in which he portrayed himself explicitly as an exponent of the information society, but it is also a paper which has been anthologised – a true sign of quality – and widely cited. It will now be very closely examined with a view to finding out whether it does in reality add anything to the case for an information society, understood in the present context as a society in which the knowledge or information sector is dominant. I have just shown how, in *The Coming of Post-Industrial Society*, Bell had tried to accommodate two quite different and even contradictory senses of informatisation. By the time of 'The social framework of the information society', a decision seems to have been made. Bell has apparently made up his mind that the most plausible way of making the case for the information society is not by magnifying the sociological significance of a minute section of the workforce, but by proving that a simple numerical majority of the workforce is engaged in information work: this is the way he now wishes to go, or, put more tendentiously (and somewhat colloquially), this is the fashionable intellectual bandwagon to which he now, in the late 1970s, wants to fasten his post-industrialism. I will argue, however, that while 'The social framework of the information society' does report some relevant new material which had not been available at the time of *The Coming of Post-Industrial Society*, it still does not really succeed in improving Bell's essential case for an information workforce.

The first point which cries out to be made is that the title of this paper has exceedingly strong echoes of the title of the section of *The Coming of Post-Industrial Society* discussed above, i.e. 'The structure of the knowledge society'. Waters has recently accused Bell of indulging in 'replicated publication' and 'cut and paste' techniques (1996: 166), and here we seem to have a good example of such.[5] There are, however, some small but highly significant differences in the wording of the two versions. To start with, in the title of the article the word 'information' has replaced 'knowledge', and, as will become apparent, this verbal change connotes a material development in Bell's thought. Second, the attitude to Machlup has changed. 'The social framework of the information society' pays homage to the man who 'made the first efforts to measure the production and distribution of knowledge' (1980c: 516). In the equivalent passage in *The Coming of Post-Industrial Society*, these efforts had been hailed as 'heroic': the paean is not here repeated and yet, paradoxically, it is clear that Bell has essentially become *more* partial to Machlupism. He still maintains that he regards Machlup's definition of knowledge as too broad, but the crucial caveat about 'any meaningful figure about the "knowledge society" ' being 'much smaller' is now conspicuously absent. Third, whereas in the earlier text Bell had abruptly dropped Machlup almost as soon as he had corrected him, in the later one he uses him as a stepping-stone to a full-blooded endorsement of the information economy and society. The precise development of the argument will now be traced and, where appropriate, criticised.

Having quoted Machlup's 'discovery' about 29 per cent of 1958 US GNP and 31 per cent of the labour force being given over to knowledge, Bell appeals to various more recent sources which allegedly buttress the Machlupian case for an expanding knowledge or information sector. First, he cites an article in *Fortune* by Gilbert Burck (1964) which had replicated Machlup's methodology and put the proportion of US GNP in 1963 at 33 per cent, or two per cent up. Bell cites this as though it were an incontrovertible authority, but certain epistemological issues need to be considered. First, *Fortune* is not an academic journal but a 'middle-brow' business magazine: can we really trust statistics from such a source? Second, Burck was an editor of the magazine as well as the author of the article: again this mildly weakens any case for the article's authoritativeness. Third, Bell, in a previous vocational incarnation, was *himself* a staff writer for *Fortune*, which again does little for notions of objectivity. But these are merely formal points, perhaps just insinuations. The most important point is that Burck, by faithfully replicating Machlup's methodology, would of course be replicating the methodological flaws which existed in Machlup's pioneering work. One does not, as Ludwig Wittgenstein famously pointed out, buy another copy of the same newspaper in order to corroborate a story.

Bell's next ally is admittedly rather stronger. Jacob Marschak, introduced as 'one of the most eminent economists of the United States' (Bell 1980c: 517), is cited to the effect that the knowledge sector would increase to nearly 40 per cent in the 1970s. The paper in question, namely 'Economics of inquiring, communicating, deciding' (1968), was published in the *American Economic Review*, which – unlike *Fortune* – is a refereed scholarly journal, and indeed one of the most highly regarded journals in economics. That does not of course entail that the paper is correct, only that it is worthy of the serious attention of the economics community. Epistemologically, then, we *may* be further forward. Yet all along Bell gives the impression that he is arguing more from authority than from a personal engagement with facts or evidence. His citation of Marschak is one sentence in length, and does nothing to show *how* this 'eminent economist' set about proving that the US knowledge industries were bound to expand.

After endorsing Burck and Marschak, Bell thinks that he is now ready to invoke the 'information economy'. 'The last decade since Marschak wrote,' he states, 'has in fact seen enormous growth in the "information economy" ' (Bell 1980c: 517), singling out for mention the expansion of adult education, health services, information and data processing, telecommunications, and television. Surprisingly, Bell then suddenly stops to acknowledge some of the methodological problems inherent in such claims:

> If one wanted to measure the actual economic magnitudes of the information economy [note that this term has already shed its inverted commas], the difficulty is that there is no comprehensive conceptual scheme that can divide the sector logically into neatly distinct units, making it possible to measure the trends in each unit over time. A logical set of

categories might consist of the following: knowledge (which would include situses – locations or social positions – such as education, research and development, libraries and occupations that apply knowledge, such as lawyers, doctors and accountants); entertainment (which would include motion pictures, television, the music industry); economic transactions and records (banking, insurance, brokerage); and infrastructure services (telecommunications, computers and programs and so on).

(Bell 1980c: 517–18)

This alternative scheme actually has many virtues. Instead of imposing a counter-intuitive homogeneity on wildly disparate activities, it makes some appropriate distinctions, between knowledge and entertainment, and between data processing and infrastructure. It was argued in Chapter 2 that the health professions (including medicine) cannot credibly be regarded as information or knowledge work, but the other items listed by Bell are surely acceptable components of a putative information sector, assuming of course that knowledge and data are defined as modes of information. However, instead of developing his own rather promising theory of the information economy, Bell makes the fateful lurch, so familiar in Information Society Studies, to Marc Uri Porat.

'Porat's work,' Bell tells us in a ringing endorsement, 'is the first empirical demonstration of the scope of information activities since Machlup, but it goes far beyond Machlup's work…' (1980c: 518–19). Although Bell mentions certain technical respects in which Porat is thought to have outdone Machlup, notably his use of input–output matrices and some other relatively sophisticated econometric tools, it transpires very quickly that he – like the majority of information society theorists – believes that the 'most interesting and novel aspect of Porat's work is the definition and measurement of the secondary information sector' (1980c: 520). To recall, this refers to the internal information activities of organisations which are not directly engaged in information work, such as the libraries of pharmaceutical companies or the public relations desks of car manufacturing firms. Bell quotes Porat's figures, according to which the primary and secondary information sectors in 1967 accounted for nearly 50 per cent of US GNP and more than 50 per cent of wages and salaries, and affirms that 'it is in *that sense* that we have become an information economy' (1980c: 521, my italic).

Figure 5.1, whose source is given in a footnote as 'a briefing packet' which Porat had disseminated at 'an OECD conference' – an egregious example of what librarians call a 'soft reference' – divides the workforce into four sectors, i.e. information, agriculture, industry, and services. As can be seen from the figure, there is no longer any conflation of the information and services sectors: they are absolutely distinct, and the former has outstripped the latter. Table 5.7, also taken straight from Porat, throws Bell's new perspective into sharp relief by splitting the labour force into just two groups, information workers and non-information workers. It presents two sets of statistics, one using an 'inclusive definition', the other a 'restrictive definition'. Bell does not explain

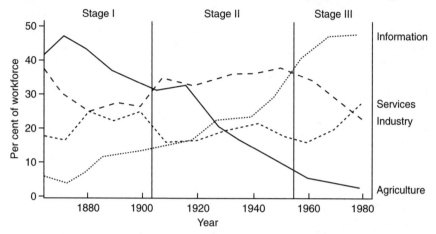

Figure 5.1 Four-sector aggregation of the US workforce, 1860–1980 (from Bell 1980c: 521).
Source: Porat 1977

the distinction, or say why neither set seems to tally with the statistics used in Figure 5.1 – for example, information workers according to the figure will be 46.6 per cent of the workforce, while the table projects 41.7 per cent (restricted) or 51.3 per cent (inclusive) – but this does not prevent him from arriving at the dogmatic conclusion that 'by 1975, the information workers had surpassed the noninformation group as a whole' (Bell 1980c: 523).

Table 5.7 Two-sector aggregation of the US workforce (in per cent) (from Bell 1980c: 523)

	Experienced civilian workforce			
	Inclusive definition		Restrictive definition	
Year	Information workers	Non-information workers	Information workers	Non-information workers
1860	7.0	93.0	4.5	95.5
1870	6.3	93.7	4.0	96.0
1880	7.7	92.3	5.1	94.9
1890	13.1	86.9	10.9	89.1
1900	14.7	85.3	10.7	89.3
1910	18.3	81.7	11.4	88.6
1920	22.0	78.0	13.3	86.7
1930	31.4	68.6	17.4	82.6
1940	30.7	69.3	18.4	81.6
1950	37.5	62.5	24.1	75.9
1960	45.5	54.5	28.4	71.6
1970	50.6	49.4	36.8	63.2
1980 (proj.)	51.3	48.7	41.7	58.3

Source: *Bureau of Labor Statistics Bulletins*

It is vital to register that what we are dealing with here is a methodological *fait accompli*. Like so many other writers in the field of Information Society Studies, Daniel Bell, no less, has been entirely captivated by Porat's thesis. This is evident from the tone of his delivery as well as from the content of his argument. Initially, he keeps things reasonably objective, his exposition framed in standard scholarly phrases such as 'as Porat points out' and 'according to Porat' (Bell 1980c: 520–1). However, within a remarkably short time, it is no longer 'according to Porat' or according to any other authority: it is unqualified assertion, accepted fact, seasoned history, dogma. Moreover, it has become a subjective matter, one in which Bell seems to feel that he has a personal stake. 'It is in that sense that *we* have become an information economy' (Bell 1980c: 521, my italic): *we* – not the United States, nor the economy, nor advanced societies, but we, the first person plural – have become an information economy. If such an epistemic stance were the end-result of a sustained sequence of logic and evidence it might be credible or at least creditable. But it is not. It is based wholly on second-hand figures from Porat and one or two other Machlupians. As Schement writes, 'after Porat's study was published, Bell endorsed Porat's position [and] retranslated Porat's data within the context of his own theory of post-industrialism' (Schement 1990: 461). The lure of Porat's sensational 50 per cent figure for the US information sector clearly proved too much even for Harvard's Henry Ford II Professor of Social Sciences. But if the critique in Chapter 2 was at all valid, and the Machlupian position is indeed riddled with ambiguities and errors, ought we not to be dismayed at the ease with which it has gained the Bellian *imprimatur*? Could we not have expected a more searching analysis than that which has been witnessed in the present commentary? Was the 'Machlup–Porat' school not imposing enough as it stood, without being turned into 'Machlup–Porat–Bell' – an awesome triumvirate against which few would dare to speak?

Evidence of regression in later writings

After such an enthusiastic endorsement of the Machlup–Porat way of quantification, one might expect that Bell's subsequent writings would be overflowing with references to the now-defined information economy and its concomitant information society. However, as was pointed out above, Bell instead seemed to grow cool to the whole idea. Two illustrations will suffice here. In 'The world in 2013' (1987), a paper the title of which suggests we might be vouchsafed a glowing portrait of a fully fledged world-wide information economy, there is not a single allusion either to Machlup or to Porat, or to any other author in the information sector tradition. Post-industrialism is still there – Japan, Bell informs us, will have graduated as a post-industrial society in his sense – but it has reverted to being largely a function of the *service* economy which had been marginalised in 'The social framework of the information society'. There is a solitary reference to 'information-based industries' (1987: 33), but such industries are now construed as species of *manufacturing* – computers and telecommunications are listed alongside pharmaceuticals – clearly implying a dissociation from the broader concept of an information sector.

Similarly, in 'The third technological revolution and its possible socioeconomic consequences' (1989), Bell has regressed to the pre-Porat formulations of *The Coming of Post-Industrial Society*. Dividing societies again into pre-industrial, industrial, and post-industrial, and reaffirming that the post-industrial stage is 'a society of services', he identifies the United States as a country where 'more than 70 percent of the labor force is engaged in services' (Bell 1989: 168). There is no mention any more of the information economy or of the famous 50 per cent figure. Moreover, of the post-industrial services alluded to, i.e. the 'human' services of education, health, and social services, and the 'professional' services involved in planning, analysis, design, and programming, at least half are self-evidently far from being straightforwardly informational, and those that *are* tolerably informational are hardly enormous parts of any nation's GNP or labour force. In other words, the information workforce concept pioneered by Machlup, developed by Porat, and embraced so wholeheartedly by Bell in 'The social framework of the information society' had by the mid- to late 1980s been unceremoniously abandoned. After a short-lived heyday, Bell lost his way as an information society theorist, or rather lost it in so far as the information society thesis is predicated on the expansion of an information sector.

The information flows element

From the beginning – from as far back, at least, as *Work and its Discontents* (1956) – the occupational setup has been Bell's chief theoretical interest, his main 'angle' on the social world. Despite the decisive rejection of Marxist politics for which he is often vilified (e.g. Webster and Robins 1986: 34), Bell seems to have inherited from Marx's philosophical legacy the idea that the economic setup, and particularly the nature of work, is the fundamental factor shaping societies. It is perhaps therefore understandable that he is often neatly categorised, *qua* information society theorist, as an exponent of the Machlupian information sector version of the information society thesis. This is, nevertheless, a hermeneutical error. In the present section, it will be argued that a second important strand can be found in Bell's thought, reflecting the quite distinct information flows version of the information society thesis. Moreover, it will be argued that Bell identifies *both* aspects of that approach, that is to say the expansion of scientific knowledge and the growth of the mass media. I will also suggest, however, that his theory fails to articulate a proper *balance* between these two elements, and that it therefore should not be regarded as a 'finished' information society thesis. (A thorough investigation requires a re-examination of some of the books and articles already looked at, which may occasionally leave an impression of repetitiveness.)

The expansion of scientific knowledge

An account of the expansion of the flow of knowledge fits very naturally into what we already know of Bell's position. As was explained in detail in the previous section, he had from an early stage identified the growth of a class of knowledge *workers* as a feature of the post-industrial economic setup, and an increase in knowledge *flows* would seem to follow from this as a corollary. Thus it comes as no surprise that initially, when Bell began to express interest in 'the idea of the information explosion' (1965: 122), scientific knowledge was really what he had in mind. He was contending in his early writings that 'what has now become decisive for society is the new centrality of *theoretical* knowledge, the primacy of theory over empiricism, and the codification of knowledge into abstract systems of symbols that can be translated into many different and varied circumstances' (1971: 4–5, italics in original). *The Coming of Post-Industrial Society* similarly declares, now with the gusto of an intellectual manifesto, that 'the concept "post-industrial society" emphasizes the centrality of theoretical knowledge as the axis around which new technology, economic growth and the stratification of society will be organized' (1974: 112).[6] A formulation in 'The social framework of the information society' (1980c: 501–2) identifies 'talented tinkerers' with their 'trial-and-error empiricism' as a trait of the industrial era, portraying them as having given way to the knowledge-based technology of the information society. Today Bell can be found making exactly the same point about 'the new relation of science to technology in the centrality of theoretical knowledge' (Bell and Graubard 1997: xiv–xv). Clearly, this particular claim is a strong feature of Bell's position.

Now Bell propounds a very precise conception of knowledge:

> I would propose a restricted definition: Knowledge is that which is objectively known, an *intellectual property*, attached to a name or a group of names and certified by copyright or some other form of social recognition (e.g. publication). This knowledge is paid for – in the time spent in writing and research; in the monetary compensation by the communication and educational media. It is subject to a judgment by the market, by administrative or political decisions of superiors, or by peers as to the worth of the result, and as to its claim on social resources, where such claims are made.
>
> (Bell 1974: 176)

As I argued in Chapter 2, there is much to be said for thus construing knowledge as socially new, publicly communicated, documented knowledge – in short, more or less, as science. It is intuitively prepossessing: if asked how much the world's stock of knowledge has increased, a typical way of answering would surely be to cite scientific discoveries and developments. Moreover, from a practical perspective, a construal of the information explosion in terms of 'intellectual property' enables accumulation to be quantified by common bibliometric and scientometric methods such as copyright and patent issues, online searches of research journal databases, and the like. Bell himself cites the standard statistics – Fremont Rider's calculations concerning the expansion of academic libraries and Derek Price's work on the exponential growth of scientific journals – and explains – again reflecting the received wisdom – that this twentieth-century phenomenon is largely due to the splitting of science into more and more fields, each with its own documentational apparatus (1974: 186–7; cf. 1980c: 527–8). Bell's views changed only very slightly over the years. In *The Coming of Post-Industrial Society*, he believed, or perhaps just hoped, that 'any growth which is exponential must at some point level off, or we would reach a point of absurdity' (1974: 181); but by the time of 'The social framework of the information society' he was attacking the claim that a saturation point had been reached, and speculating darkly on 'the end of the Alexandrian library' – that is, of the kind of library which can house every published work (1980c: 527–8). Either way, this is the stuff of routine information science, although Bell's formulations are as usual distinguished by the eloquent prose in which they are clothed, such as his allusion to the knowledge explosion as a 'torrential flood' or 'onslaught' of 'Babel' (1980b: 57; 1980c: 528).

Various scholars (e.g. Gould 1974: 37; Kumar 1978: 220; Badham 1984: 59) have pointed out that Bell allocates a leading role to science, but few, if any, have registered the important fact that the idea is not his own. In a revealing section of *The Coming of Post-Industrial Society* entitled 'The history of an idea', Bell identifies from his 'inventory of influences' an article by physicist Gerald Holton in *Daedalus*, house journal of the American Academy of Arts and Sciences. Holton's paper seems to have completely convinced him of 'the significance of theoretical knowledge in its changing relation to technology' (1974: 35). Now this must be disconcerting, and for precisely the same kind of reason that Bell's heavy reliance on Machlup's and Porat's controversial statistics was (or so it was argued) worrying. Is a single essay, albeit one by an eminent scholar in a prestigious journal, a sufficient basis for the work it is made to do in Bell's adaptation? Just as Bell's position on the information sector is founded in the final analysis on a markedly slender empirical base, so his views on the central role of science are now seen to originate in one uncorroborated piece of science history. *Prima facie*, it would appear that we again have the makings of a *radical mismatch* between the weight placed on an aspect of a theory and the knowledge base from which it is derived. Moreover, it is arguable that Bell simply overemphasises the role of science in twentieth-century invention. After all, what are Apple's Steve Wozniak and Steve Jobs, the college dropouts who created 'user-friendly' computing in a garage laboratory, if not shining examples of the supposedly extinct 'talented tinkerer'? Conversely, it is debatable whether science really was so marginal to pre-modern technology. Margaret Rose, for example (1991: 35), cites the inventions of the nineteenth-century mathematician Charles Babbage as proof that the dependence of technological innovation on theoretical knowledge is not a peculiarity of the twentieth century; and it would surely not be difficult to find many other such illustrations.

A conceptual issue which arises is that of where, if 'knowledge' is reserved for the lofty heights of theoretical knowledge or science, ordinary information flows fit into the picture. As the idea of the information society gained momentum in the 1980s, Bell began to turn his thoughts to this very question. In 'Gutenberg and the computer: on information, knowledge and other distinctions', he staked out his position thus:

> Note that I distinguish between information and knowledge ... Information is news, facts, statistics, reports, legislation, tax-codes, judicial decisions, resolutions and the like ... Knowledge is interpretation in context, exegesis, relatedness and conceptualisation, the forms of argument. The results of knowledge are theories: the effort to establish relevant relationships or connections between facts, data and other information in some coherent form and to explain the reasons for those generalisations.
>
> (Bell 1985: 15, 17)

These definitions are highly compatible with the position sketched in Chapter 2 in response to Machlup's conflation of information and knowledge. Bell is positing an *epistemological hierarchy* in which knowledge, ranking higher than information, requires an analysis or synthesis – an 'effort' of the mind – of disparate units of information and data. Such gradations are deeply embedded in ordinary language, explaining why, for example, the man on the Clapham omnibus finds it strange when archives or academic libraries, those supposed temples of *knowledge*, are said to be part of the *information* industry, or when research *scientists* are classified as *information* workers. In short, Bell is to be commended for drawing a thick line between information and knowledge. Indeed, one of the overarching conclusions of this book will be that such distinctions are critical for a disambiguation of the information society thesis.

However, if this is the case, if a clear-cut distinction between knowledge and information is indeed intuitively correct, we are obliged to ask Bell whether he is theorising about the information society or the knowledge society or both? Unfortunately, he equivocates. As was noted above, he had mused at the start of *The Coming of Post-Industrial Society* as to whether he should call his construct 'the "post-industrial" society, rather than the knowledge society, or the information society, or...', thereby implying that 'knowledge society' and 'information society' were just alternative descriptors with little to choose between them; but his more formal epistemology seems to suggest otherwise. Questioned on this point by the author, Bell declined to give a direct answer. Instead he said that 'knowledge is the hub of the matter', and that while information systems are important, 'the more important elements in a society remain the character of our knowledge systems, the conflicts in the polity and the changes in culture' (1996a). The role of information technology in Bell's thought will be taken up below. For our present purposes, however, the message so far seems to be that, despite his use of the term 'information explosion', Bell sees himself as in essence a theorist not of the information society but of the knowledge society; or, put another way, that he is a social theorist only of information *qua knowledge*: knowledge, not information, is the hub of social structure.

The mass media explosion

It was demonstrated in Chapter 3 that there is another side of the 'information explosion'. This one deals not with the frontiers of science, nor even, particularly, with information in the precise sense of facts, news, or statistics, but rather with the whole range of flows passing through society's media, and especially, of course, the mass media. Most bibliometric work on the information explosion studiously ignores the latter, but I argued that the totality of items flowing with terrifying abundance through such media, including entertainment and advertisements and many other 'vulgar' communications, should be accommodated, or at least discussed, in any contemporary theory of information worth its salt. Everyone, not just scientists and other white-collar professionals, feels that they are being overloaded with information, with the 'onslaught of Babel'; but, of course, what most people have in mind is television, radio, and other mass media, and now also that unique merger of mass and point-to-point communication, the Internet. It is therefore pleasing to discover that Bell, while he focuses on the higher epistemological modes, is perceptive enough to acknowledge – albeit too briefly – the social role of the lower modes.

Bell had intimated in *The Coming of Post-Industrial Society* that 'an effort to deal with comprehensive societal change' would need to embrace a plurality of information flows (1974: 176). Again, however, the benchmark text for understanding his views on the subject is 'The social framework of the information society'. Here, in fact, we encounter the most illuminating and well-rounded definition of the information explosion in the literature of Information Society Studies:

> The information explosion is a set of reciprocal relations between the expansion of science, the hitching of that science to a new technology, and the growing demand for news, entertainment and instrumental knowledge, all in the context of a rapidly increasing population, more literate and more educated, living in a vastly enlarged world that is now tied together, almost in real time, by cable, telephone and international satellite, whose inhabitants are made aware of each other by the vivid pictorial imagery of television, and that has at its disposal large data banks of computerized information.
>
> (Bell 1980c: 525–6)

Much exegetical energy could be devoted to such a rich passage, but the important point for present purposes is that it manifestly incorporates, in addition to the expansion of science and its relation to technology, the popular dimension of the information explosion. Elsewhere Bell gives striking proofs of the power of the televised image, such as the national broadcast of police dogs snarling at the great Martin Luther King in Birmingham, Alabama, which prompted ten thousand sympathisers to fly to his aid (1980b: 60). As an illustration of the profound significance of communication flows in a growing 'information society', the sensationalisation of the civil rights struggle could not be bettered.

One would expect that, having thus factored the mass media into the information equation, an evaluation of their social impact, or at least a presentation of some quantitative data or trends, might follow. In the event, however, mass media flows disappear from the Bellian script straight after making their dramatic appearance. The reason for their marginalisation is not very clear. Bell laments that, with the exception of science, 'it is almost impossible to provide any set of measurements to chart [the] growth [of the information explosion]' (1980c: 526). The exposition of Joho Shakai in Chapter 3 – we saw thirty years of painstaking quantification of the volume of information in a society – shows that this is simply incorrect. It is indeed mildly surprising that Bell never came across this research, since, in addition to being one of the great modern eclectics, he has always taken a special interest in Japan – even in retirement he has written for the periodical *Shukan Diamond*. In another context, Laurence Veysey has claimed that Bell 'derives all his evidence from narrow elites' and demonstrates 'almost no interest in the larger society beyond these elites' (1982: 59). 'He casts a wider net,' Veysey continues, 'only in a relatively brief discussion of shifts in the occupational structure'. However, as has now been shown, the 'wider net' is actually also visible, albeit fleetingly, in Bell's masterly definition of the information explosion in 'The social framework of the information society'. In any case, there is really no need to accost Bell with the extremely serious charge of snobbery. His selectivity can be explained more satisfactorily as the result of sheer desultoriness. Like Manuel Castells and other would-be encyclopaedic thinkers who strive for the conceptual high ground of the information society thesis, Bell just covers too many fields and too many themes to be able to do them all justice. If non-scientific information flows have slipped through his 'net' soon after being 'caught', this is disappointing but hardly a legitimate pretext for political diatribes.

It is fairer to conclude that so far as its treatment of the mass media is concerned, the Bellian synthesis is promising, but unconsummated. We may or may not agree with Castells's striking statement in *The Rise of the Network Society* that 'a few years after its development television became the cultural epicenter of our societies' (1996: 332–3), but we are certainly owed a fuller treatment of TV, and other mass media, than Bell vouchsafes. Just as he arguably *overplays* the uniqueness of theoretical knowledge, so he *underplays* the role of other contemporary modes of information such as entertainment. In addition, Bell neglects to articulate a position on how the two different aspects of the information explosion might be related. This is self-evidently a necessary move, because they apparently point in quite different, even opposite, directions. That is to say, we can easily imagine a society that is awash with entertainment and other (arguably) inferior modes of information, but which is woefully short of the higher form of information called knowledge; indeed, it could very well be argued that this is precisely what some Western media magnates are currently doing to many developing countries by means of satellite television. Anyway, the hermeneutical issue here is that, while Bell's theory is large enough to embrace a plurality of elements of information society thinking, i.e. not just the growth of post-industrial occupations but also the growth of information flows, and again not just scientific knowledge but mass media flows as well, it does not always *fuse* these elements in a convincing manner. The result is that the Bellian synthesis appears unshapely, obese in some parts and skeletal in others.

The information technology element

In addition to information work and information flows, Bell incorporates information technology (IT) into his theory of the information society. It would be exceedingly odd if he had not done so. As was noted in Chapter 1, 'information society as IT-pervaded society' is the popular conception. Furthermore, as was argued in Chapter 4, an account of the diffusion of IT is intrinsically a promising empirical basis for the information society thesis, at least where it receives a sophisticated formulation like that of Ian Miles. As will now be seen, Bell too presents a positive doctrine of the social role of computers and telecommunications. One question which will be to the fore in the following discussion is whether his treatment of this element of information society thinking effects a successful synthesis, or whether, instead, it gives the impression – as does so much work on the information society by lesser writers – of a hastily executed and dislocated response to the rapid advancement of the information revolution.

The generic philosophy of technology

For the record, computers were mentioned very early on in Bell's *oeuvre*, notably in an article on 'The study of the future' which cited predictions of a 'new, automated economy' featuring a robotised service sector (1965: 121, 130). However, before further pursuing Bell's views on IT, it is helpful briefly to review some of his statements on the nature of technology *in general*. Information technology is presumably merely a species of the genus technology: if so, one could expect to learn much from an information society theorist's doctrine concerning the nature of technology in general – if they have one. It is a salutary fact that few information society theorists do, in fact, have anything remotely approximating a generic philosophy of technology. The more careful among them, notably Miles, will try to specify what is meant by 'IT' but rarely, if ever, is a more generic account forthcoming. One of the qualities which marks Bell out from the majority of information society theorists is that he is willing and able to theorise at levels of abstraction. These engagements are not necessarily finally convincing, but they are always worthy of serious philosophical attention, and this holds true for his philosophy of technology.[7] As an academic field the philosophy of technology remains, as one exponent puts it, 'in its early stages', but Bell's pioneering contribution to this specialism has already been recognised (Mitcham 1994: 17, 249, 324).

Perhaps the best source for Bell's general theory of technology is his paper on 'Technology, nature, and society: the vicissitudes of three world views and the confusion of realms' (1980a; first published 1973). 'Technology, like art,' we are advised (Bell 1980a: 20), 'is a soaring exercise of the human imagination'. A comparison with art is one of the highest possible notes on which to begin, and demonstrates that Bell is very positively predisposed to technology; in a sense, one could say, much of his thought, and especially the much-criticised 'optimism' that pervades it, could be seen as an outworking of this stance. Unlike art, however, technology must be largely an exercise of *instrumental reason* rather than imagination, a point Bell concedes by formally defining technology in the same paper as 'the instrumental ordering of human experience within a logic of efficient means, and the direction of nature to use its powers for material gain' (1980a: 20). Rhetoric aside, concepts such as instrumentality, order, logic, efficiency, means, power, and material gain must be constitutive of any cogent doctrine of technology, for they are indeed, as Bell states here, its 'essence'.

Technology, Bell continues, transforms the social structure, by providing sources of energy, by enabling mass production, by facilitating communication and control, and – in the case of what he calls 'intellectual technology' – by substituting algorithms for human judgements. The premise that there can be *intellectual* technology as well as *machine technology* is one of Bell's major innovations in the philosophy of technology, and one which orientates his theory of *information* technology. 'The new intellectual technology,' he explains (Bell 1980a: 21), 'marks the last half of the twentieth century, as the machine was the symbol of the first half', and the computer, being the tool which carries out the required calculations, is its concrete manifestation; more than that, information processing devices seek nothing less than 'the compass of rationality itself'. Bell does not substantiate the latter, massive, claim; no doubt he realises that so doing would require a volume of philosophical apologetics, opening up, *inter alia*, complex issues relating to 'artificial intelligence' and even the venerable 'mind–body problem'. But he has already said enough for our present need, which is to acquire a sense of the kind of pivotal role that technology in general and IT in particular was destined to play in his thinking. Some of the finer ramifications are explored below.

Mainframes: computers for social alchemy

In correspondence with the author, Bell (1996a) referred to *The Coming of Post-Industrial Society* as 'my book on post-industrial technology', and it is certainly the case that new technology is one of the main themes of this canonical work of Information Society Studies. However, I wish to suggest that it plays there a rather different, and in some ways less significant, role from the one assigned to it in Bell's subsequent writings. The first reference to information processors occurs in the middle of the book's introduction. Expatiating on his notion of the primacy of theoretical knowledge, Bell writes that 'the development of modern economics ... has been possible because of the computer' (1974: 24). *The Coming of Post-Industrial Society* was, as its subtitle says, 'a venture in social forecasting', and social-scientific forecasting is, of course, precisely the kind of activity facilitated by information processing. More generally, computers are implicated in 'the rise of [the] new intellectual technology' (Bell 1974: 27), spelled out here as information theory, cybernetics, decision theory, game theory, utility theory, maximin strategies, and stochastic processes: all such techniques are deemed by Bell to be distinctive tools of the modern mind, and they all share the quality of being necessarily computational, in the sense of requiring, for the mega-calculations – 'feats' (1974: 30) – they involve, the services of information machines. Indeed, computers help us, in Bell's optimistic prognosis, to 'realize a social alchemist's dream: the dream of "ordering" the mass society' (1974: 33).

It would seem that the role which the computer was playing in Bell's thinking at this stage was an esoteric and technocratic one. What could be more esoteric than high-tech 'social alchemy', a formula resembling nothing so much as an amalgamation of Fabianism and freemasonry? At any rate, Bell was clearly *not* envisaging the diffusion of the user-friendly personal computer, nor the microcomputer revolution, nor informatisation in the popular sense. In line with state-of-the-art computing at the time at which *The Coming of Post-Industrial Society* was written, he basically had in mind mainframes and their characteristic academic and governmental applications. Now there is no *a priori* reason why an information technology version of the information society thesis should not take this narrow approach, but it is important to realise that such a version would engender a very different thesis from the kind examined in Chapter 4. The one, predicated on mainframes, yields a 'top-down', primarily qualitative, thesis emphasising the wide significance of a narrow base of powerful IT; the other, predicated on microcomputers, yields a much more quantitative, 'bottom-up' thesis stressing the wide distribution of (relatively) cheap IT.

Indeed, a little further into the introduction, Bell seems deliberately to downplay the information revolution, stating that 'in terms of technology, probably more substantial change was introduced in the lives of individuals in the nineteenth century by the railroad, steamship, electricity, and telephone, and in the early twentieth century by radio, automobiles, motion pictures, aviation, and high-speed vertical elevators, than by television and computers, the main technological items introduced in the last twenty-five years' (1974: 42). Lifts have changed the world more than computers: there is little ammunition *there* for the kind of message that many IT-intoxicated information society theorists are today propagating, with their rhetoric of total social reconstruction! Bell admittedly does refer in the same passage to a 'revolution in communications', but again this is immediately diluted by being set alongside another revolution, namely that taking place in transportation systems. Similarly, in the later chapter devoted to 'The dimensions of knowledge and technology', computers are listed with atomic energy and jet engines as among the more spectacular innovations which give purchase to talk of a 'constantly accelerating rate of technological change' (Bell 1974: 191–2); but they do not enjoy the role of a *prima donna*.

In fact, the whole of Bell's treatment of technology in chapter 3 of *The Coming of Post-Industrial Society* turns out to be of a general nature, with nothing to suggest that he regards the diffusion of IT as specially noteworthy. On the contrary, the sole specific mention of an IT-related process, namely automation, is one which positively militates against the kind of mindset espoused by so many information society theorists:

> No large-scale society changes with a flick of a wrist or the twist of a rhetorical phrase. There are the constraints of nature (weather and resources), established customs, habits and institutions, and simply the recalcitrance of large numbers. Those, for example, who made sweeping predictions about the radical impact of automation, based on a few spectacular examples, forgot the simple fact that even when a new industry, such as data processing or numerical control, is introduced, the impact of industries with sales mounting quickly even to several billion dollars is small compared to an economy which annually generates a trillion in goods.
>
> (Bell 1974: 211)

With its repudiation of the notion of a radical impact, this passage would automatically disqualify Bell from Miles's 'transformist' camp, and perhaps even from his middle-of-the-road structuralist camp. It is strongly playing down the social impact of IT and mocking those who were predicting a computerised leisure-filled utopia. A later footnote identifies Alvin Toffler's bestseller *Future Shock* as typical of the self-deceived claims of the information revolutionaries: computers have, Bell counters, had comparatively little effect on the *'daily life* of individuals' (1974: 318).

Thus, unpalatable though some may find it, much of the textual evidence suggests that Bell was *not*, in 1973, able to envisage a singular epoch-making capability for information technology. However, having noted all of the foregoing, it must also be conceded that there is another – thinner – strand which emerges suddenly in the final chapter of *The Coming of Post-Industrial Society*, and which appears on the surface to give more comfort to the information revolutionaries. '1945 to 1950 were,' Bell states on page 346, 'the "birth-years", symbolically, of the post-industrial society'. Second only to atomic power in this particular list of key symbols of the new epoch was ENIAC, the world's first mainframe electronic computer. What is particularly interesting here is Bell's accompanying remark that 'never in the history of invention has a new discovery taken hold so quickly and spread into so many areas of use as the computer'. He does not develop the point, and he goes on, as usual, to enumerate several other technological benefits of the period 1945–50, but he has said enough to suggest that he is now, as he apparently was not in earlier chapters of *The Coming of Post-Industrial Society*, wanting to ascribe to IT a large measure of epoch-making significance. Essentially, this is a claim about *diffusion*, the rapid spreading of a technology across society and the economy, and this is of course precisely the type of claim about IT *qua* enabling or revolutionary technology that Toffler and many other like-minded information society theorists have been in the habit of making. The difference is that Bell is making ENIAC not *the*, but only *a*, symbol of the new age, and yet even this difference can be dissolved if we emphasise, as we very plausibly might, that it is really the diffusion that makes a technology important. Atom bombs, after all, have not 'spread into so many areas of use', and so it could be argued that they must be of less societal significance than computers. And yet this line of argument seems to be a direct contradiction of Bell's very school-masterly points against Toffler and Tofflerism noted above.

It is not pleasant to have to confront an eminent thinker with a charge of inconsistency, but, not for the first time (Machlup was granted the same treatment in Chapter 2), this methodological journey to the roots of the information society thesis now requires it. For one cannot have the thing both ways. Either computers are widely diffused in society or computers are not widely diffused in society. Either ENIAC symbolised the coming of post-industrial society or ENIAC did not symbolise the coming of post-industrial society. Either *The Coming of Post-Industrial Society* is a legitimate benchmark text for claims concerning the information revolution or it is a bogus text for such claims. The most charitable way of dealing with this difficulty would perhaps be to say that where canonical writings are concerned the hermeneutical task is rarely straightforward. If that is obsequious or evasive, one might point out that Bell's interests are so wide-ranging that they can hardly not be inconsistent – although one does not expect this particular problem between the covers of a single book, even if that book is a compilation of separately published papers rather than a genuine monograph (Waters 1996: 24). However, I will return to the issue of consistency in the concluding section. The point here is that, despite his self-styled vocation as a sociological seer, Bell was certainly not *wholly* alive to the technological trajectories which information processing was beginning to prefigure at the time *The Coming of Post-Industrial Society* was published. But all that was soon to change.

Microcomputers: information revolution and home informatics

If there was even a faint glimmer of information-revolutionary thinking in Bell's work of the early 1970s, it is reasonable to assume that it would become considerably brighter as the years went by. For it is well known that the main stimulus for the information technology version of the information society thesis was not ENIAC and the other mainframes it spawned, but rather the spread of microcomputers in the late 1970s and early 1980s. The first genuine microcomputer – actually still described as a 'minicomputer' – the self-assembly Altair 8800, was advertised for sale in *Popular Electronics* in January 1975; Apple II appeared in 1977, followed by IBM's personal computer (PC) in 1981. This was a critical period for the information revolution – a term which was, and often still is, used synonymously with '*micro*computer revolution' – so we must expect the IT element in Bell's post-*Coming* writings to be considerably more salient. The opening sentences from 'The social framework of the information society' bear out such expectations:

> In the coming century, the emergence of a new social framework based on telecommunications may be decisive for the way in which economic and social exchanges are conducted, the way knowledge is created and retrieved and the character of the occupations and work in which men engage. This revolution in the organization and processing of information and knowledge, in which the computer plays a central role, has as its context the development of what I have called the postindustrial society.
>
> (Bell 1980c: 500–1)

The information revolution had now suddenly gripped Bell's sociological imagination: the two main species of IT, namely telecommunications and information processing, are implicated in a scenario (the 'may be' simply means that it is not quite a formal prediction – a typical Bellian caveat) in which a new social structure has come forth, and the computer, rather than sharing the limelight with other outstanding twentieth-century technologies, now plays *the*, rather than merely *a*, central role in the post-industrialist drama. The definite article is apposite, for Bell goes on to state that 'technological revolutions, even if intellectual in their foundations, become symbolized if not embodied in some tangible "thing", and in the postindustrial society that "thing" is the computer' (1980c: 509). Such reification, not to say iconisation, of the microcomputer has, of course, become integral to a certain level of discourse about the information society. 'If,' he proceeds, 'electricity was the agent that transformed the second half of the nineteenth century, in a similar vein the computer has been the "analytical engine" that has transformed the second half of the twentieth century'.

Bell also argues, and this is a distinctive feature of his new position, that a merging of technologies had taken place – that, while communications media could in the past be divided into print-on-paper on the one hand, and non-print media like telegraph, telephone, radio, and television on the other, now the technologies and their respective industries were coming together. 'The really major social change of the next two decades,' he writes, '*will* come in the [communications] infrastructure, as the merging technologies of telephone, computer, facsimile, cable television and video discs lead to a vast reorganisation in the modes of communication between persons' (1980c: 533, my italic: no 'may be' now). Following Antony Oettinger, Bell calls this process 'compunications'. Now, of course, it would be called 'convergence', a concept which we encountered in the work of Miles, and which lies at the heart of any theory of information technology in the late 1990s. By all accounts, the age of the 'standalone' gadget is gone.

Tom Forester, one of the most prolific anthologists in Information Society Studies, introduced his reprint of 'The social framework of the information society' with the gloss that 'Bell has developed his ideas further in the light of the microelectronic revolution' (Forester 1980: 500). With the benefit of hindsight, Margaret Archer (1990: 107) has recently opined that 'by 1980 Daniel Bell had ... joined in the celebration of the new axial principle – computer-assisted "theoretical knowledge" universalized by telecommunications'. The truth is even starker than that: Bell's thinking had actually made a major new departure, taking him deeply into Miles's transformist camp. This is evident in his explicit use of the word 'transformed', in his comparison of compunications with a wholly pervasive nineteenth-century technology (electricity), and also in the technological determinism embedded in the claim that the computer has acted as a single-handed agent or 'engine' of change. Bell denies that he is any kind of determinist, but if we were to judge his position solely by 'The social framework of the information society', the case for the prosecution would surely be overwhelming.

While this article thus contained a material development in Bell's theory of the socio-technical world, it is necessary to discover whether, despite his subsequent abandonment of the term 'information society', his intoxication with information technology persisted. Again, a rather unsettling turn awaits the close reader. 'Gutenberg and the computer' (1985) constitutes a General Defence of The Book Against The Computer, and dismisses David Bolter's *Turing's Man: Western Culture in the Computer Age* – then arousing much interest among the arts and humanities intelligentsia – as 'a shallow work which makes extravagant claims for the consequences of the computer on modes of thought' (Bell 1985: 19). However, this contribution to *Encounter* can perhaps be ignored as an aberration, a playful excursion designed to appeal to the self-conscious and cyberphobic clientele of a 'high-brow' literary magazine of the mid-1980s: Bell is, after all, a consummate man of letters as well as a scientist, and must occasionally be allowed whatever may be the prose equivalent of 'poetic licence'. Only two years later, in 'The world in 2013', he restores to computers a leading role, and even speaks excitedly, albeit in inverted commas, of the 'wired nation' (1987: 34) – at that time a buzz word of IT theorists.

Then in 'The third technological revolution and its possible socioeconomic consequences' (1989), an important paper which has not received enough attention from commentators, Bell demonstrates that he was now able, as he evidently had not been only a decade and a half earlier, to believe in the triumph of personal computing:

> The industrial revolution produced an age of motors – something we take
> for granted. Motors are everywhere, from automobiles to boats to power

tools and even household devices (such as electric toothbrushes and electric carving knives) that can run on fractional horsepower – motors of one-half and one-quarter horsepower. Similarly, in the coming decades, we shall be 'pervaded' by computers – not just the large ones, but the 'computer on a chip', the microcomputer, which will transform all our equipment and homes. For automobiles, appliances, tools, home computers and the like, microcomputers will operate with computing power of ten MIPS (millions of instructions per second) per computer.

(Bell 1989: 167)

'We have,' as the opening paragraph puts it, 'passed into the crucial period of diffusion' (1989: 164). Such passages might have been authored by an Alvin Toffler or a Yoneji Masuda, or indeed by a Bill Gates. Social alchemy has transmuted into what Miles would call home informatics. It is obvious, in other words, that by the end of the 1980s Bell was embracing a thesis about the general alteration of social life – the *daily life* of the average individual.

The statement about the pervasiveness of microcomputers in 'The third technological revolution and its possible socioeconomic consequences' is, however, the last strong piece of evidence for an IT element in Bell's information society thesis. In a more recent paper, 'Social science: an imperfect art', he writes that 'the fundamental sociological difficulty today, if one seeks to build theory, is the radical break-up of the institutional structures of society – in the economy and the polity – because of technology and telecommunications, and the changes in scale in the arenas where all these activities are played out' (Bell 1995a: 19). Telecommunications are obviously still important to him, but technology has gone back to being generic: there is nothing here to suggest that he sees *information* technology in particular as being axial to the construction of 'theory'. Except for a passing allusion to IBM – in its capacity, ironically, as a manufacturer of mainframes as opposed to microcomputers (1995a: 20) – there is nothing now of either the spirit or the letter of the information revolution.

The apparent disenchantment was confirmed in private correspondence:

Information becomes important in three ways: as a control system in the coded direction of production; as an ordering principle for scheduling, and other recording functions, as in management information systems; and in communications, as in the Internet. But important as these changes are, the more important elements in a society remain the character of our knowledge systems, the conflicts in the polity and the changes in culture.

(Bell 1996a)

Such a passage is a long way from transformism. Computer-controlled production, management information systems, and the Internet: these are now the sum total of Bell's computerised society, the only non-negligible applications of what he had called, at the height of the putative information revolution, an 'analytical engine' destined to 'transform' the social frameworks of the twentieth century. An even more emphatic message was given in another letter:

> The idea of 'information society' is a sub-set of the technological dimension of 'society' and often subordinated to larger organizational structures in the way an information technology officer in a corporation is subordinated to other managerial officers in the firm.
>
> (Bell 1996c)

Bell would not have spoken this way a few years earlier. IT now has no special purchase on the nature of society; it has been subordinated, downsized, relegated to a middle-ranking position in the scheme of things. Bearing in mind that Bell is referring here to only one aspect of the information society thesis, i.e. information technology, he seems very unwilling, in these revealing recent statements, to be identified any longer with the information society cause.

What then should be the verdict on the evolution of Bell's thinking about IT? Is the information revolution woven naturally into his thought, or merely stuck on to it syncretistically, perhaps as a result of the 'bandwagon effect' of majority opinion? The harshest interpretation would be to accuse him of naked intellectual opportunism, to allege that he was not particularly concerned with IT until it became prestigious to be considered an authority on the subject, and that he later distanced himself from the information society thesis because he became embarrassed at finding himself in sociologically unsophisticated company. This is Frank Webster's view, although even Webster has to acknowledge that the background of rapid microcomputer proliferation in the 1980s made Bell's 'opportunism' more understandable (1995: 30–1). It is certainly hard to deny that Bell's account was largely reactive. He was for too long strangely lacking in insights into the technological and social trajectories of computing, and sometimes, at least, his work leaves the impression of an *ad hoc* response to the acceleration of informationisation. There is no doubt also that, as a former journalist, it is in Bell's nature to write for 'effect'. He has always been, as Michael Miller puts it, 'a victim of his laudable desire to be relevant to contemporary discussions' (1975: 18) – and a willing, open-eyed victim at that. He would not, for example, have published almost exclusively in wide circulation non-specialist periodicals if he were seeking purely to assemble a scientifically impeccable theory. Nevertheless, Bell's interest in technology is genuine and profound and, however many inadequacies his analysis contains, it should not be lightly dismissed, nor tarred with the same brush as that deserved by his epigones. Bell did temporarily lose the sense of perspective we should expect of an eminent social theorist, and he is certainly sometimes inconsistent. However, if we take his writings as a whole, and resist the temptation to focus on the hyperbolic material which provided such easy pickings for information revolutionaries (and targets for their critics), we can learn much from his evolving understanding of the social role of information technology.

Conclusion: prospects for a mature synthesis

Steinfield and Salvaggio, who are virtually alone in noticing the complex nature of the Bellian contribution to Information Society Studies, have affirmed that 'perhaps the most influential work describing the nature of information societies is that of Daniel Bell' (1989: 9). There is no need for the 'perhaps'. Bell is incontrovertibly the most influential theorist of the information society, and I am arguing that he is also the ablest. This chapter has not negotiated every aspect of his position. It has omitted his controversial doctrine of the three 'realms' of society, which would have taken us too far into doctrinaire sociology.[8] It has largely left aside his account of the nature of the relations between technology and society, in this case because of the extensive treatment of such matters in Chapter 4. It has also prescinded from Bell's not implausible theory of the Just Meritocracy as the appropriate form of social democracy for post-industrial societies (outlined in the coda of *The Coming of Post-Industrial Society*). My project has been ruthlessly self-disciplined and forensic. I have tried to show exactly what Bell understands by the term 'information society', to identify the main influences on his thought, and to register the ways in which he can be said to have progressed the information society thesis. In particular, this chapter has assiduously *disaggregated* Bell's thought, interpreting it as a compound of three strands, elements, or versions of the information society thesis – in a sense, as a synthesis of three different, but not necessarily mutually exclusive, 'information society theses'. I wish now briefly to recapitulate Bell's treatment of each element, before moving on to a definitive judgement as to whether his synthesis can be regarded as successful.

The dominant version of the information society thesis, at least in Anglo-American circles, is the one predicated on an alleged inexorable growth of an information sector. This approach, of which Machlup was the great founder and Porat and others the developers, was shown to have been a major influence on Bell's thought, converging apparently very neatly with his own famous thesis about the preponderance of post-industrial services in modern societies. It was demonstrated that Bell, at one stage, accepted Machlup's and Porat's statistical materials in their entirety. However, Machlupism was strongly contested in Chapter 2, and if the criticisms marshalled there were valid Bell must as a consequence have adopted some cardinal methodological errors and ambiguities. Given that Machlupism is so prevalent in Information Society Studies, it is not surprising that Bell should wish to negotiate its potential for his theory of the modern world. But it *is* surprising – and surely also blameworthy – that a theorist of his stature should have adopted it so uncritically. The kinds of methodological rigour for which this book has been an extended plea were, regrettably, not to be found in the places where they were most sorely needed. Indeed, it is debatable whether the information society thesis ought to accommodate the information sector version at all. While I have not claimed that it is definitely false, I have suggested that this version is inherently weak and somewhat futile. If Bell has done nothing to change this appraisal of it, and he has not, then surely his incorporation of the information sector element is not something which should be applauded? Should he not, in fact, stand accused of adding his very considerable authority to a shaky hypothesis?

Bell's position, thankfully, does not stand or fall with claims concerning the information sector. It also involves a doctrine of information flows, whose overall role in Information Society Studies was evaluated in Chapter 3. Foremost in his doctrine of the information explosion is an account of the exponential growth of scientific knowledge and its impact on technological development. Close exegesis disclosed that Bell's account, especially as formulated in classic form in his key paper 'The social framework of the information society', also identified the more general social information flows which Joho Shakai theorists have endeavoured to measure. But in contrast with his full treatment of STM flows, Bell underplays the social role of the mass media, even unwisely asserting that such flows are inherently unmeasurable. This oversight, though typical of Western information society theorists, is disappointing in a diligent, learned, and eclectic thinker like Bell. Nevertheless, he is to be commended for his clarification of the epistemology of Information Society Studies, and especially for making clear-cut distinctions between entertainment, information, and knowledge. Henceforth, any tolerable information society thesis must give sufficient emphasis to the fact that STM flows – for example, flows of the physics proposition '$E = mc^2$' – are different from flows of the television programme *Dallas*. This might appear to be an elementary truth, but we have now seen enough information society theorising to know that it is one which has been forgotten all too often.

Finally, Bell accommodates information technology. The argument was made in Chapter 4 that, since IT is generally what the man on the Clapham omnibus has in mind if and when he thinks of the information society, the information revolution is probably the most sensible starting-point for Information Society Studies; it was also argued that Milesianism is the most promising expression of this approach available. The present chapter has charted the permutations in Bell's thinking about technology during the years in which the information revolution unfolded, and particularly the transition from mainframes to microcomputers. The computer was observed assuming a larger and larger role in the 1970s and 1980s, and then receding from centre-stage as the general excitement over microelectronics abated. While Bell's evolving treatment of the information technology element was, in broad terms, defended, I also argued that he sometimes fell prey to the hyperbole for which 'information revolutionaries' are notorious.

The problem remains of determining whether Bell's overall synthesis, that is to say the manner in which he fuses the separate elements, is convincing. It should be stressed here that the reading of Bell as a synthesiser is a *construal*, an interpretation which has been placed upon textual evidence. It has not been argued that Bell is a self-conscious synthesiser. Mid-way through our correspondence I brought this very issue into focus, putting the following questions to him:

Do you agree that there are in fact several 'information society theses': one that, following Machlup, talks about information work and sectors; another that is interested in the 'information explosion'; and a third that emphasises the diffusion of information technology (e.g. Nora and Minc)[9]? In your own writings on the information society you seem to endorse all three variants: is this the case and, if so, could you say a word or two about how your position – a synthesis? – relates to each variant?

Bell completely bypassed this query in subsequent communications, strongly implying that he had not really thought things through in such a way.

However, in the last analysis, the question of how Bell sees himself is less important than that of whether, objectively speaking, he actually produced a successful synthesis – and the answer to this, unfortunately, has to be negative. Its great weakness lies not at all in its range but in its *shape*: it fails to *assimilate* each of the elements properly, leaving some parts of the theory overblown and others underdeveloped. Discussing some other areas of Bell's thought, Laurence Veysey arrived at a similar conclusion:

> A major trouble with Bell is that too many things for him turn out to be primary. It is as if he cannot write about a particular subject without being pulled into a declaration that it is absolutely central to the whole society so long as he is choosing to fasten his attention upon it. This means we should distrust Bell's capacity to achieve a sense of proportion as he views any particular subject.
>
> (Veysey 1982: 53)

Veysey suggests bluntly that 'much of this may come down to the realization that Bell does not seem to care to go through the pains of editing himself'. This chapter has presented additional evidence, such as the sometimes inconsistent treatment of IT and the 'salami-slicing' of pieces of his writing, which indicates that more self-editing would indeed have been of benefit to Bell's cause. However, it is not idleness which stops him from staying in some fields long enough to do a proper workmanlike job: it is *scientific curiosity*, or perhaps, at worst, what Bell himself called his 'restless vanity' (cited in Webster and Robins 1986: 33). But whatever causes lie behind it, and notwithstanding the fact that Bell has shed far more light than any other information society theorist, the unavoidable conclusion must be that he fails to produce a streamlined synthesis. Bell was always the theorist most likely to succeed; since, in the end, even he falls well short of the goal, we are forced to wonder whether a completely adequate synthetic theory of the information society can soon be achieved.[10]

Notes

1   A version of the present chapter has appeared in the *Journal of Information Science* (Duff 1998a).

2 Tsay's co-citation analysis supplies hard evidence for Apostle and Raymond's submission that 'sociological work, particularly Daniel Bell's, occupied a central place in the professional disputes [over the nature of librarianship and information studies]' (Apostle and Raymond 1997: preface).

3 It would be wrong to claim that this interpretation is unprecedented, since Steinfield and Salvaggio (1989: 9) have noted that 'Bell's conception is explicitly multidimensional'. However, their analysis, amounting to merely one page and involving no textual exegesis at all, cannot be described as anything other than introductory. It is one thing to *say* that Bell's theory is synthetic, quite another to *show* that it is so.

4 I wish to acknowledge Professor Bell's courtesy in entering into dialogue with me by letter during 1996, and later, on the occasion of the conferring of his honorary doctorate at Napier University (10–11 July 1997), face-to-face. I am also very grateful to him for sending me an unpublished paper he had read to the American Sociological Association, 'The break-up of space and time: technology and society in a post-industrial age' (1992). This has not been quoted because Bell, at the time, was intending to revise it for subsequent publication.

5 Indeed, a very large proportion of the same material was 'salami-sliced' into a third outlet, namely 'Teletext and technology: new networks of knowledge and information in postindustrial society' (1980b).

6 'The crux of my argument [in *The Coming of Post-Industrial Society*],' Bell confirmed in private correspondence, 'was the new role of the codification of theoretical knowledge in becoming directive of changes in science and technology' (1996a).

7 The coda of *The Coming of Post-Industrial Society*, to take one example, contains some philosophising about the concept of distributive justice. Bell gets things wrong – he misdescribes (1974: 444) John Rawls's *magnum opus*, *A Theory of Justice*, as 'the most comprehensive effort in modern philosophy to justify a socialist ethic', when it is in fact a defence not of socialism but of liberal egalitarianism – but he always does so in a way which nevertheless demonstrates his philosophical prowess. It is indeed a matter for regret that professional Anglo-American political philosophers are not more widely aware of his contributions. However, political philosophy proper lies well outside the scope of the present study (cf. Duff 1990).

8 Bell divides society into three realms, i.e. socio-economic structure, polity, and culture, and maintains, *contra* Marxism and much sociological orthodoxy, that they are largely independent of one another. A superb exposition of the doctrine can be found in chapter 2 of Waters (1996). The information society thesis has been analysed in my own book solely with regard to its proper home, the socio-economic realm.

9 I cited Nora and Minc as exponents of the information technology version rather than Ian Miles because it is on record that Bell has read their work: he contributed a foreword to their famous report, *The Computerization of Society* (1980).

10 People I respect highly have assured me that Manuel Castells's trilogy achieves just that. While applauding much in Castells's work, not least its energy and scope, this is a view with which I beg to differ. The trilogy may succeed on Castells's own terms, but it does not succeed on the terms articulated in my book. That is to say, it does not contain a measured calibration of diverse truth-claims from the three chief schools of thought, nor their fusion into a shapely macrolevel synthesis. However, perhaps I have yet to see the light on this matter.

6   Overall conclusions

Chapter 5 discussed the foremost synthesis of the various strands of information society thinking, that of Daniel Bell. Bell's position was found to be a complex formation which, while successful or at least promising in some respects, was also weak in others: the conclusion had to be that the theory of the information society has still not been finally constructed. Here, at the end of our investigation, it is necessary to summarise the main findings and, where appropriate, to suggest the directions in which the information society thesis might wish to go if it is to overcome its current limitations. For this book does not aspire to be an obituary of the information society thesis; on the contrary, while it has been largely an exposure of methodological shortcomings, and while it certainly implies that a great deal of speculative sociological and socio-philosophical work on the information society builds on unstable conceptual and empirical foundations, its aim has always been to clear the way for a chastened, more cogent thesis to emerge. The following conclusions present the essential findings of the critique of methodology. In the Coda, the outlines of a new variant of a synthetic information society thesis will then be offered.

There are several information society theses

Scholars tend to speak of the information society and the information society thesis as though it were a single, well-defined matter. This methodological critique has proved that that is very far from being the case. Three distinct theses were identified. First, there is one according to which modern societies are characterised by a preponderance of information work; it is also known as the 'information economy thesis'. This set of claims dates back to the economist Fritz Machlup and is the dominant version (by any bibliometric standards) of the information society thesis. Second, there is the thesis that modern societies are characterised by an information explosion, an exponential increase in information flows. This version, much less well known in the West, was traced to the Japanese Joho Shakai research tradition. Third, there is the technological approach, which defines information societies in terms of the 'information (technology) revolution' and the pervasive impact of IT: the methodological assumptions underlying Ian Miles's sophisticated formulation of 'the information society *qua* computerised society' were analysed. These are the three main basic approaches discernible in the information society literature, but more often than not they are conflated and confused. Most information society theorists do not seem to be aware that there is more than one thesis at work, or, as I have put it, that there is a plurality of *versions* of the information society thesis. This is true even of scholars who espouse a 'synthetic' approach, one which combines some or all of the various strands. Even Daniel Bell, no mean social theorist, seemed to equivocate and obfuscate in his treatment of the different themes; indeed, he apparently does not even recognise himself as a synthesiser. To have unravelled these different strands can only, therefore, enhance the prospects for a more cogent theory of the information society.

A cogent information society thesis will be synthetic

Society is multifaceted; so is information. Information work and the makeup of the gross national product are important to society. Information flows are important to society. Information technology is important to society. It is hard to see, therefore, how an adequate theory of the information society can be one-dimensional. The lodestar of Information Society Studies should be a *synthetic* information society thesis, one which fuses the manifold elements of informationisation in a balanced way. As Chapter 5 indicated, achievement of this goal is evidently still a long way off.

All societies are information societies

Attention has been drawn to various 'demarcation' problems. The general point is that it is very difficult to prove – and since it is counter-intuitive there is a heavy burden of proof in the matter – that modern societies are more information-based than other societies. There is something *prima facie* suspect, perhaps even arrogant, about the assertion that *we* are now, while *they* were not then, living in information societies. The computer programmer works with information; so did the railway clerk. The executive at IBM works with information; so too, no doubt, did the chief butler at Chatsworth. The information scientist at Aslib is an information worker; so was the curator at the Bodleian and, no doubt, the tablet cataloguer at Ebla. To be sure, a plausible case can be made that the contemporary USA, or Japan, or Britain, is an information society, but it is not nearly so easy to argue convincingly that other societies are non-informational. As in theology and most other arts and sciences, 'proving a negative' is an uphill methodological struggle. This is a truism which seems to have been overlooked by the majority of information society theorists; indeed, it is very rare for an information society theorist to produce facts and figures which could even in principle bear out such a claim. As we saw, substantive diachronic data are rare: for the most part, the statistical series we are presented with do not go back further than the beginning of the twentieth century, hardly long enough for a thesis which in most formulations puts the information epoch on a par with the industrial and agrarian eras. A wiser way forward, it is suggested, is to concede that, of course, all societies are and were information societies. Access to information has always been a condition of social power, and the economy of even the most primitive societies must have been to a significant extent dependent on information flows. A little objective reflection should tell us that all societies are information societies, *but also that they are information societies in different ways*. What is special about some advanced societies is that they are dependent upon computerised and telecommunicated information, and especially nowadays upon what Joho Shakai researchers called 'segmented' (bunshu) electronic information. If this were what the information society thesis were claiming then it would surely command much more respect from its critics.

The dominant version is methodologically challenged

The information society thesis is weakened by its over-reliance on the Machlupian version. This conclusion is not likely to be well received in many information society circles, precisely because it flies in the face of a current favourite of the information and social sciences. However, it is not necessarily being suggested that Machlupism should be abandoned completely. That the nature of work is central to the nature of a society is a truism. We split history into agrarian eras and industrial eras precisely because of it. Therefore, if societies are indeed moving into a new era in which information processing has displaced manufacturing as the main occupation and source of GNP, then that would be a development of great significance. However, it must at last be admitted that there are serious difficulties with the verification of this claim, difficulties which, without quite wholly impugning the thesis, make dogmatic assertions on its behalf unwise. I am not defending the extreme view that the measurement of information work is so intractable that the whole project is misconceived. While difficult, complex, and tendentious one cannot go so far as to say that information sector metrics are doomed to failure. While it may be impossible to say that past societies were *not* information societies, it must be possible in principle to work out a tolerably serviceable metric to show that current societies *are* information societies, in the information sector sense. But while possible in theory the state-of-the-art is in practice rather unconvincing, and is certainly not worthy of the kind of fanfare trumpeted by many information society theorists. Is it really too heterodox to conclude that the future for Information Society Studies might lie less in this methodological direction than has hitherto been thought?

The potential of Joho Shakai

Conversely, it is suggested that the potential of the information flows version has not been sufficiently exploited. It is often stated that there has been an exponential increase in information, but the statement is usually supported only by tired old formulas based on the work of Derek Price, or by simplistic allusions to the contents of *Ulrich's Union List of Periodicals* or the physical weight of, say, *Index Medicus*. There is a shockingly widespread ignorance of Joho Shakai, the Japanese research tradition which alone has systematically addressed the problem of measuring information flows in society. Information society theorists in the West could do much worse than investigate this work and begin planning similar information flow censuses for their own societies. As argued in Chapter 3, one great strength of this version is its intuitiveness, its congruence with the perceptions of the man on the Clapham omnibus about 'information overload'; in stark contrast, to tell the average secretary or television repair man – not to mention the average dancer or doctor – that he or she is an information worker is to cause a reaction approximating consternation. The question which must be faced is this: why does the information society thesis insist on continuing in its current counter-intuitive tracks when a much more promising methodology is available?

The problem of the mass media

There is here, however, a problem concerning the role the conventional mass media should play in the information society thesis. The Joho Shakai researchers measure all information flows, including those transmitted by the mass media – which, given the nature of the beast, make up the bulk of flows. But surely if information society theorists do have something distinctive to say, they will not want to collapse their information society thesis into older theses about the social impact of television, or into even older theses about the social impact of newspapers? We need to be able to distinguish computers from television even though television is undoubtedly a transmitter of information. The Internet throws this problem into sharp relief, since it is in some respects, such as its growing function as an entertainment tool, more akin to television than to computers. If the mass media do converge completely with computers and telecommunications, what will become of the distinctive insights about modernity that information society theorists have produced? Will the mass media theorists and the information society theorists join together? Will the departments of 'film and television studies' (and photography, and radio, and journalism studies) merge with the departments of information science? And if so, what retrospective judgement will be made on the information society thesis of the 1970s–1990s? This cluster of questions can perhaps only be resolved when trends have unfolded more fully. However, all the equivocation must stop now.

The definition of information technology

Computers and allied telecommunications technologies undoubtedly have a place in the information society thesis (ideally couched in a generic philosophy of technology). This is the most common lay perception and there are strong grounds for accepting it. But there is a specific definitional issue which needs to be addressed with more rigour. The information revolution is a phenomenon of the 1970s and 1980s but electronic computers, not to mention telephones, pre-dated these decades by a substantial stretch. What is required is a more *nuanced* account which recognises that information technology is as old as civilisation itself, and which perhaps casts the convergence of digital computing and telecommunications as merely a current mode of IT. Milesianism is the only formulation of the information technology version of the information society thesis to have addressed this problem in any detail, but it has not produced the final word. There is a need for more work on essentialism: on what is to count as the 'essence' of IT, and what as its various forms or 'appearances'. Such work would clearly also be relevant to the issues raised in connection with the potential of Joho Shakai.

The distinction between knowledge and information

An even more fundamental definitional issue which needs to be settled is how the terms 'knowledge' and 'information' are to be understood. In Chapter 2, Machlup was sharply criticised for his championing of synonymity. As was emphasised there and throughout this book, ordinary language, far from making these terms synonymous, puts them in a clear-cut conceptual hierarchy as follows:

Wisdom
Knowledge (including Science)
Information
Data.

Knowledge is higher than information, as Bell, for one, clearly recognised. One can say that knowledge is a mode of information in the sense that it is higher-order information, but unless this qualification is made one is simply engaging in equivocation and mystification. A knowledge society must be a different entity from an information society, and this will be the case whatever metric is used. Objectively speaking, it is surely an extraordinary fact that information society theorists routinely equate the two. Moreover, it has become increasingly clear that more than one concept of information is at work: in the Coda I will explore this matter, drawing a new distinction between the *de jure* information society and the *de facto* information society.

The falsity of the traditional trajectory

The information society thesis must relinquish one of its most characteristic conceptual frameworks, namely the trajectory of agrarian–industrial–information epoch. The information revolution is almost always compared with the industrial revolution, which is compared in its turn with the transition from the primitive to the agrarian way of life. However, there is simply not enough evidence yet to suggest, still less prove, that societies are undergoing changes on such a scale. To fall into the habit of equating the information and industrial revolutions is dubious social science, and is unlikely to augment the credibility of the information society thesis. I defended the Milesian account, according to which the information revolution is a mini-revolution – one might say, with double meaning, a micro-revolution – within the ongoing industrial revolution. It is possible that it will one day turn out to be of full epoch-making significance, although I have suggested that this is highly improbable. But in any case the data currently at our disposal do not allow us to go beyond a moderate Miles-type formulation. Scholarship ought to be a lifelong quest for *objectivity*: information society enthusiasts should understand that their views on modern developments might be just a little partisan – chronologically as well as geographically.

The under-conceptualisation of information–society relations

The information society is in some sense an outcome of the Boolean equation Information AND (Work OR Flows OR Technology) AND Society. It is incumbent on information society theorists to articulate the nature of the relationship between information and society, and in this matter, too, they have for the most part been remiss. Miles is an exception. By supplying us with mediating concepts such as 'techno-economic paradigm' and 'socio-technical system', he has illuminated the ways in which information and IT permeate the economy and society. Henceforth information society theorists should either work with these concepts or give a good explanation as to why not. However, while Milesianism has thus provided an invaluable service in deepening the conceptuality of the information society thesis, it skirts around the critical issue of technological determinism. I suggest, *pace* Miles and other sophisticated information society theorists, that a strong measure of technological determinism is actually essential if we are to get very far with the explanation of modernity.

The under-conceptualisation of communication

The intersection of the information society thesis with media and communication studies has been noted at appropriate points above. However, even where the version of the information society thesis was overtly communicational, in the sense of being the work of telecommunication researchers, it was found that the conceptual relations between information and communication were left opaque. The Information Flow Census measures all transmissions of information, that is to say it measures *communication* flows, and it might therefore be better understood as yielding a dynamic 'communicating society' (or perhaps 'info-communicating society') thesis rather than a static 'information society' thesis. By contrast, both the information sector and the information technology versions focus on nodes, the situses of information work or technology. Machlup complicated matters by defining the production and distribution of information (which of course he miscalled knowledge) as any change in the state of mind of anyone, thereby largely obliterating the dividing-line between information and communication. In ordinary language, however, a communication can be new even when the information is old: this distinction, and the differing models and measurements to which it gives rise, ought surely to be more closely observed in Information Society Studies.[1]

Bibliometrics: the pedigree problem

The critique has frequently drawn attention to bibliometric aspects of the information society thesis. It was shown that few of the 'canonical works', the early texts upon which traditions have been built, were published in fully accredited modes or calibrated in the proper ways. The primary source of the information sector version was released as a monograph by a reputable press, but, in spite of being an essay in intrepid interdisciplinary adventurism, it met with *ad hominem*, indulgent reviews. The information flow censuses largely reside in workaday government reports and have never been rigorously evaluated, at least by Western scholars: this book aspires to have made a small beginning in that respect, albeit relying mainly on translations. The information technology approach has been so amorphous that Milesianism, also partly a report phenomenon, may be its only cogent expression. Admittedly, innovation in the social sciences is often brokered by reports in the first instance, but one must expect the proper media of scholarly publication to come to the fore subsequently. Even Bell's writings have for the most part bypassed the normative modes of academic quality assurance, notably the journal peer review process. This is not to cast a slur on any of these pioneering thinkers, only to suggest that some of their ideas and propositions concerning, specifically, the information society may have had too easy a passage. A question mark thus hangs threateningly over the pedigree of the information society thesis. Surely the best way to proceed is to be candid about this and, where possible, to make good the congenital methodological defects which have entered the established wisdom?

Post-dogmatism: towards a new epistemic modality

Perhaps the key underlying point in all of the above is one of epistemic modality. The main problem with the information society thesis in its current forms is the dogmatism with which it is advanced. The thesis has been shown to be methodologically inadequate in many ways, but it is not thereby necessarily misconceived. If more qualifications and caveats were introduced around the claim that 'society x is an information society', and if it were stated *sotto voce* instead of shouted emphatically from the rooftops, then the information society thesis might hope to find more acceptance among the seriously erudite. If the *methodology* is improved in the ways suggested here, Information Society Studies will have a happier future in the academy.

Note

1 I wish to thank Professor A.J. Meadows of Loughborough University for drawing my attention to this poorly understood dimension of the information society thesis. The present work makes only a small beginning at articulating the rich conceptuality of communication and its relations with information and society.

Coda

An agenda for Information Society Studies

In the light of the foregoing critique of methodology, this Coda attempts to sketch a way forward for Information Society Studies. It does not claim to present a fully worked-out new position, but instead suggests some of the main parameters within which subsequent reflection could take place. This task is conceived of as being two-fold: first, the nature of the field of Information Society Studies needs to be somewhat clarified; second, the outlines of a cogent synthesis of the information society thesis should be offered as a positive contribution to that field. Metaphorically, the jungle of information society discourse was systematically cleared in Chapters 1 to 6. Now, the enclosure is fenced and plans for a new construction are laid.

The field of Information Society Studies

In a marvellous essay on 'The science of bibliography', Michael Keresztesi argues that new disciplines go through three critical phases. They start with Phase I, the 'pioneering phase'. 'The birth of many scientific disciplines,' Keresztesi writes, 'can be traced to some great thinkers, or a pioneering intellectual who burst upon the scene with original ideas, profound insights, startling propositions, or illuminating new theories' (1982: 13–14). There is often a struggle for attention and recognition, and a desire to win over other scholars to the emerging doctrine. Bibliographically, Phase I used to be marked by a flurry of pamphlets, but nowadays 'every conceivable medium becomes involved – lectures, articles, interviews, books, conference and seminar papers'. If successful, the pioneering phase generates widespread interest and a powerful momentum is created. Phase II is thus the 'elaboration and proliferation stage'. The new ideas pass out of the monopolistic control of a single institution or coterie, to be developed by an international community of scholars of differing organisational and perhaps disciplinary allegiances. National and international associations or committees are formed, and the bibliographic apparatus is expanded to include such items as *Who's Who*s, directories, and an official journal. There is also at Phase II what Keresztesi calls an 'excessive preoccupation with methodology', although no rationale is offered for this curious observation. Finally, there is Phase III, the 'establishment phase'. All doubts about intellectual legitimacy have been dealt with, and the discipline is now granted full admission to academia. It is organised into university departments, and undergraduate and graduate courses are offered in it. Standards become formalised institutionally by means of official curricula and professional or scholarly accreditation procedures. At Phase III, the bibliographic apparatus is further augmented by media as diverse as catalogues, textbooks, syllabi, and dissertations.

It is illuminating to try to place Information Society Studies on Keresztesi's trajectory. I argued in Chapter 1 that Information Society Studies does not yet exist, in the sense that what the literature presents is an unsystematic and inchoate agglomeration of theories rather than a soundly based, circumscribed academic area. It was even suggested that the present critique of comparative methodology can be regarded as a basic contribution to a *new* field, i.e. *Information Society Studies*. But in another sense, of course, Information Society Studies has existed for several decades. Chapter 1 showed that the term 'information society' was coined as long ago as 1964, and that articles, books, and even a dictionary on the subject were appearing by the late 1960s and early 1970s. In Keresztesian terms, the present situation actually seems to have features germane to all of the evolutionary phases. Clearly, we have 'a pioneering intellectual who burst upon the scene with original ideas', namely Fritz Machlup. We also have the international armies of followers (witness Porat and all the other Machlupians cited in Chapter 2), the competing schools of thought (Joho Shakai and the information technology version), and the interdisciplinarity characteristic of the elaboration and proliferation phase. There is no longer, in some circles at least, a struggle for acceptance. On the other hand, there are no international committees or associations, and even scholarly conferences on the information society are hard to find. Have the academic authorities given the new field ('field' is preferred here to the stronger term 'discipline') the level of respectability associated with Phase III – the establishment phase? The answer to this must be negative. There are no departments of Information Society Studies, hardly any undergraduate[1] or graduate courses wholly dedicated to Information Society Studies, and no standards for scholarly or professional accreditation. Meadows has pointed out that 'to some extent, the appearance of specialisms on the intellectual scene can be identified from the dates at which university chairs in the subject have been founded' (1998: 45). In that respect as well, the field in question has not yet arrived, for there are no chairs of Information Society Studies.

When looked at bibliographically the same disarray is evident. Much work on the information society can be found in pamphlets, public lectures, and reports, all the paraphernalia of Phase I. But we also have the key Phase II organ of journals. *The Information Society: An International Journal* is now deeply inside its second decade. New journals with an identical or near-identical mission are constantly appearing, two recent examples being *Convergence: The Journal of Research into New Media Technologies* and *Information, Communication and Society*. Moreover, as the bibliometric study in Chapter 1 showed, the editorial policy of a leading established information science journal, *Journal of Information Science*, has also strongly favoured information society research latterly. Whether any one of these will become an 'official journal' of Information Society Studies remains to be seen. However, they are all excellent scholarly productions, and so some of the norms of peer review are obviously already being observed. On the other hand, there is no *Who's Who* or directory in existence, and 'information society' is not yet an accepted subject heading in many of the databases of the information and social sciences. Similarly, we have some Phase III media, such as PhD dissertations, and textbooks already in their second edition (e.g. Feather 1998), but not others – syllabi, catalogues, and the like.

Thus, there is confusion: much activity but little regularisation or affiliation. It is hoped that the present work will help to move the situation forward by focusing scholarly attention on neglected definitional and methodological issues. In addition, the following five practical suggestions are offered:

1. *The field should be named Information Society Studies*

There are those who have started suggesting that 'social informatics' is a better name for the emerging field. Against this, I would point out that the term 'informatics' has an unavoidable technical connotation, whereas non-negligible strands of thought in the field – not least the Machlupian school – do not emphasise information technology. Information Society Studies is a broader and less misleading rubric. The word 'studies' also adds a desirable academic flavour.

2. *Information Society Studies should be recognised as an interdisciplinary field*

The field is no more a monopoly of sociology than it is an exclusive preserve of information science. The truth is that it is a specialism of interest to researchers from a wide range of disciplines, as the bibliometric survey in Chapter 1 demonstrated. Since the information society is *ex hypothesi* an emergent social formation, the sociological perspective is certainly fundamental, but other classic disciplines like economics and philosophy should also have a stake in its explanation and evaluation, as should younger fields such as communication studies and information science. Interdisciplinarity rather than academic territorialism should be the norm.

3. *Information Society Studies should be accepted as a branch of information science,* inter alia

If information scientists are to make a major contribution to Information Society Studies their efforts need to be recognised by their own colleagues. We often say that information scientists are either 'retrievalists' or 'bibliometricians' or 'scientific communication specialists'. It is being proposed that 'information society specialists' should now be added. Alan Gilchrist, editor of the *Journal of Information Science*, has led the way in this respect by publishing many articles on the information society; perhaps other key organs like the *Journal of Documentation* need to open their doors. (To say that Information Society Studies should be seen as a branch of information science is not of course to imply that it cannot also be a specialism of sociology, economics, etc.)

4. The journal situation should be kept under control

It was mentioned that there are already at least three interdisciplinary journals devoted to the study of the information society: *The Information Society*, *Convergence*, and now *Information, Communication and Society*. There is the *Journal of Information Science*. There are also literally scores of other periodicals (see Appendix 3) which have expressed at least a passing interest in the information society. In bibliometric terms, therefore, there is a high level of 'scatter', and if the field is to develop a degree of rationalisation may be necessary. It is particularly difficult to understand the rationale for the creation of *Information, Communication and Society*, whose mission seems to be identical to that of the well-established (at least in the United States) *The Information Society*. If too many 'core' journals occupy the same market, the standard of research is likely to go down as editorial demand for papers increases relative to authorial supply. This is a delicate matter, but it is being suggested that the journal situation needs to be looked at dispassionately – and some hard decisions made.

5. Scholarly conferences should be organised

Finally, Information Society Studies requires more practical organisation. *Who's Who*s and membership lists are not necessary: inventing such paraphernalia at this stage would be premature, and might even play into the hands of a 'clique' (perhaps one associated with a particular journal or university or discipline). The field should be allowed to develop naturally and in a cosmopolitan spirit. However, a mild centripetal force would be conducive to progress, and some scholarly conferences should therefore be organised. What is envisaged here is not large convocations trying to cover every topic or technology which can loosely be related to the information society – such meetings already take place, many of them organised by one or other tentacle of the European Commission – but rather highly focused learned symposia whose objective is solely the advancement of learning. The prospects of success would be enhanced if these were hosted by institutions with established reputations in a cognate field: a university department of sociology or a graduate school of information science would be ideal. The aim in all this should be not to create a tightly knit 'movement' or 'cause', but simply to facilitate an epistemologically cumulative dialogue across disciplinary and national barriers.

The *de jure* information society thesis

As a material contribution to Information Society Studies, the very rough outlines of a new variant of a synthetic information society thesis will now be supplied. Much of the methodological confusion identified in the foregoing critique reduces in the final analysis to misleading definitions of information. As we saw, Machlup started the downward semantic slide as far back as 1962. His 'terminological proposals' were no doubt made with the best of intentions, but by including every alteration in anyone's epistemic state he was imputing an extremely wide meaning to 'information'; even worse, he spoke of 'knowledge' rather than 'information'. His disciple Porat helped somewhat by reclaiming the term 'information', but Porat still included in his 'information economy' thesis much of what Machlup had called 'knowledge', and the tradition has followed suit. Joho Shakai researchers have also operated with an all-encompassing definition: for them, everything which is transmitted across telephone lines or other communication media counts as information. Even a sophisticated and methodologically self-aware information technology version of the information society thesis runs into semantic impasses – as was seen with Ian Miles. Daniel Bell, the synthesiser, moved unconsciously between narrow and wide definitions, never really achieving a consistent position.

Given such a background, it is suggested here that Information Society Studies needs henceforth to make a basic distinction between the *de facto* information society thesis and the *de jure* information society thesis. The *de facto* information society thesis measures everything that is actually referred to, however loosely, as information. Thus, it might embrace some or all of Machlup's five meta-industries, some or all of what is accommodated under the rubric 'joho', and some or all of what is being processed by 'information processing' devices such as computers. That is to say, it makes no distinction, either semantically or axiologically, between a newly worked-out mathematical equation, a string of jumbled characters, a theological axiom, a phatic spoken on a telephone, a pornographic film, and an accurate, up-to-date list of planetary longitudes. All of this is 'information' in the sense that it can all be digitised or telecommunicated or forced into a Machlupian accounting framework. The *de jure* information society thesis, by contrast, rejects the amorphous approach, assigning a strict meaning to the key word. It reverts to the norms of ordinary language. For the *de jure* information society thesis, information is facts rather than rumours or fictions, organised data as opposed to jumbled-up characters, valid statistics as opposed to soap operas on satellite television; it is 'hard' information in contradistinction to misinformation or pseudo-information. Its paradigm is the reliable timetable or the set of directions which is of practical utility in getting from A to B. It is what the man on the Clapham omnibus expects to receive from an official when he asks for information about his next journey.

The *de jure* information society has much in common with the knowledge society, where the latter is allowed its natural meaning of a society based on scientific knowledge. Knowledge is higher-order information. One cannot build knowledge on inaccurate data or inadequate information, but if one synthesises sufficient information in certain ways one can sometimes produce the intellectual systems typically referred to as 'knowledge'. Thus while not all information qualifies as knowledge, all knowledge is made up of information. An electoral register is information; a successful psephological theory, incorporating such registers among other components, is knowledge. No doubt different accounts of the information–knowledge axis can be given – we saw plenty in Chapters 1 to 5 – but this one has much to commend it from an ordinary language point of view. Anyway, the corollary is that the *de jure* information society is a society which is conducive to knowledge formation. Practically speaking, one could not easily distinguish a *de jure* information society from a knowledge society: in both, information, in the *de jure* sense of facts and figures and statistics and useful data, would be abundant.

The *de jure* information society thesis will also tend to converge with the information technology version. Where information and knowledge are driving forces, the promotion of 'compunications' is likely to be a high priority. The *de jure* information society might be characterised by networks of huge databanks, an electronic social intelligence or memory. However, there is no logical necessity that information should exist in any particular form, electronic or otherwise. A society with a well-developed public library system might come closer to the *de jure* information society than a society awash with technical gadgetry. The main question is: can real information be found? If it can be found in conventional printed volumes in library reference sections but not on the Internet or on satellite television, then the more conventional situation may be closer to the ideal. Joho Shakai measures all communication flows: the *de jure* information society is interested only in genuinely informative flows. And as regards the occupational setup, the professional librarian *is* at the vanguard of the *de jure* information society, because her mission is precisely to disseminate real information – assuming, of course, that she is not merely propagating crime novels and other information-poor forms of light entertainment. The archivist is also an information worker in the present sense, as is the information officer in the Citizens' Advice Bureau. But much if not most of Machlup's overpopulated knowledge sector would have to be written off as having nothing to do with the *de jure* information society.

Finally, and inevitably, the problem of social justice must be faced. The *de jure* information society thesis is already semantically prescriptive in the sense that it admits only a small fraction – the 'hard core' – of *de facto* information flows; but it needs to be prescriptive in an ethical sense too. Information should be not only *abundant* but also *available* – to all members of society. Like the *de facto* information society of Machlup or the Ministry of Posts and Telecommunications, the *de jure* information society brings the whole population into its frame. Thus a strong distributional condition has to be built into our thesis. How exactly this is articulated is a matter which cannot be taken up here, but we may expect that in the *de jure* information society the gap between 'info rich' and 'info poor' is reduced if not obliterated.[2] And while the information society itself cannot be confined to the higher education sector or to scientists – Bell's 300,000 talented persons – it seems likely that information 'professionals' of many kinds would indeed play a key role in *delivering* such a society. We should continue to chart *de facto* informationisation using the best of the available methodologies, but our ultimate ambition should be to bring about the *de jure* information society.

Notes

1   The University of Teesside is believed to have recently introduced a BA Information Society.
2   A very rough outline of a Rawlsian theory of informational justice is offered in Duff (1998b).

Appendix 1

Database searches

Using the search strategy 'informat? (w) (societ? or industr?)', the following bibliographic databases were interrogated via the DIALOG host:

Conference Papers Index 1973–
Dissertation Abstracts Online 1861–
Economic Literature Index 1969–
Information Science Abstracts 1966–
Inspec 1969–
Magazine Index 1959–
Philosophers Index 1940–
Sociological Abstracts 1963–

As stated in Chapter 1, these searches appeared to confirm that there were no relevant 'information society' references prior to 1970, or 'information industry' references prior to 1963.

Appendix 2

Telephone interview with Youichi Ito

The following is a transcript of a telephone interview with Youichi Ito of Keio University, Fujisawa, Japan, which took place on 22 June 1995. I am grateful to the Japanese speaker David McNeill, now at Liverpool John Moores University, for contacting Professor Ito with my questions.

Whom do you credit with inventing the term 'information society'? In your article you say that Umesao was responsible for the 'information society boom'. But you also cite Professor Kamishima's article, which the editors of the journal Hoso Asahi *entitled 'Sociology in information societies'. Who is ultimately responsible for coining the term?*

Umesao is generally credited with inventing the term. The contribution of the editors of *Hoso Asahi* would not have been especially important.

To your knowledge, was this the first appearance of the term in the world?

Yes. Of course, in parallel similar ideas were emerging at the same time in other parts of the world, but the term first appeared in Japan.

If this was the first appearance of the term, do you think that the authors (Umesao, Kamishima, etc.) were influenced by the work of Fritz Machlup, whose The Production and Distribution of Knowledge in the United States *was published in 1962 – a year before the* Hoso Asahi *article?*

No, I don't think so. Umesao was an anthropologist and probably would not have had much interest in Machlup's work. Machlup of course was an economist. So the two of them were coming from different fields of study. Did Machlup use the term 'information society' in his book? I'm not sure.

Internationally, Yujiro Hayashi is credited with being the inventor of the 'information society'. Yet his book Johoka Shakai: Hado no Shakai Kara Sofuto no Shakai e *was published in 1969. Why is he so famous for inventing the concept if his book was published five or six years after its first mention in Japan?*

Because his book was a bestseller in Japan and was probably the first book to actually use the term 'information society' in the title. Umesao's and other people's work appeared in journals or newspaper articles. So Hayashi is best known outside Japan.

Appendix 3

Periodicals carrying articles on the information society between 1984 and 1997

(One paper per periodical unless otherwise indicated)

AEU: Journal of the Asia Electronics Union
AI and Society
American Archivist
American Behavioral Scientist
American Cartographer
Annals of the American Academy of Political and Social Science
Archives and Manuscripts
Asian Survey (2)
Aslib Proceedings (2)
British Telecommunications Engineering
Bulletin of Science, Technology and Society
Bulletin of the American Society for Information Science
Cataloguing and Classification Quarterly
Change
Common Market Law Review
Communicate for the Telecommunications User
Communications Engineering International
Computer Networks and ISDN Systems (2)
Computers and Society
Critical Studies in Mass Communication
Critique of Anthropology (3)
Cultures
Current Contents
Digest of Japanese Industry and Technology (2)
East European Politics and Societies
Economic Development Quarterly
Education and Computing
Education for Information
Educational Leadership
Educational Technology
EDUCOM Bulletin
Electronic Library (3)

Electronic Publishing Review
Electronics and Wireless World (4)
European Cancer News
Fujitsu Scientific and Technical Journal
Futures (2)
Futurist
Government Publications Review (2)
IFIP Transactions A – Computer Science and Technology (3)
IFLA Journal
Information Age
Information Processing and Management (2)
Information Services and Use (2)
Information Technology and People
Informatologia Yugoslavica
International Forum on Information and Documentation
International Journal of Micrographics and Optical Technology
International Journal of Technology Management
International Labour Review
International Library Review
Internet Research
Javnost – The Public
JIPDEC Report
Journal of Communication (2)
Journal of Consumer Policy
Journal of Economic Issues
Journal of Family Practice
Journal of Information and Image Management
Journal of Information Science (12)
Journal of Systems Management
Journal of Telecommunication Networks
Journal of the Copyright Society of the USA
Journal of the Operational Research Society
Library Review
Library Science with a Slant to Documentation
Literary and Linguistic Computing
Management Decision
Media, Culture and Society (3)
Media in Education and Development
NEC Research and Development
New Left Review
New Library World
New Zealand Libraries
NTT Review
Online
Online and CDROM Review

Operational Geographer
Optical Information Systems
Personnel Training and Education
Political Quarterly
Proceedings of the American Society for Information Science
Prometheus
Public Administration Review
Scholarly Publishing
School Library Journal
Science Education
Scientometrics
Search
Social Science Computer Review
Society
Sociology
South African Journal for Librarianship and Information Science
Special Libraries (2)
Systems Research
Technological Forecasting and Social Change (3)
Telecommunication Journal
Telecommunication Journal of Australia
Telecommunications Policy (2)
Telematics and Informatics (7)
Telephony
The Economic and Social Review (5)
The Information Society: An International Journal (24)
Theory and Society
Theory, Culture and Society
Tijdschrift voor Economische en Social Geografie
Tolley's Communication Law
Transportation
University Computing
University of Pennsylvania Law Review
Wilson Library Bulletin
World Futures

Bibliography

American Society for Information Science (1970) *The Information Conscious Society: Proceedings of the ASIS Annual Meeting, October 11–15, 1970, Philadelphia, Pa.*, Washington, DC: ASIS.

Apostle, Richard and Raymond, Boris (1997) *Librarianship and the Information Paradigm*, Lanham, MD: The Scarecrow Press.

Archer, Margaret S. (1990) 'Theory, culture and post-industrial society', in Mike Featherstone (ed.) *Global Culture: Nationalism, Globalization and Modernity*, London: Sage, pp. 97–119.

Arriaga, Patricia (1985) 'Toward a critique of the information economy', *Media, Culture and Society* 7(3): 271–96.

Association for Economic Planning, Information Study Group (1969) *Johoka Shakai no Keisei* [*The Formation of an Informationised Society*], Tokyo: AEP.

Badham, Richard (1984) 'The sociology of industrial and post-industrial societies', *Current Sociology* 32(1): 1–141.

Bannon, Liam (1997) 'Conceptualising "the information society" ', *The Economic and Social Review* 28(3): 301–5.

Bell, Daniel (1956) *Work and its Discontents*, Boston: Beacon.

—— (1960) *The End of Ideology: On the Exhaustion of Political Ideas in the Fifties*, Glencoe: Free Press.

—— (1965) 'The study of the future', *The Public Interest* 1, Fall: 119–30.

—— (1967) 'Notes on the post-industrial society (1)', *The Public Interest* 6, Winter: 24–35.

—— (1971) 'Technocracy and politics', *Survey: A Journal of East & West Studies* 17(1): 1–24.

—— (1974) *The Coming of Post-Industrial Society: A Venture in Social Forecasting*, London: Heinemann Educational Books; first published by Basic Books, New York, 1973.

—— (1976) *The Cultural Contradictions of Capitalism*, New York: Basic Books.

—— (1980a) 'Technology, nature, and society: the vicissitudes of three world views and the confusion of realms', in Daniel Bell, *The Winding Passage: Essays and Sociological Journeys 1960–1980*, Cambridge, MA: Basic Books, pp. 3–33; first published in *Technology and the Frontiers of Knowledge: The Frank Nelson Doubleday Lectures*, Doubleday and Co., 1973.

—— (1980b) 'Teletext and technology: new networks of knowledge and information in postindustrial society', in Daniel Bell, *The Winding Passage: Essays and Sociological Journeys 1960–1980*, Cambridge, MA: Basic Books, pp. 34–65; first published in *Encounter* XLVIII, June 1977.

—— (1980c) 'The social framework of the information society', in Tom Forester (ed.) *The Microelectronics Revolution*, Oxford: Blackwell, pp. 500–49; first published in Michael L. Dertouzos and Joel Moses (eds) *The Computer Age: A Twenty-Year View*, Cambridge, MA: The MIT Press, 1979.

—— (1985) 'Gutenberg and the computer: on information, knowledge and other distinctions', *Encounter* LXIV, May: 15–20.

—— (1987) 'The world in 2013', *New Society* 18 December: 31–41.

—— (1989) 'The third technological revolution and its possible socioeconomic consequences', *Dissent* 36(2): 164–76.

—— (1992) 'The break-up of space and time: technology and society in a post-industrial age', unpublished paper read to the American Sociological Association, Pittsburgh, 20 August 1992.

—— (1995a) 'Social science: an imperfect art', *The Tocqueville Review* XVI(1): 3–24.

—— (1995b) 'The cultural contradictions of Newt Gingrich', *New Perspectives Quarterly* Spring: 7–9.

—— (1996a) Letter to the author, 12 February.

—— (1996b) Letter to the author, 12 August.

—— (1996c) Letter to the author, 16 October.

Bell, Daniel and Graubard, Stephen R. (eds) (1997) *Toward the Year 2000: Work in Progress*, Cambridge, MA: The MIT Press.

Beniger, James R. (1986) *The Control Revolution: Technological and Economic Origins of the Information Society*, Cambridge, MA: Harvard University Press.

Besselaar, Peter van den (1997) 'The future of employment in the information society: a comparative, longitudinal and multi-level study', *Journal of Information Science* 23(5): 373–92.

Blaug, Mark (1982) Review of *Knowledge: Its Creation, Distribution and Economic Significance, Vol. I: Knowledge and Knowledge Production*, in *British Journal for the Philosophy of Science* 33(3): 323–4.

Bolter, J. David (1984) *Turing's Man: Western Culture in the Computer Age*, London: Duckworth.

Boulding, Kenneth E. (1963) Review of *The Production and Distribution of Knowledge in the United States*, in *Challenge* May: 38.

Bowes, John E. (1981) 'Japan's approach to an information society: a critical perspective', in G. Cleveland Wilhoit and Harold de Bock (eds) *Mass Communication Review Yearbook Volume 2*, Beverly Hills, CA: Sage, pp. 699–710.

Burck, Gilbert (1964) 'Knowledge: the biggest growth industry of them all', *Fortune* November: 128–270.

Burgelman, Jean-Claude (1994) 'Assessing information technologies in the information society: the relevance of communication science', in Slavko Splichal, Andrew Calabrese, and Colin Sparks (eds) *Information Society and Civil Society: Contemporary Perspectives on the Changing World Order*, West Lafayette, IN: Purdue University Press, pp. 185–207.

Burton, Paul (1992) *Information Technology and Society: Implications for the Information Professions*, London: Library Association Publishing.

Bush, Vannevar (1945) *Science, the Endless Frontier: A Report to the President*, Washington, DC: Public Affairs Press.

Castells, Manuel (1996) *The Information Age: Economy, Society and Culture, Vol. I: The Rise of the Network Society*, Oxford: Blackwell.

Cawkell, A.E. (1984) 'The information society 1: technology, politics and infrastructures', *Electronics and Wireless World* 90 (No. 1580): 62–6.

—— (1986) 'The real information society: present situation and some forecasts', *Journal of Information Science* 12(3): 87–95.

—— (1998) 'The information age – for better or for worse', *Journal of Information Science* 24(1): 56–8.

Chang, Shan-Ju (1995) 'Concepts of information society, cultural assumptions and government information policy: a case study of [the] USA', *Journal of Information, Communication and Library Science* 2(1): 25–49.

Coats, A.W. (1982) Review of *Knowledge: Its Creation, Distribution and Economic Significance, Vol. I: Knowledge and Knowledge Production*, in *The Economic Journal* 92(365): 210–11.

Cooper, Michael D. (1983) 'The structure and future of the information economy', *Information Processing and Management* 19(1): 9–26.

Crawford, Susan (1983) 'The origin and development of a concept: the information society', *Bulletin of the Medical Library Association* 71(4): 380–5.

Cronin, Blaise, Snyder, Herbert, and Atkins, Helen (1997) 'Comparative citation rankings of authors in monographic and journal literature: a study of sociology', *Journal of Documentation* 53(3): 263–73.

Danjczek, Michael H. (1987) 'Perceptions of the impact of the information society on the poor', unpublished Ed.D. dissertation, Lehigh University.

Dedijer, Stevan (1996) 'Development and management by intelligence: Japan', in Blaise Cronin (ed.) *Information, Development and Social Intelligence*, London: Taylor Graham, pp. 304–23.

Devlin, Patrick (1965) *The Enforcement of Morals*, Oxford: Oxford University Press.

Dordick, Herbert S. and Wang, Georgette (1993) *The Information Society: A Retrospective View*, Newbury Park, CA: Sage.

Downs, Anthony (1957) *An Economic Theory of Democracy*, New York: Harper.

Dreyer, Jacob S. (ed.) (1978) *Breadth and Depth in Economics: Fritz Machlup: The Man and His Ideas*, Lexington, MA: D.C. Heath & Co.

Duff, Alistair S. (1990) ' "Revolution of the fixed wheel"? Left critiques of the information society thesis', unpublished M.Sc. dissertation, University of Strathclyde.

—— (1995) 'The "information society" as paradigm: a bibliometric inquiry', *Journal of Information Science* 21(5): 390–5.

—— (1998a) 'Daniel Bell's theory of the information society', *Journal of Information Science* 24(6): 373–93.

—— (1998b) 'Information gaps: social justice in the information society', *International Journal on Information Theories and Applications* 5(4): 134–42.

Duff, Alistair S., Craig, David, and McNeill, David A. (1996) 'A note on the origins of the "information society" ', *Journal of Information Science* 22(2): 117–22.

Edelstein, Alex S., Bowes, John E., and Harsel, Sheldon M. (eds) (1978) *Information Societies: Comparing the Japanese and American Experiences*, Seattle, WA: International Communication Center, University of Washington.

Feather, John (1998) *The Information Society: A Study of Continuity and Change*, 2nd edn, London: Library Association Publishing.

Ferkiss, Victor (1979) 'Daniel Bell's concept of post-industrial society: theory, myth and ideology', *The Political Science Reviewer* IX: 61–102.

Fincham, Robin (1987) 'From "post-industrialism" to "information society": comment on Lyon', *Sociology* 21(3): 463–6.

Forester, Tom (ed.) (1980) *The Microelectronics Revolution*, Oxford: Blackwell.

—— (ed.) (1989) *Computers in the Human Context: Information Technology, Productivity and People*, Oxford: Blackwell.

—— (1993) 'Information technology and theory', in William Outhwaite and Tom Bottomore (eds) *The Blackwell Dictionary of Twentieth-Century Social Thought*, Oxford: Blackwell, pp. 287–8.

Fortner, Robert S. (1995) 'Excommunication in the information society', *Critical Studies in Mass Communication* 12(2): 133–54.

Freeman, Christopher, Clark, John, and Soete, Luc (1982) *Unemployment and Technical Innovation: A Study of Long Waves and Economic Development*, London: Frances Pinter.

Freeman, Christopher and Soete, Luc (1990) 'Information technology and the global economy', in Jacques Berleur, Andrew Clement, Richard Sizer, and Diane Whitehouse (eds) *The Information Society: Evolving Landscapes*, New York: Springer-Verlag/Captus University Publications, pp. 278–94.

Garfield, Eugene (1979) '2001: an information society?', *Journal of Information Science* 1(4): 209–15.

Garnham, Nicholas (1996) 'Constraints on multimedia convergence', in William H. Dutton (ed.) *Information and Communication Technologies: Visions and Realities*, Oxford: Oxford University Press, pp. 103–19.

Gill, Harjinder S. and Yates-Mercer, Penelope (1998) 'The dissemination of information by local authorities on the World Wide Web', *Journal of Information Science* 24(2): 105–12.

Goffman, William and Warren, Kenneth S. (1980) *Scientific Information Systems and the Principle of Selectivity*, New York: Praeger Scientific.

Goldstein, Leon J. (1981) Review of *Knowledge: Its Creation, Distribution and Economic Significance, Vol. I: Knowledge and Knowledge Production*, in *American Historical Review* 86(5): 1063–4.

Gould, Julius (1974) 'Shapes of things to come: Daniel Bell's "Post-Industrial Society" ', *Encounter* XLII, May: 36–40.

Harris, Michael H. and Hannah, Stan A. (1993) *Into the Future: The Foundations of Library and Information Services in the Post-Industrial Era*, Norwood, NJ: Ablex.

Harsel, Sheldon M. (1981) 'Communication research in information societies: a comparative view of Japan and the United States', in G. Cleveland Wilhoit and Harold de Bock (eds) *Mass Communication Review Yearbook Volume 2*, Beverly Hills, CA: Sage, pp. 711–16.

Hayashi, Yujiro (1969) *Johoka Shakai: Hado no Shakai Kara Sofuto no Shakai e [The Informationised Society: From Hard to Soft Society]*, Tokyo: Kodansha Gendai Shinso.

Haywood, Trevor (1995) *Info-Rich–Info-Poor: Access and Exchange in the Global Information Society*, London: Bowker-Saur.

—— (1997) *Praise the Net and Pass the Modem: Revolutionaries and Captives in the Information Society*. The First Ameritech Information Society Lecture, Edinburgh: Merchiston Publishing; first published in *Library Review* 46(7): 472–89 (1997).

Holzner, Burkart (1982) 'Towards the economics of knowledge': review essay on Machlup's *Knowledge: Its Creation, Distribution and Economic Significance, Vol. I: Knowledge and Knowledge Production*, in *Contemporary Sociology: A Journal of Reviews* 11(3): 295–8.

Horowitz, Irving L. (1986) *Communicating Ideas: The Crisis of Publishing in a Post-Industrial Society*, Oxford: Oxford University Press.

Hunt, Shane (1965) Review of *The Production and Distribution of Knowledge in the United States*, in *Journal of Political Economy* 73, June: 311–12.

Ito, Youichi (1978) 'Report at the final plenary session: cross cultural perspectives on the concept of an information society', in Alex S. Edelstein, John E. Bowes, and Sheldon M. Harsel (eds) *Information Societies: Comparing the Japanese and American Experiences*, Seattle, WA: International Communication Center, University of Washington, pp. 253–8.

—— (1981) 'The *"Johoka Shakai"* approach to the study of communication in Japan', in G. Cleveland Wilhoit and Harold de Bock (eds) *Mass Communication Review Yearbook Volume 2*, Beverly Hills, CA: Sage, pp. 671–98.

—— (1991a) 'Birth of *joho shakai* and *johoka* concepts in Japan and their diffusion outside Japan', *Keio Communication Review* 13: 3–12.

—— (1991b) *'Johoka* as a driving force of social change', *Keio Communication Review* 12: 35–58.

—— (1994) 'Information societies with strong and weak civil society traditions', in Slavko Splichal, Andrew Calabrese, and Colin Sparks (eds) *Information Society and Civil Society: Contemporary Perspectives on the Changing World Order*, West Lafayette, IN: Purdue University Press, pp. 233–53.

Johnson, Orace (1982) Review of *Knowledge: Its Creation, Distribution and Economic Significance, Vol. I: Knowledge and Knowledge Production*, in *The Accounting Review* 57(1): 223–5.

Johnson, Richard D. (1987) 'Machlup and the information age', *Scholarly Publishing* 18(4): 271–6.

Johoka Shakai Jiten [*Dictionary for Informationised Societies*] (1971), Tokyo: Mainichi Shimbun-sha.

Jones, Steven G. (ed.) (1995) *CyberSociety: Computer-Mediated Communication and Community*, Thousand Oaks, CA: Sage.

Kadushin, Charles (1974) *The American Intellectual Elite*, Boston, MA: Little, Brown, & Co.

Katz, Raul L. (1988) *The Information Society: An International Perspective*, New York: Praeger.

Keizai Shingikai Joho Sangyo Bukai (1969) *Nihon no Johoka Shakai: Sono Kadai to Bijon* [*Japan's Informationised Society: Themes and Visions*], Tokyo: Keizai Shingikai Joho Sangyo Bukai.

Keresztesi, Michael (1982) 'The science of bibliography: theoretical implications for bibliographic instruction', in Cerise Oberman and Katina Strauch (eds) *Theories of Bibliographic Education: Designs for Teaching*, New York: R.R. Bowker, pp. 1–26.

Kitahara, Yasusada (1984) 'Telecommunications for the advanced information society in Japan: Information Network System', *Journal of Telecommunication Networks* 3(4): 339–43.

Klapp, Orrin E. (1986) *Overload and Boredom: Essays on the Quality of Life in the Information Society*, London: Greenwood Press.

Kling, Rob (1994) 'Reading "all about" computerization: how genre conventions shape nonfiction social analysis', *The Information Society* 10(3): 147–72.

Komatsuzaki, S., Tanimitsu, T., Ohira, G., and Yamamoto, K. (n.d.) *An Analysis of the Information Economy in Japan from 1960 to 1980*, Tokyo: Research Institute of Telecommunications and Economics.

Kumar, Krishan (1978) *Prophecy and Progress: The Sociology of Industrial and Post-Industrial Society*, Harmondsworth: Penguin.

Kuwahara, Takao, Kamishima, Jiro, and Komatsu, Sakyo (1964) 'Joho shakai no soshiorogii' ['Sociology in information societies'], *Hoso Asahi* January: 19–39.

Lancaster, F.W. (1978) *Toward Paperless Information Systems*, New York: Academic Press.

Laudon, Kenneth C., Traver, Carol G., and Laudon, Jane P. (1994) *Information Technology and Society*, Belmont, CA: Wadsworth.

Lehtonen, Jaako (1988) 'The information society and the new competence', *American Behavioral Scientist* 32(2): 104–11.

Lekachman, Robert (1963) Review of *The Production and Distribution of Knowledge in the United States*, in *Political Science Quarterly* 78(3): 467–9.

Lyon, David (1987) 'Information technology and information society: response to Fincham', *Sociology* 21(3): 467–8.

—— (1988) *The Information Society: Issues and Illusions*, Cambridge: Polity Press.

McAnlis, Mark L. (1986) 'Cogent preaching: effective ministry in an information society', unpublished D.Min. dissertation, Fuller Theological Seminary.

Machlup, Fritz (1962) *The Production and Distribution of Knowledge in the United States*, Princeton, NJ: Princeton University Press.

—— (1978) *Methodology of Economics and Other Social Sciences*, New York: Academic Press.

—— (1980) *Knowledge: Its Creation, Distribution and Economic Significance, Vol. I: Knowledge and Knowledge Production*, Princeton, NJ: Princeton University Press.

—— (1982) *Knowledge: Its Creation, Distribution and Economic Significance, Vol. II: The Branches of Learning*, Princeton, NJ: Princeton University Press.

—— (1983) *Knowledge: Its Creation, Distribution and Economic Significance, Vol. III: The Economics of Information and Human Capital*, Princeton, NJ: Princeton University Press.

Machlup, Fritz, Leeson, Kenneth, and associates (1978) *Information through the Printed Word: The Dissemination of Scholarly, Scientific, and Intellectual Knowledge, Vol. 1: Book Publishing; Vol. 2: Journals; Vol. 3: Libraries*, New York: Praeger Publishers.

Machlup, Fritz and Mansfield, Una (eds) (1983) *Knowledge: Its Creation, Distribution and Economic Significance, Vol. IV: The Study of Information: Interdisciplinary Messages*, Princeton, NJ: Princeton University Press.

McLean, Mick (ed.) (1985) *The Information Explosion: The New Electronic Media in Japan and Europe*, London: Frances Pinter.

Mandi, P. (1983) Review of *Knowledge: Its Creation, Distribution and Economic Significance, Vol. I: Knowledge and Knowledge Production*, in *Acta Oeconomica* 31(1–2): 149–52.

Marschak, Jacob (1968) 'Economics of inquiring, communicating, deciding', *American Economic Review* 58(2): 1–8.

Martin, William J. (1995) *The Global Information Society*, Aldershot: Aslib Gower.

Masuda, Yoneji (1968) *Joho Shakai Nyumon* [*Introduction to an Information Society*], Tokyo: Perikan-Sha.

—— (1970) 'Social impact of computerization: an application of the pattern model for industrial society', in *Challenges from the Future: Proceedings of the International Future Research Conference, Vol. 2*, Tokyo: Japan Society of Futurology/Kodansha, pp. 13–24.

—— (1981) *The Information Society as Post-Industrial Society*, Washington, DC: The World Future Society.

Meadows, A.J. (1996) Review of William J. Martin, *The Global Information Society*, in *The Electronic Library* 14(3): 278–9.

—— (1998) *Communicating Research*, San Diego, CA: Academic Press.

Melody, William H. (1996) 'The strategic value of policy research in the information economy', in William H. Dutton (ed.) *Information and Communication Technologies: Visions and Realities*, Oxford: Oxford University Press, pp. 303–17.

Miksa, Francis L. (1985) 'Machlup's categories of knowledge as a framework for viewing library and information science history', *Journal of Library History, Philosophy and Comparative Librarianship* 20(2): 157–72.

Miles, Ian (1985) 'The new post-industrial state', *Futures* 17(6): 588–617.

—— (1988a) *Home Informatics: Information Technology and the Transformation of Everyday Life*, London: Pinter.

—— (1988b) *Information Technology and Information Society: Options for the Future*, London: Economic and Social Research Council. Programme on Information and Communication Technologies [Policy Research Papers No. 2]; reprinted in William H. Dutton (ed.) *Information and Communication Technologies: Visions and Realities*, Oxford: Oxford University Press, 1996, pp. 37–52.

—— (1991) 'Measuring the future: statistics and the information age', *Futures* 23(9): 915–34.

—— (1997) 'Cyberspace as product space: interactive learning about interactive media', *Futures* 29(9): 769–89.

Miles, Ian and Gershuny, Jonathan (1987) 'The social economics of information technology', in Ruth Finnegan, Graeme Salaman, and Kenneth Thompson (eds) *Information Technology: Social Issues: A Reader*, London: Hodder & Stoughton/The Open University, pp. 209–24.

Miles, Ian and Robins, Kevin (1992) 'Making sense of information', in Kevin Robins (ed.) *Understanding Information: Business, Technology and Geography*, London: Belhaven Press, pp. 1–26.

Miles, Ian, Rush, Howard, Turner, Kevin, and Bessant, John (1988) *Information Horizons: The Long-Term Social Implications of New Information Technologies*, Aldershot: Edward Elgar.

Miles, Ian, with Brady, Tim, Davies, Andy, Haddon, Leslie, Jagger, Nick, Matthews, Mark, Rush, Howard, and Wyatt, Sally (1990) *Mapping and Measuring the Information Economy: A Report Produced for the Economic and Social Research Council's Programme on Information and Communication Technologies* [Library and Information Research Report No. 77], London: British Library.

Miller, S. Michael (1975) 'Notes on neo-capitalism', *Theory and Society* 2(1): 1–35.

Minc, Alain (1987) 'The informatisation of society', in A.E. Cawkell (ed.) *Evolution of an Information Society*, London: Aslib, pp. 134–40.

Ministry of Posts and Telecommunications, Research Committee on the Information Flow Census (1972) *Joho wa Bakuhatsu Shite Iruke* [*Is Information Exploding?*], Tokyo: MPT.

Ministry of Posts and Telecommunications (1975) *Joho Ryutsu no Keiryo Shuho* [*The Methods for the Measurement of Information Flow*], Tokyo: MPT.

—— (1978) *Tsushin Hakusho* [*White Paper on Communications in Japan*], Tokyo: MPT.

—— (1995) *Tsushin Hakusho* [*White Paper on Communications in Japan*], Tokyo: MPT.

—— (1998) *Tsushin Hakusho* [*White Paper on Communications in Japan*], Tokyo: MPT.

Mitcham, Carl (1994) *Thinking Through Technology: The Path between Engineering and Philosophy*, Chicago: University of Chicago Press.

Moore, Nick (1997) 'Neo-liberal or dirigiste? Policies for an information society', *Political Quarterly* 68(3): 276–83.

Morris-Suzuki, Tessa (1988) *Beyond Computopia: Information, Automation and Democracy in Japan*, London: Kegan Paul International.

Nass, Clifford I. (1987) 'Following the money trail: 25 years of measuring the information economy', *Communication Research* 14(6): 698–708.

—— (1988) 'Work, information, and information work: a retrospective and prospective framework', *Research in the Sociology of Work* 4: 311–33.

Newman, Julian and Newman, Rhona (1985) 'Information work: the new divorce?', *British Journal of Sociology* 36(4): 497–515.

Nora, Simon and Minc, Alain (1980) *The Computerization of Society: A Report to the President of France*, Cambridge, MA: The MIT Press; first published as *L'Informatisation de la Société*, Paris: La Documentation Française, 1978.

Okada, Naoyuki (1978) 'Some aspects of Japan as an information society', in Alex S. Edelstein, John E. Bowes, and Sheldon M. Harsel (eds) *Information Societies: Comparing the Japanese and American Experiences*, Seattle, WA: International Communication Center, University of Washington, pp. 153–60.

Organization for Economic Cooperation and Development (1981) *Information Activities, Electronics and Telecommunications Technologies: Impact on Employment, Growth and Trade*, Paris: OECD.

Paisley, William (1986) 'The convergence of communication and information science', in Hendrik Edelman (ed.) *Libraries and Information Science in the Electronic Age*, Philadelphia, PA: ISI Press, pp. 122–53.

Parker, Edwin B. with Porat, Marc U. (1975) *OECD Informatics Studies: Proceedings of the OECD Conference on Computer and Telecommunications Policy, Paris, February 1975: Background Report*, Paris: OECD, pp. 87–129.

Poirier, René (1990) 'The information economy approach: characteristics, limitations, and future prospects', *The Information Society* 7(4): 245–85.

Pool, Ithiel de Sola, Inose, Hiroshi, Takasaki, Nozumo, and Hurwitz, Roger (1984) *Communications Flows: A Census in the United States and Japan*, Amsterdam: North-Holland and University of Tokyo Press.

Porat, Marc Uri (1977) *The Information Economy, Vol. 1: Definition and Measurement; Vol. 2: Sources and Methods for Measuring the Primary Information Sector (Detailed Industry Reports)*; [with Michael R. Rubin] *Vol. 3: The Interindustry Transactions Matrices, 1967*; [with Michael R. Rubin] *Vol. 4: The Technology Matrices, 1967*; [with Michael R. Rubin] *Vol. 5: The 'Total Effect' Matrices, 1967*; [with Michael R. Rubin] *Vol. 6: The Labor Income by Industry Matrix of Employee Compensation, 1967*; [with Michael R. Rubin] *Vol. 7: The Labor Income by Industry Matrix of Employee Compensation, 1970*; [with Michael R. Rubin] *Vol. 8: National Income, Workforce, and Input-Output Accounts*; [with Michael R. Rubin] *Vol. 9: User's Guide to the Complete Database*, Washington, DC: US Department of Commerce, Office of Telecommunications.

Poster, Mark (1990) *The Mode of Information: Poststructuralism and Social Context*, Cambridge: Polity Press.

Preston, Paschal (1997) 'Beyond the "information society": selected atoms and bits of a national strategy in Ireland', *The Economic and Social Review* 28(3): 185–211.

Preston, Paschal and Wickham, James (1997) Editorial [in Special Issue devoted to Ireland, Europe and the global information society], *The Economic and Social Review* 28(3): v–viii.

Price, Derek de Solla (1963) *Little Science, Big Science*, New York: Columbia University Press.

Research Institute of Telecommunications and Economics (1968) *Sangyoka Igo no Shakai ni Okeru Joho to Tsushin [Information and Communication in a Post-Industrial Society]*, Tokyo: RITE.

—— (1970) *Sangyoka Igo no Shakai ni Okeru Denki Tsushin no Yakuwari [The Role of Telecommunications in a Post-Industrial Society]*, Tokyo: RITE.

Rich, Robert F. (1982) In memory of Fritz Machlup, *Knowledge: Creation, Diffusion, Utilization* 4(2): 331–2.

Robinson, Sherman (1986) 'Analyzing the information economy: tools and techniques', *Information Processing and Management* 22(3): 183–202.

Rose, Margaret A. (1991) *The Post-Modern and the Post-Industrial: A Critical Analysis*, Cambridge: Cambridge University Press.

Rosen, Sherwin (1986) Review of *Knowledge: Its Creation, Distribution and Economic Significance, Vol. III: The Economics of Information and Human Capital*, in *Journal of Economic Literature* 24, March: 141–3.

Roszak, Theodore (1994) *The Cult of Information: A Neo-Luddite Treatise on High Tech, Artificial Intelligence, and the True Art of Thinking*, 2nd edn, Berkeley, CA: University of California Press.

Rubin, Michael R. and Huber, Mary T. (1986) *The Knowledge Industry in the United States 1960–1980*, Princeton, NJ: Princeton University Press.

Sangyo Koso Shingikai Joho Sangyo Bukai (1969) *Nihon Shakai Johoka Sokushin no tame no Seisaku Yoko [Policy Outlines for Promoting the Informationisation of Japanese Society]*, Tokyo: Sangyo Koso Shingikai Joho Sangyo Bukai.

Savage, Caroline (1994) 'Optical disc technology in bank customer service units', *Information Management and Technology* 27(3): 107–11.

Schement, Jorge R. (1990) 'Porat, Bell, and the information society reconsidered: the growth of information work in the early twentieth century', *Information Processing and Management* 26(4): 449–65.

Schement, Jorge R. and Curtis, Terry (1995) *Tendencies and Tensions of the Information Age: The Production and Distribution of Knowledge in the United States*, New Brunswick, NJ: Transaction Publishers.

Shultz, T.W. (1963) Review of *The Production and Distribution of Knowledge in the United States*, in *American Economic Review* 53, September: 836–8.

Sigismund, Charles G. (1980) 'Trading in the marketplace of ideas: a contribution to the theory of production of knowledge', unpublished Ph.D. dissertation, Stanford University.

Simon, Herbert A. (1987) 'What computers mean for man and society', in A.E. Cawkell (ed.) *Evolution of an Information Society*, London: Aslib, pp. 111–22.

Sowell, Thomas (1986) *Marxism: Philosophy and Economics*, London: Unwin Paperbacks.

Splichal, Slavko, Calabrese, Andrew, and Sparks, Colin (eds) (1994) *Information Society and Civil Society: Contemporary Perspectives on the Changing World Order*, West Lafayette, IN: Purdue University Press.

Stehr, Nico (1994) *Knowledge Societies*, London: Sage.

Steinbuch, Karl (1966) *Die Informierte Gesellschaft: Geschichte und Zukunft der Nachrichtentechnik* [*The Informing Society: The History and Prospects for Technical Communication*], Stuttgart: Deutsche Verlags-Anstalt.

Steiner, George (1975) *After Babel: Aspects of Language and Translation*, London: Oxford University Press.

Steinfield, Charles and Salvaggio, Jerry L. (1989) 'Toward a definition of the information society', in Jerry L. Salvaggio (ed.) *The Information Society: Economic, Social and Structural Issues*, Hillsdale, NJ: Lawrence Erlbaum Associates, pp. 1–14.

Stonier, Tom (1985) *The Communicative Society: A New Era in Human History*, London: Foundation for Public Relations Research and Education.

Takahashi, Tatsuo and Kida, Hiroshi (eds) (1969) *Chishiki Sangyo* [*Knowledge Industry*], Tokyo: Sangyo Nohritsu Tanki Daigaku.

Tanaka, Yasumasa (1978) 'Proliferating technology and the structure of information space', in Alex S. Edelstein, John E. Bowes, and Sheldon M. Harsel (eds) *Information Societies: Comparing the Japanese and American Experiences*, Seattle, WA: International Communication Center, University of Washington, pp. 195–209.

Tateno, Tadao (1978) 'Telecommunications administration in Japan', in Alex S. Edelstein, John E. Bowes, and Sheldon M. Harsel (eds) *Information Societies: Comparing the Japanese and American Experiences*, Seattle, WA: International Communication Center, University of Washington, pp. 9–12.

Time (1962) 'The knowledge industry', 21 December (No. 80): 55.

Times Literary Supplement (1995) 'The hundred most influential books since the war', 6 October: 39.

Toffler, Alvin (1970) *Future Shock*, London: The Bodley Head.

—— (1980) *The Third Wave*, London: Pan.

Tomita, Tetsuro (1975) 'The volume of information flow and the quantum evaluation of media', *Telecommunication Journal* 42(6): 339–49.

—— (1978) 'Information and communication policies in an age oversupplied with information', in Alex S. Edelstein, John E. Bowes, and Sheldon M. Harsel (eds) *Information Societies: Comparing the Japanese and American Experiences*, Seattle, WA: International Communication Center, University of Washington, pp. 19–23.

Traue, J.E. (1990) 'Five thousand years of the information society', *New Zealand Libraries* 46(6): 17–18.

Tsay, Ming-Yueh (1995) 'The impact of the concept of post-industrial society and information society: a citation analysis study', *Scientometrics* 33(3): 329–50.

Turner, J.S. (ed.) (1958) *Conventions: An American Institution*, Cincinnati, OH: International Association of Convention Bureaus.

Umesao, Tadao (1963) 'Joho sangyo ron' ['On information industries'], *Hoso Asahi* January: 4–17.

Valencia, Rosita P. (1986) 'Knowledge and information occupations in Singapore: a country case study', unpublished Ph.D. dissertation, University of Southern California.

Veysey, Laurence (1982) 'A postmortem on Daniel Bell's postindustrialism', *American Quarterly* 34(1): 49–69.

Waters, Malcolm (1996) *Daniel Bell*, London: Routledge.

Weaver, Warren (1955) 'The mathematics of information', in *Automatic Control*, New York: Simon and Schuster for *Scientific American*.

Webster, Frank (1994) 'What information society?', *The Information Society* 10(1): 1–23.

—— (1995) *Theories of the Information Society*, London: Routledge.

Webster, Frank and Robins, Kevin (1986) *Information Technology: A Luddite Analysis*, Norwood, NJ: Ablex.

Wersig, Gernot (1973) *Informationssoziologie: Hinweise zu Einem Informationswissenschaftlichen Teilbereich [The Sociology of Information: An Introduction to a Scientific Approach]*, Frankfurt: Athenäum Verlag.

Wiio, Osmo A. (1985) 'Information economy and the information society', *Media in Education and Development* 18(4): 187–91.

Williams, Frederick (ed.) (1988) *Measuring the Information Society*, Newbury Park, CA: Sage.

Wrong, Dennis (1996) 'The sense of an ending', *Times Literary Supplement* 29 March: 8–9.

Yamaguchi, Kaoru (1990) 'Fundamentals of a new economic paradigm in the information age', *Futures* 22(10): 1023–36.

Yeong, Dong Y. (1990a) 'A sectoral analysis of the information sector in the information economy', unpublished Ph.D. dissertation, Rutgers University.

—— (1990b) 'The nature of the information sector in the information society: an economic and societal perspective', *Special Libraries* 81(3): 230–5.

Yoshizoe, Yasuto (1988) 'An economic interpretation of "Information Flow Census" data', *Keio Communication Review* 9: 53–83.

Young, Michael (1958) *The Rise of the Meritocracy*, Harmondsworth: Penguin.

Index